THE
LAST FLIGHT
OF THE
LUFTWAFFE

THE
LAST FLIGHT
OF THE
LUFTWAFFE

The Fate of Schulungslehrgang Elbe
7 April 1945

ADRIAN WEIR

ARMS AND
ARMOUR

ARMS & ARMOUR PRESS
An imprint of the Cassell Group
Wellington House, 125 Strand, London WC2R 0BB

ISBN 1 85409 300 2

Edited and designed by Roger Chesneau/DAG
Publications Ltd

CONTENTS

MAPS

PREFACE

The research which led to this book began as a simple attempt to find out more about the events which took place over Germany on 7 April 1945. Many works which examine *Luftwaffe* activity during the closing stages of the war in Europe give vague details regarding a special operation mounted that day against US Eighth Air Force bombers. All these accounts give enough detail to interest the reader but little more. After more than fifty years, and with so many facts revealed about the 1939–45 war, surely it would prove a simple task to find a full account of this operation.

In fact it proved to be almost impossible using existing references. As more sources were examined, more conflicting evidence was revealed. How large had this operation been? How had it been formed? Was the unit—as had been frequently been suggested—a suicide formation linked somehow to the so-called *Selbstopfermänner* (literally, 'self-sacrifice men')? Even the name of the unit was in doubt. Was it *Rammkommando 'Elbe'* or *Lehrgang 'Elbe'*, or did it carry the evocative name which has been linked to many late-war operations—'*Wehrwolf*'? The account which appeared to offer the most help was that in the book written by *Herr* Hajo Herrmann, the *Luftwaffe* officer whose name was linked with the planning behind the unit and its operation. However, *Herr* Herrmann does not dwell in detail upon the battle fought over Germany on 7 April 1945, allocating a mere handful of pages to the subject.

So began a time-consuming and often confusing search for the truth. Through good fortune, two early contacts were to prove the most valuable. The first was the German author *Herr* Ulrich Saft, who had already spent much of his time researching similar subject matter and had been able to meet with many of those involved. Much of the information relating to the *Luftwaffe* operations has been confirmed by *Herr* Saft in his book *Das Bittere Ende der Luftwaffe*. The detailed investigation carried out by *Herr* Saft has provided a source of information which would otherwise have been unavailable.

The second contact was to prove even more important. The author was informed by *Herr* Herrmann that a veterans' group had been established for those involved in the *'Elbe'* operation and was then pleased to be put in touch with *Herr* Werner Zell, who was closely linked to the founding and running of this group. By means of a lengthy correspondence with an ever-patient Herr Zell, himself a survivor from 7 April 1945, the author was able to find answers to many of the remaining questions. Without the starting point provided by *Herr* Saft's book and without the kind help offered by *Herr* Zell, the present work would not have been possible, and the author is indebted to these two gentlemen.

In preparing this work the author also returned to unpublished official records of the Eighth Air Force's operations of 7 April 1945. This has allowed a list of events to be built up using first-hand information, prepared only a matter of hours after the events themselves took place. It has, then, been possible to assemble the framework, as it were, around the picture of the mission flown by the 'Elbe' force. Wherever possible, combats have been described from the point of view of each side, although of course the individual incidents were confused and much detail has proved difficult to confirm. However, in these instances the author has avoided the temptation simply to follow the narratives provided by earlier works—even that by *Herr* Saft. By examining the reports prepared by bomber crews and staff of the Eighth Air Force and from contacts made with the survivors, it has proved possible to match some of the events and actions. Where the chaotic skirmishes clouded the story some assumptions have been made, but in other cases the reader is provided only with confirmed facts. To many readers the events described in the early chapters will be well known, but it is felt that in order to understand the formation and operation of 'Elbe' such background information—for example, *General* Galland's *'Grosse Schlag'* and the career of Hajo Herrmann—needs to be re-stated.

A word of thanks must go to all those who have helped in the research for this book, and to one further person—the author's wife Gillian, who supported the project and provided the necessary encouragement for it to be completed.

ACKNOWLEDGEMENTS
The following is a list of all those who provided help, advice or encouragement during the preparation of this book. In Belgium: P. J. Martin. In Germany: Hajo Herrmann; Gunter Herz; Wolfdietrich Hoeveler, Editor, *Flug Revue*; Rainer Laabs, Ullstein GmbH; Johannes Mohn, Editor, *Jägerblatt*, Gemeinschaft der Jagdflieger; *Generalleutnant* Günther Rall; Lilo Rubberts; Ulrich Saft; *Frau* Scholl, Bundesarchiv, Freiburg; Hansjurgen von Reigen; Bruno Waltert, Editor, *Berliner Morgenpost*; Hans-Joachim Wicht, Editor, *Altmark-Zeitung*, Salzwedel; and Werner Zell. In the United Kingdom: John Armstrong; Colin Durrant, 390th BG Memorial Museum, Ipswich; P. J. V. Elliott, The Royal Air Force Museum, Hendon; Jacqui Etheridge, The British Film Institute; Ken Everett, 100th BG Memorial Museum, Diss, Norfolk; Paul Goodman, National Museum of Photography, Film & Television, Bradford; Paul Kemp, Imperial War Museum, London; Rita Klapper, for valuable help in translating seemingly endless streams of material; Ian F. Mason, for his

expert knowledge of the Bf 109G, gained from his work on 'Black 6'; Kathy Moran, The Fighter Collection; Alan Parker, Frank Smith Books, Newcastle-upon-Tyne, for always finding the titles I needed; Doris E. Pullen; Richard S. Robinson, for help in finding the needle in the haystack; David Tappin; and H. J. Woodend, Ministry of Defence, Pattern Room, Nottingham. In the USA: Lieutenant-Colonel Richard Asbury; Dr Fred Beck, USAF History Support Center, Bolling AFB, DC; Colonel Ward Boyce, American Fighter Aces Museum, Mesa, Arizona; Jim Carlisle, USAF AFMPC, Randolf AFB, Texas; Robin E. Cookson, US National Archives, Maryland; Timothy J. Cronen, Smithsonian Institution, NASM, Washington, DC; Colonel Louis H. Cummings, USAF Historical Foundation, Andrews AFB, Maryland; Jeffrey L. Ethell; Garry L. Fry, for allowing me access to his records and for his friendly advice; William E. Howard, former 100th BG pilot; James H. Kitchens III, USAF Historical Research Agency, Maxwell AFB, Alabama; Rebecca Lentz Collier, US National Archives, Washington, DC; and Major Joe T. Reams, USAF Historical Research Agency, Maxwell AFB. Finally, special thanks go to Peter Burton and Roderick Dymott of Arms & Armour Press, who both showed surprising confidence in this project, and to Roger Chesneau, for turning my words into this book.

A.W.

INTRODUCTION

Throughout mankind's unending commitment to, and long fascination with, warfare, many actions during the ages have stood as memorials to the ultimate in courage and sacrifice. When examined in retrospect, how such actions are judged depends very much on the side with which one's alliances lie. Deeds of self-sacrifice can be described simultaneously as displaying both courage and stupidity—even a misguided fanaticism.

In the all too numerous conflicts which have touched the lands occupied by man, time and again examples can be found of the few standing fast against the many. In the ancient world, the courage of a small number of Spartan warriors, led by their king Leonidas, in defending the strategic pass of Thermopylae in 480 BC against the greater numerical strength of a Persian army became a symbol of determined resistance. By an act of self-sacrifice these troops provided a valuable breathing space, which facilitated the successful evacuation of Athens, until that moment threatened by the invading Persian forces. By their refusal to yield to superior numbers and by their disciplined resistance, the warriors of Sparta provided the standard against which all future defending forces would be judged.

At Mesada in AD 73 the resistance of a Jewish fortress besieged by a large formation from the all-conquering legions of Rome provides an example of the refusal to yield to an army of occupation. Even in the knowledge that their resistance was doomed to failure, the occupants of Mesada remained immovable. After two years of siege, with the Roman forces about to breach the walls of their fortress, over 960 men, women and children committed suicide rather than relinquish their independence to Rome.

In examining the worldwide conflict of 1939–45 it is the kamikaze pilots of Imperial Japan which are most often used to illustrate such ultimate actions. However, whilst these pilots were following an ancient military code which taught that such actions were right and proper, it is also possible to make a comparison with the actions of Royal Air Force pilots. Such pilots flying as a part of the Advanced Air Striking Force who flew their outclassed Fairey Battles against the Sedan bridges in May 1940, and even Fighter Command's daring 'Few' who protected the skies over Britain in later months, could be judged to have displayed similar courage and self-sacrifice. During the final frantic weeks of the dying Third Reich a comparable, though much less well documented, commitment was made by young pilots of the *Luftwaffe*.

By September 1944 Allied forces were exerting what was to prove fatal pressure in their stranglehold of the Reich. Within the increasingly desperate remains of the Third Reich many proposals were considered by German commanders—plans which would stop or even repel the invading enemy forces. Whilst facing the unending onslaught from the feared Soviets in the East, the Reich was being forced to endure a ceaseless bombardment by the aircraft of both the RAF and the United States Army Air Forces, whose aircraft roamed at the head of the relentlessly advancing Allied formations.

The once mighty *Luftwaffe* had been reduced by both combat attrition and bombardment to a mere shadow of its former glory. With the seemingly invincible Allied air forces visible daily over what remained of the Reich, civilians and ground forces alike had come to view the remnants of *Reichsmarschall* Göring's force, especially the fighters of the *Jagdwaffe*, with distaste and scorn. The promise of 'wonder weapons' offered the only encouragement to those still involved in the daily battle of survival. Plans for counter-attacks or a concentration of forces to repel these invaders existed in profusion, but all such hopes depended on one vital ingredient—a *Luftwaffe* force able to gain the upper hand over its adversaries.

To both members of the armed forces and their leaders, a means to gain this vital control did exist: the *Luftwaffe*'s jet aircraft. What was needed was a breathing space in which this force could be built, strengthened and fully trained. Having endured over six years of continued combat, the *Luftwaffe* was left with few experienced leaders. Those who had survived through exceptional skill and excessive good fortune would be required to lead any rebuilt force. It was therefore essential that the proposals being drafted allowed this nucleus to pass on their knowledge.

How could this be accomplished, whilst still providing the means to stop the Allied air bombardment and gain some form of air superiority? To complicate matters further the *Luftwaffe* suffered two further shortages, firstly of fuel and secondly of ammunition. It was therefore clear that any renewed attempt to use the *Jagdwaffe* had to rely upon action of a very limited scale.

This limitation ruled out any attempt to remove the threat from Allied fighter-bombers and medium bombers based on the European mainland. Such an operation, '*Bodenplatte*'(Baseplate), had been attempted on 1 January 1945 and resulted in a carefully collected fighter force being wasted in a costly ground-attack mission. The requirements for a further series of operations against the Allies' forward air bases could not be met within the required time scale. Whilst the *Jagdwaffe* was able to offer some protection to its own bases, greatly enhanced by still effective flak units, it was incapable of turning its surviving *Geschwader* to offensive operations. The aircraft from both the US Ninth Air Force and the RAF's 2nd Tactical Air Force would have to be allowed to continue their operations until the *Jagdwaffe* was able to turn its jets against them.

The options had therefore become limited to some form of small-scale operation, requiring limited quantities of fuel and weapons and reliant upon relatively inexperienced air crews. The target would have to be concentrated, the results obtained from, if possible, a single mission. Highly developed fighter tactics would not be essential and extended combat was to be avoided

The spring skies over Europe were to provide the inspiration. Daily the massed formations of four-engine Eighth Air Force bombers, the hated *Viermöte*, left their trails as they flew on towards targets within the remaining German-controlled areas. Flying virtually unchallenged, this force was able to destroy production facilities and supply networks essential to future plans. If the intruding aircraft could be stopped, it would be possible to carry out the required rebuilding and the transportation system could be used to move the essential supplies.

An attack upon one such Eighth Air Force raid seemed to offer a large target, would require only a single operation and would provide a highly visible success. What remained uncertain was the means by which this could be accomplished, while to ensure some form of survival for the remaining forces it had to be carried out at the earliest opportunity.

1. THE OPPOSITION

The *Luftwaffe* of 1945 was not the seemingly invincible force with which Adolf Hitler launched his *Blitzkreig* upon Europe in 1939. As an essential part of the Reich's war machine, it had been blooded over Spain during the Civil War, and many of the tactics and weapons with which it would fight the forthcoming conflict had been tried and tested in support of General Franco's forces.

Having grown from a strength of 1,100 officers and 17,000 men in 1935, by 1939 the *Luftwaffe* had expanded to some 15,000 officers and 370,000 men. This expansion, and the demands placed upon the service, led to a lack of cohesion in decision-making, planning and what has been called 'strategic competence'. Although those in command of the force were often quick to seek the required expertise in the various disciplines required within a modern air force, the circumstances of its birth and its formative years were to lead to the *Luftwaffe* possessing a collection of experts in their own limited fields, with limited vision. According to Murray, '[The *Luftwaffe*] officer corps showed a lack of understanding of the larger issues involving the interrelation between air power and national strategy, defects which may indeed have been nothing less than fatal.'

Following the death in 1936 of *General* Walther Wever, the *Luftwaffe's* first Chief of Staff (and an officer whose First World War service had led to his being considered as a possible Army Commander-in-Chief prior to his appointment in 1937), the force was led by a succession of officers who lacked the vision and strategic insight required to command such a vital organization. Despite the image conveyed to the rest of the world, the *Luftwaffe* of 1939 was already limited to reactive operations, missions which were forced upon it by daily political demands and increasingly by urgent operational requirements.

Having itself been convinced by the effectiveness and decisiveness of its *Blitzkreig* tactics, the *Luftwaffe* was ill-prepared for a lengthy period of combat. With the small-scale production plans of 1939 behind schedule and with a limited number of trained air crews, its leadership believed that both German technical expertise and the qualitative superiority of its equipment would prove more than enough to cope quickly with any enemy it encountered. For an air force finding itself required to support the operations of a leader with Europe-wide or even world-wide ambitions, these deficiencies would prove fatal. The scale of the conflict ensured that the *Luftwaffe* of 1939 faced a steady attrition, resulting in a decline in both its numerical superiority and also in its combat capability.

Many of those involved in the *Luftwaffe* tried as best they could to awaken their leaders to the dangers about to descend upon them. In 1943 the growth of the combined Allied bomber forces was clearly understood by many to be the greatest danger facing Germany, but when in October 1943 *Generalfeldmarschall* Milch attempted to build up fighter strength in order to protect the Reich he was severely criticized by *Reichsmarschall* Göring, who even went so far as to dismiss the forecast build-up in USAAF strength as being totally fanciful and beyond American industrial capacity. When Milch attempted to carry his concern to his *Führer* he was again rebuffed: both senior men refused to accept that defence demanded any urgent attention. At a time when the USAAF were still learning the lessons of long-range operations and had yet to find their perfect escort fighter, the *Luftwaffe* found itself constantly hindered by its commanders. In an 'Ultra' transmission intercepted in October 1943, the *Reichsmarschall* personally criticized what he saw as a wasteful experiment being carried out by fighter units. The measure he referred to was the introduction of drop tanks, which allowed the fighters to range further in their battle against the bombers. These tanks were being jettisoned before combat, and Göring saw this as an example of extravagance and deserving of a personal reproach. It is true that by 1943 Göring had already begun his slide from power and his detachment from the realities facing Germany. The bold fighter ace of 1918 was finding it difficult to come to terms with the technical side of modern warfare and to accept the growing costs of Hitler's war. In his account of events, Albert Speer records that he had already begun to dismiss the value of the *Reichsmarschall*: 'Göring had relapsed into his lethargy, and for good. He did not wake up again until he was on trial in Nuremberg.'

By the summer of 1944 the *Luftwaffe*, designed to support the operations of an offensive Panzer force, had been placed on the defensive. With the Allied foothold in Normandy, it was now required to fight a war on four fronts: the skies over Normandy, the Mediterranean, the Eastern Front and, increasingly, the skies over the Reich.

Despite the increasing demands for protection from both industry and the Fatherland itself, Hitler demanded that a offensive bomber capability be retained. The maintenance of this force, together with a desire to expand its capabilities, placed a growing strain upon the finite resources available. However, even with the planned introduction of revolutionary aircraft types, it is doubtful if the bomber force, the *Kampfgruppen*, would have been able to achieve any form of strategic victory. With Allied forces holding such a dominant position in the skies over Europe, to rebuild the bomber force would have required a *Luftwaffe* able to achieve some measure of air superiority to remove the constant threat imposed by roving Allied fighters and bombers. It is clear that, even to establish a force able to achieve the hoped-for retaliation, a strong and sizable defensive fighter force was demanded. Not until September 1944, when the desperate fuel shortages became impossible to ignore, did Hitler finally concede that the bomber force should be replaced as the most urgent priority. Ultimately it was not to be the requirements of offering protection to his borders or even defending his cities which forced Hitler to alter his priorities. It was instead a belated realization of the effect of the Allied bombing offensive upon the Reich's vital industry and its transportation infrastructure.

When called upon, the *Luftwaffe* was unable to provide a defensive force capable of meeting the now critical requirements of its leaders. Its fighters were already attempting to protect too large an area with too few resources. The scale of operations and the relentless campaign had forced the *Luftwaffe* to depend upon the proven fighters: in order to maintain a force to face the continued Allied offensive, the fighter units had no breathing space to develop and then introduce new types. This led to the *Jagdwaffe* remaining a force equipped with the Focke-Wulf Fw 190 and Messerschmitt Bf 109, the latter a type which had reached the limits of its development. By 1943 this had led to a position where the Allies, even the Soviet Union, had caught up and overtaken the *Luftwaffe* in standards of equipment and levels of trained crews.

When this inadequacy became apparent, it brought upon the leadership of the *Luftwaffe* the full wrath of an enraged Hitler. Summoned to a meeting on 3 September 1944, *General der Flieger* Werner Kreipe, the successor to *Generaloberst* Korton, was forced to endure a torrent of abuse from his *Führer*, who dismissed all those in the *Luftwaffe* whom he considered had shown an inability to defend the country. The meeting ended with the announcement that henceforth all *Luftwaffe* units, except those equipped with the new jets, were to be disbanded. The defence of the Reich from that point forward was to be concentrated upon a flak force, which was to be tripled in size. Although this pronouncement was never carried through, it illustrates the tightrope walked daily by those who, in theory at least, had the task of commanding the *Luftwaffe*. Failure in the eyes of Hitler could not be excused, and, as many were to find to their cost, that failure carried a very high price. For the *Luftwaffe*, already operating with minimal stockpiles of fuel, the failure to provide Hitler with the victories he demanded also resulted in the force having to compete for continued supplies. With the Panzer armies occupying pride of place, the *Luftwaffe*, which had once operated so closely with the Army, was forced to curtail even the reconnaissance flights which were so vital to ground operations.

To understand how the *Luftwaffe*, especially the *Jagdwaffe* fighter force, found itself in such a grave position it is necessary to examine the forces it was required to operate against. Although the battles fought against Polish,

Dutch and French forces cannot be ignored, it was to be the combat operations in what became daily battles of attrition with the Royal Air Force and the United States Army Air Forces which determined its ultimate fate. It is important to remember that, even by the end of 1939, the battles had started to extract a considerable cost. Both the scale of the war which erupted and the increasing levels of attrition reduced any advantages that may have existedin the *Luftwaffe's* technical expertise and in the qualitative superiority of its aircraft. Valuable pilots and vital aircraft were lost during the initial phase of operations in Europe. Even more importantly, the support infrastructure essential to replace such losses was ill-prepared for the demands now placed upon it by war.

The Royal Air Force

Of all the battles fought by the *Luftwaffe* during the period 1939–45, its fight against the bombers, launched from the airfields of England, was to prove the most crucial to the survival of the Adolf Hitler's 'Thousand-Year Reich'. Having gone to war in 1939 with a bomber arm that was intended to act as its principle weapon, the Royal Air Force in fact possessed a force which quickly proved to be inadequate for the massive task now required of it. In its first operation of the war, Bomber Command launched 29 aircraft, a mix force of twin-engine Bristol Blenheims and Vickers Wellingtons, in a daylight raid against German shipping in Wilhelmshaven harbour. Only fifteen of these aircraft found their intended target, and although two ships were damaged seven of the bombers were shot down.

Despite the initial limitations imposed by both its aircraft and its existing navigation systems, Bomber Command was by May 1940 at last able to strike back at Germany. Application of the theory of strategic bombing had until then been restricted by the British War Cabinet. In a desperate attempt to limit the scale of the European conflict, both France and the United States had requested that Britain mount no attacks against German land targets. Not until Hitler launched his attack upon the West on 10 May was the RAF finally freed from its shackles.

During the inter-war years the RAF had been built upon the principal that any future war would be won by the bomber. The introduction of monoplane designs in the 1930s reinforced the idea that a fast bomber could not be stopped by defending fighters. It was this thinking that was to lead to the almost fatal shortages of fighter aircraft for the defence of Britain. The designs that were in service—the Supermarine Spitfire, Hawker Hurricane and Boulton-Paul Defiant—were short-range defensive aircraft, while the accepted invincibility of the bombers meant that their own missions were to be flown unescorted. Early attacks against German naval targets inflicted heavy losses upon Bomber Command and quickly led to the realization that unescorted daylight raids were not practical.

The alternative was to continue the nocturnal raids which until that time had been restricted to dropping propaganda leaflets over German cities. On the night of 15/16 May a force of 99 bombers, consisting of Vickers Wellingtons, Armstrong Whitworth Whitleys and Handley Page Hampdens, was at last unleashed to attack strategic targets in the industrial Ruhr. However, with only 30 of the crews claiming to have identified their assigned targets, it proved to be an insubstantial beginning to the bombing campaign against Germany.

The failings of the initial RAF attacks to inflict the expected damage, on both material and morale, was not fully realized until 1941. These failings resulted from the problems experienced by Bomber Command crews in finding the intended targets and hitting them both accurately and decisively, together with an unexpectedly strong defence from the *Luftwaffe*'s flak units. Advances in technology would eventually provide the solutions to many of the RAF's navigational difficulties, and the introduction of the first true 'heavy' bombers would allow Bomber Command to inflict the size of blows it considered necessary. The more capable aircraft began to make their mark on the evening of 12 March 1941, when a force of Avro Manchesters and Handley Page Halifaxes was dispatched to Hamburg. However, the period 1939–41 found Bomber Command ill-prepared for the task expected of it: the missions were seemingly flown by a group of individuals using their own methods of attacking the same target. According to Middlebrook, 'There was an air of amateurism and individuality about these raids that a bomber-crew member of 1944 or 1945 would find hard to imagine.'

The solution to Bomber Command's failing fortunes was to be found not only through advances provided by technology but also because of the efforts of one man, Air Chief Marshal Sir Arthur Harris. On 22 February 1942 Harris was appointed as Air Officer Commanding-in-Chief of Bomber Command, a post he was to hold until the end of hostilities. He was to pursue his work with an almost fanatical purpose.

By early 1943, under Harris's protective eye, RAF Bomber Command had grown by a massive proportion. It now possessed almost 700 four-engine bombers, capable of reaching any target in Germany. Its main weapons were the Avro Lancaster and Handley Page Halifax, forming the main force together with the Short Stirling. However, the fast twin-engine bomber was destined to retain a central role in Bomber Command, which in the form of the magnificent de Havilland Mosquito possessed a extremely capable and versatile aircraft. New techniques necessary to attack targets successfully had also been introduced. Although the RAF continued to develop precision bombing techniques, the limitations in navigation and target identification had led to the adoption of less demanding area-bombing. Raids were now planned with meticulous care, the bombers being concentrated over their target in an attempt to swamp the defenders and inflict the maximum amount of damage. In March 1943 Bomber Command began a period later called its Main Offensive against Germany. Having built his force, Air Chief Marshal Harris was allowed to launch a campaign aimed at the destruction of German industry and the resistance of the German people. Beginning in May 1943, this campaign included phases which later became known as the Battle of the Ruhr, the Battle of Hamburg and the Battle of Berlin. Harris's ultimate goal was stated in unambiguous fashion in a letter of December 1943 when he wrote to the Air Ministry that 'The Lancaster force alone should be sufficient, but only just sufficient, to produce in Germany by 1 April 1944 a state of devastation in which surrender is inevitable.'

The Air Chief Marshal's bold ambition was not to be achieved, despite the best efforts and sacrifice of Bomber Command's crews. In April 1944 the war had yet to reach its peak: the European conflict was destined to continue for a over a year. Victory was to require the liberation of Europe by Allied ground forces, forced to fight for every inch of rubble which by then covered much of the Continent. Bomber Command was to be in almost continuous operation until 2 May 1945, when 125 Mosquitos attacked their very last targets in Kiel. Despite the growth of Bomber Command during the campaign, final victory was to require further developments in the employment of air power, achieved with a combined bomber force, of a scale unimaginable in 1939, consisting of RAF Bomber Command together with the USAAF.

The United States Army Air Forces
As in Britain during the inter-war years, the theory of strategic bombing had been readily adopted in the United States. This resulted from a desire to possess a far reaching and invincible bomber force. However, the United States Army Air Forces had adopted an alternative role for their aircraft. Rather than directly attacking civilian targets, the role of the USAAF was driven by a desire to achieve victory whist inflicting the minimum damage upon civilian targets. It was thought that a small force of advanced bombers could be employed with precision to strike at essential industrial targets. This would cripple an enemy and lead in turn to the collapse of civilian morale. As a form of self-protection, the high-flying bombers were to attack in tight formations, able to concentrate their bombs upon a target and their defensive weapons upon any enemy fighters. Incorporating the latest technology of the day, the bombers were to fly in daylight in order to increase their ability to identify the selected targets.

By 1937 the USAAF possessed the aircraft and the technology capable of meeting these requirements: the Boeing B-17, equipped with the Norden bomb sight, was to become its principle offensive weapon. It was assumed that the bombers would be able to fly above the enemy defences, outside the reach of defending fighters, and achieve almost surgical accuracy with their bombs. Again, it was to be the grim reality of war which forced the USAAF to rethink this policy—a war which could not have been imagined by the pre-war planners.

The entry into the war by the United States in December 1941 enabled a military and industrial capacity on a massive scale to be harnessed in support of the Allied cause. On the same day that Arthur Harris assumed control of Bomber Command, 22 February 1942, the initial elements of the US VIII Bomber Command arrived in England. Under the command of Major-General Carl A. Spaatz, the advance party established the necessary administrative systems to support the combat elements which were to follow. The first combat aircraft to arrive in Britain was a B-17E, flown over 3,000 miles from Maine via Greenland and Iceland to Prestwick in Scotland. The first mission by crews from the VIIIth was not, however, to be flown in either the B-17 or its stable-mate the Consolidated B-24 Liberator. On 4 July 1942 six American crews joined the RAF's No 226 Squadron and flew in their Douglas Bostons to attack *Luftwaffe* airfields in the Low Countries.

The first true USAAF raid was to be carried out the following month. To allow crews some support during the mission, it was decided to provide an RAF escort, in the form of Spitfires. Whilst not intended to be a feature of future raids, this support stemmed from Bomber Command's hard-earned experience and should perhaps have served as a warning to Spaatz and his commanders of the ultimate fate of USAAF operations. On 17 August 1942 a token force of eleven B-17Es attacked the Rouen-Sotteville marshalling yards, a short distance inland from the French coast. Whilst the value of this raid was perhaps limited, it served to mark the official combat début of American forces. By January 1943 these forces had grown in size and experience so that they were at last ready to begin their raids upon Germany.

On 27 January over 60 bombers were launched against targets along the River Weser, but, encountering bad weather en route, the aircraft were forced to divert to their secondary target, Wilhelmshaven. Already wary of German defences, the US crews followed a route across the North Sea selected to avoid overflying the European mainland. On this occasion, however, even over the target area only a light flak defence was encountered, and a series of uncoordinated attacks by enemy fighters resulted in the loss of only three Fortresses. This first raid on Germany was followed by a series of missions during which the USAAF began to suffer a growing number of losses as the defending fighters established tactics to combat its formations. In addition, the selection of more important targets resulted in the crews being forced to fly through more heavily defended flak zones.

A contributing factor which was to shape the role of the Eighth Air Force was the Casablanca Conference, a series of meetings held by the Allied leadership in January 1943. These were intended to provide Britain and America with a blueprint for the defeat of Hitler. Under extreme pressure from Stalin, who called for the opening of a second front in Europe by the spring of

1943, it was decided that Allied forces based in England would launch an invasion of the European continent 'as soon as practicable'. Both Churchill and Roosevelt had decided that the earliest possible date for this invasion would be August 1943, after the success of operations in Tunisia and Sicily and even then only after extensive cross-Channel operations to prepare the way for the Allied invasion forces. An angry Stalin, not pleased by the decisions of Casablanca, felt that he that was fighting Hitler alone and that Britain and America were not prepared to match the sacrifices being made by Russia.

For the RAF and USAAF the sacrifices were only just beginning. Following Casablanca the bomber forces were provided with a list of priority targets which were deemed essential to achieve the eventual goal of a return to the mainland of Europe. To enable the targets to be defeated in the required time, a Combined Bomber Offensive was officially launched in June 1943 with the issue of the 'Point Blank' directive. As 'Point Blank' provided the Eighth Air Force with a mission to attack German aircraft manufacturing plants and their associated component industries, it was perhaps inevitable that the bombers would encounter a *Luftwaffe* attempting to protect these targets. With the list also including rubber and ball-bearing factories, the bombers would be forced to run the gauntlet of defending forces on longer-ranging missions to targets well protected by both ground-based flak units and the *Jagdwaffe*. Whilst RAF Bomber Command was embarked upon its nocturnal mission stalked by an unseen enemy, the crews of the Eighth Air Force were to face their opponents in the daylight hours with all the associated horrors of the battle.

The missions launched by the Eighth Air Force led to a growing number of encounters with the *Jagdwaffe*, which began to bring into question the USAAF's policy of flying self-defending bomber formations. The aircraft were now within range of the defending fighters for longer and longer periods, and bomber casualties began to escalate.

It was the scale of these mounting costs during the Eighth Air Force's operations of 1943 which sowed a seed of doubt in the minds of many involved in the campaign. Despite the initial warnings given by the RAF, who had already attempted daylight missions, it proved necessary for the USAAF to experience the realities of such missions and re-learn the same hard facts. Without a strong escort, even heavily armed bombers such as the B-17 were proving incapable of withstanding a determined and continued attack by opposing fighters. The missions to which the Eighth Air Force were committed demanded a fighter escort capable of providing protection to and from the targets, which often lay at the furthest corners of the Reich. A long-range fighter did exist and was indeed in service, but this aircraft, the Lockheed P-38 Lightning, had not been designed for the conditions encountered in the skies over Europe, its twin engines and fuel systems proving incapable of meeting operational demands. With the limits of the P-38 becoming apparent, and with greater success for the type being found in other roles and other theatres, a new fighter arrived in England to attempt the escort mission. The Republic P-47 Thunderbolt soon revealed its own shortcomings: a large and heavy aircraft, it was further handicapped by the additional weight of external tanks, essential to boost its range to the German border. The Thunderbolt would prove an outstanding and rugged aircraft in a variety of roles, but its maximum range as an escort fighter left a dangerous gap from the German border to the bombers' targets. With the P-38 the only available aircraft possessing the range required but unable to meet the demands of operations, the bombers would be alone for a very dangerous flight.

The extent of this deficiency was revealed in a most brutal fashion during the raid, on 17 August 1943, upon targets at Schweinfurt and Regensburg. When the escorting P-47s turned back, the B-17s were to endure an unprecedented series of attacks en route to their targets. By the time the final survivors landed back at their bases in England the total losses had been calculated—60 B-17s, with a further 168 suffering varying degrees of damage, the air crew fatalities from this mission alone amounting to 552. Such a cost could not be sustained by the American military and political leadership, and even if the required damage was being inflicted upon the targets, the aircraft losses replaced by industry and the air crews replaced by the training programmes, public opinion would quickly have turned against a campaign which exacted such a high price for victory. This first raid against the vital ball-bearing plants at Schweinfurt/Regensburg was to be followed by further severe blows: on 10 October 30 B-17s were lost during a raid on Münster, and a further 60 fell when the Eighth Air Force again returned to Schweinfurt on 14 October.

As the American leadership considered the future of long-range missions, the Eighth Air Force was to be allowed a fortunate breathing space by operational demands and was able to recover from the shock inflicted by these three raids. As a necessary part of the build-up to the invasion of Europe, the list of targets for the end of 1943 was concentrated in France and the Low Countries. Although the *Luftwaffe* defences had inflicted a major defeat upon the USAAF, it was the requirements of invasion planning and also the deteriorating weather over Europe during the winter of 1943/44 which led to the absence of the USAAF from the skies over Germany. When the Eighth Air Force bombers were freed from their supporting role and again turned against their primary industrial targets, they at last possessed the means to mount successful raids and to exact their revenge upon the *Jagdwaffe*.

In August 1943 command of the Eighth Air Force fighter force passed to General William Kepner, a supporter of single-engine, long-range fighters who refused to believe that the range of the P-47 could not be surpassed. Kepner was to be proved correct. Experiments carried out by the North

American Aviation company with its latest product resulted in a fighter which was to become as synonymous with USAAF operations as the Supermarine Spitfire had become with the RAF's. Originally designed and operated as a low-level fighter and fighter-bomber, the North American P-51 Mustang had been fitted with a Rolls-Royce Merlin to examine the improvements offered by this powerful engine. The resulting performance, with the Merlin engine coupled to the Mustang's aerodynamically advanced airframe, produced a fighter capable of enduring an $8^1/_2$-hour escort mission yet retaining the performance to combat any opposing fighters encountered. With growing official support and an urgent requirement existing in Europe, the new aircraft was seen as the ideal type to equip the Eighth Air Force fighter groups.

By June 1943 the P-51B was being rolled out of factories in California, to be followed in August by the first P-51C from Texas. It was decided that the first unit to re-equip with the new type would be the 354th Fighter Group, who would be responsible for establishing the capabilities of the P-51. Unable to afford a lengthy period of trials and training in America, the 354th FG would receive their new aircraft in England. As could be expected by a decision which resulted by the P-51 being 'thrown in at the deep end', the 354th FG experienced many problems with its new mounts. Whilst the airframe was advanced, the armament of four 0.50 Browning machine guns proved lightweight and the freezing conditions found at altitude over Europe producing frequent jamming. In addition, as an inexperienced group the 354th FG was perhaps not best placed to determine the full potential of the P-51. A new supporter for the P-51 was found in the leader of the combat-proven 4th FG.

Already experienced in fighter operations, having served with the RAF as a part of the original Eagle Squadron, Lieutenant-Colonel Don Blakeslee had become frustrated by the heavyweight P-47 which equipped the 4th FG. He was able to obtain secondment to the 354th FG to gain experience at first hand prior to his own unit receiving the new fighter. Before his return to the 4th FG Blakeslee flew seven missions in the P-51, which included a 960-mile round trip to Kiel on 13 December 1943, when 41 P-51s joined with P-47s and P-38s to create an escort force of 394 fighters. It was these early missions which led to praise from experienced pilots like Blakeslee, who had quickly become convinced of the potential offered by the P-51. This in turn was to lead General Kepner to demand priority in deliveries of the new fighter.

Whilst the P-47 remained the predominant type in service with Eighth Air Force fighter groups during the early months of 1944, by May the P-51 was equipping fifteen fighter groups. Improvements to both the P-38 and P-47 allowed each of these types to continue to give valuable service, the latter type being suited to providing cover for the bombers on the return leg of their long flights. However, just as the B-17 was destined to be the dominant bomber over the equally capable B-24, the long-legged P-51 was to become the fighter of choice amongst the Eighth Air Force units. As combat experience led to the early P-51B and C being replaced on the production lines by the more capable P-51D, the fighter groups found their ideal mount and the bombers their ideal protector. For the *Luftwaffe*, however, the P-51 represented a previously unimagined adversary: no longer would the skies within the borders of Germany be the undisturbed hunting grounds of German fighters, and no longer could they expect to attack the bomber formations and remain free from the attentions of USAAF fighters.

With Allied troops firmly established in France and advancing towards the Reich, the Eighth Air Force bombers returned to their targets in Germany. Their raids began to exert the required pressure upon German industry, especially the critical oil production facilities. In opposing these raids the *Jagdwaffe* was faced with the better armed B-17G and B-24G/H bombers and their escorts of P-51s, which increasingly gained the upper hand in their encounters. As the bombers continued to reach their targets, the P-51s began to encounter fewer German fighters as the *Jagdwaffe* was forced to conserve its diminishing resources. When it was found that the bombers required fewer escorts the P-51s were then unleashed, allowed to roam further afield in search of their prey. For the *Jagdwaffe* even the skies above its own bases were to become battlefields. The escorts had themselves been able to become the hunters.

In the campaign carried out by RAF Bomber Command and the USAAF Eighth Air Force both air arms experienced massive losses. While the bold claims made by bomber leaders in the early stages of the campaign were not to be achieved, the combined forces were able to weaken Germany to such a degree that victory for the Allies was inevitable. During post-war interrogation Erhard Milch was to tell his British captors that it was the USAAF daylight raids which had defeated Germany, as these raids had concentrated upon transportation and oil targets. However he was qualified this statement by saying, 'The British inflicted grievous and bloody injuries on us—but the Americans shot us in the heart.'[1]

It was the combined bomber formations which had carried the war the very heart of the Reich and struck the fatal blows. Had the offensive against Germany been limited to the Bomber Command's nocturnal battles, it is probable that the *Luftwaffe*'s night fighters, the *Nachtjägerverbände*, would have been able to defend the Reich. Even at the very end of the war in Europe, this force continued to represent a formidable foe. However, when combined with the more equal daylight battles, the sheer numerical strength of the Allies, supported by what seemed infinite resources, began to exert unyielding pressure.

---

[1]Irving, David, *The Rise and Fall of the Luftwaffe*, Purnell Book Services, p. 297.

The cost to the bomber crews flying by both day and night against targets defended by *Luftwaffe* fighter and flak units was to be high. For RAF Bomber Command the air crew losses amounted to 55,573, which equates to 12 per cent of the total British Empire and Commonwealth losses. The USAAF, whose campaign covered a shorter time period, suffered 3,030 losses. In the post-war period the bomber offensive has become the subject of much debate. The morality of an offensive which cost the lives of an estimated 600,000 German civilians has been called into question, and the leaders, especially Sir Arthur Harris, have become figures of controversy. What must be remembered is that, until the combined Allied powers were able to return to the European mainland, the bombers alone were in a position to take the fight to within Hitler's Third Reich. Even after June 1944 the Allied bombers were still required to destroy the ability of German forces to defend themselves and to deny them the opportunity to reinforce those front-line forces facing the advancing Allied ground armies. The RAF and USAAF provided the means to mount the vital campaign in the West which had been demanded by Stalin. They forced Germany to allocate resources for her defence whilst also inflicting damage to her industrial capacity which would ultimately bring an Allied victory that much nearer.

2. *GENERAL* GALLAND AND *DER GROSSE SCHLAG*

By late 1944 the *Luftwaffe* fighter force had lost its once prominent position. Despite facing massive opposition, the *Jagdwaffe* had been required to defeat both the daylight and nocturnal bombers. In failing to counter this threat, both Göring and his *Luftwaffe* lost their prestige. Whilst Göring was increasingly unable to come to terms with this rejection, the officers and crews within the *Luftwaffe* continued the fight. It was hoped that technical breakthroughs such as jet and rocket fighters, together with advanced armaments including air-to-air missiles, would ultimately counter the decline in both numbers and experience within the fighter force.

What was essential for the survival of the remaining force was that it be employed to the best possible effect. The leaders of the fighter force had formed their own plans during 1944, intending to employ their units in the most effective way. Under *General* Adolf Galland these proposals had resulted in the planned *Grosse Schlag* (Great Blow). By carefully building fighter reserves, Galland intended to assemble a force of over 3,500 aircraft. His proposal was to use this force against the USAAF bombers. Waves of fighters were to attack a raid during the length of its flight over Europe. Lost or damaged aircraft attempting to find safety in Sweden or Switzerland were to be picked off by a screen of patrolling night fighters. In preparing these plans Galland estimated that between 400 and 500 bombers could be destroyed. Such an aim could not be achieved without losses. The ever-present Allied fighter escorts and the defensive firepower of the massed bomber formations were expected to extract a cost of up to 400 *Luftwaffe* fighters and perhaps as many as 150 pilots.

Central to these plans would be the deadly jet fighter, the Messerschmitt 262. During November 1944 Galland approached his close friend *Oberst* Johannes Steinhoff, then commanding the fledgeling jet unit *JG 7*. After discussing his plans the senior officer then asked that an attack be prepared as a demonstration of a large-scale Me 262 operation. However, at this stage Steinhoff was forced to admit that his unit had insufficient strength to mount such a demonstration. As with the formation of any new organization, *JG 7* had encountered numerous difficulties in its attempt to become operational. In addition, having finally received the new jets, Steinhoff and his staff had yet to devise the best tactics for the employment of their revolutionary fighters; this problem was to remain with the jet force for the duration of its existence.

While still offering a continued resistance to the USAAF, Galland's force was trained and its plans were refined. The required reserve of aircraft and fuel was steadily built up, and by the end of November 1944 Galland awaited only favourable weather. It had been decided that the jets of *JG 7* would strike first, their high-speed attacks serving to scatter the escorts and to shake up the USAAF formations, allowing the conventional *Jagdwaffe* fighters which followed to then hit the broken bomber boxes. These plans had advanced to the stage where *Oberst* Steinhoff had selected suitable forward bases for the jets in the area north of Dortmund, straddling the frequently used bomber routes. However, the fortune of the fighter force was to be decided not by the plans of *General* Galland but by those of the *Luftwaffe* High Command (*Oberkommando der Luftwaffe*) and ultimately those of Adolf Hitler.

The *Luftwaffe* was viewed as nothing more than a force to support ground operations, and Galland's reserve was to be squandered in a very costly operation. As November turned to December the force earmarked for the 'Great Blow' was ordered to prepare for operations in support of a new ground offensive planned for the Western Front. Galland and his staff were dismayed to discover that their fighter pilots and aircraft, carefully nurtured for a massed attack on a USAAF daylight raid, were to be employed in a role for which they were ill-prepared—as a ground attack force against Allied airfields in Holland and Belgium.

The use of *General* Galland's fighter force during *'Bodenplatte'*, a four-hour operation which took place on 1 January 1945, had many consequences. The raids themselves had little lasting effect upon the Allied air forces: fewer aircraft than expected were damaged or destroyed, and such losses were easy to replace. As a result of the action, over 150 *Luftwaffe* pilots were killed or reported as missing, a total which included not only the inexperienced 'new growth' but also irreplaceable *Staffel* and *Gruppe* leaders. The entire Ardennes ground offensive during the harsh winter of 1944/45 was to fail and the cost to the *Jagdwaffe* for supporting the offensive was eventually to total some 700 pilots. The manner in which the *Jagdwaffe* had been employed was to be a major contributing factor to the so called 'Mutiny of Aces', a meeting held on 22 January (appropriately in a hunting lodge) which was attended by, amongst others, *Oberste* Hermann Graf, Günther Lützow, Günther von Maltzahn, Gustav Rödel, 'Macki' Steinhoff and 'Hannes' Trautloft, and *General* Adolf Galland. This in turn led to the fall from grace of Galland and his supporters—yet a further blow to the declining fortunes of the *Luftwaffe*.

With the existing leadership of the *Jagdwaffe* now in disgrace, others in a position to gain the ear of *Reichsmarschall* Göring were able to advance their own proposals. One such proposal had been prepared as early as September 1944 by Oberst Hajo Herrmann, but, despite support from *Generalmajor* Peltz, the officer responsible for the remaining bomber force and commander of

Jagdkorps I, it had been consigned to one of the many files in *Luftwaffe* head-quarters. Having attracted the attention of the *Reichsmarschall* with his successful *'Wilde Sau'* force, Hajo Herrmann was at times able to move in the required circles. Whether Göring was able to foresee the ultimate outcome of *'Bodenplatte'* and the entire Ardennes offensive or whether he simply continued to grasp at any hope of restoring his position with Hitler, on 1 January he consulted Herrmann on his proposals. At last the latter had the chance to push forward his plans in person with his commander, and he grasped the opportunity.

3. DESPERATE MEASURES

As early as September 1943 the problems created by the growing spectre of Allied air attacks, together with a decrease in *Luftwaffe* resources to combat this threat, had led to a number of individuals offering what they viewed as ideal solutions. Having accepted that circumstances demanded that such proposals be considered, *Generalfeldmarschall* Erhard Milch requested that *Generaloberst* Günther Korten officially launch an investigation into the various plans and report upon their validity. What Korten quickly discovered was a range of solutions to a series of problems, both existing and theoretical. It appears that the circumstances which existed had inspired theories which whilst often radical were sometimes desperate.

Amongst the plans intended to create havoc within the massed formations of USAAF bombers was one from *Oberst* Edgar Petersen. Seeking a method of destroying the tightly packed boxes of bombers, Petersen suggested that war-weary Ju 88s be packed with explosive and flown into the heart of the American bombers, the explosive charge being detonated by a timed device activated by the pilot, who was to leap from his doomed aircraft at the last instant. The combination of a short time fuse, a last-second jump to safety and flying such a lethal bomb in a what would be very hostile environment would limit the survival expectations of the brave pilot. But it was this chance of survival, however slim, which ensured that such ideas received consideration within the *Luftwaffe*. With Milch able to satisfy himself that his crews were not to become a suicide force, he dutifully reported progress to the *Reichsmarschall*. At the end of his briefing Göring found that he had been presented with another possible opportunity to re-establish his prestige within the highest circles of the Reich. Open to such possibilities, as always, the *Reichsmarschall* requested that matters be pursued further and that *Generaloberst* Korten begin to compile a list of willing volunteers. Because of the increasingly desperate military situation the appearance of such plans coincided with a series of even more extreme proposals.

The secrecy which served to restrict details of the missions from those expected to volunteer was to enmesh the various plans together into a complex and potentially lethal web. One of the latest plans had been drafted by Hanna Reitsch, the darling of the Nazi propaganda machine, who had gained fame as Germany's greatest female pilot and, because of this fame, admittance into the highest of circles. With her acceptance by the Nazi hierarchy further enhanced by her relationship with *Generaloberst* Robert *Ritter* von

Greim of the *Luftwaffe*, Hanna Reitsch was able to ensure that her plans were viewed by those with influence. She was thus able to gain support for her proposals from *Generalmajor* Walter Storp, a respected officer now serving as *General der Kampfflieger*, who was in turn in a position to place such plans before those with the ultimate powers.

The plans drafted by Hanna Reitsch, with the assistance of *Hauptmann* Heinrich Lange, called for the establishment of a group of *'Selbstopfermänner'*, literally 'self-sacrifice men', who were to forfeit their lives for the glory of the Reich in a manner similar to the men of the Japanese Imperial forces. Initially the possible weapon for this force had not been established, but once again a further proposal would provide an ideal choice. Already famous for his daring exploits, *SS-Hauptsturmführer* Otto Skorzeny had turned his attention to the employment of aircraft against important ground targets. Skorzeny had suggested that a Fieseler Fi 103 (the *Vergeltungswaffe Eins*, or V-1) be modified to accommodate a small cockpit to allow a pilot to guide the bomb to its target with pin-point accuracy. By the summer of 1944 a programme was under way to develop and test these weapons under the designation *Reichenberg*. The *Selbstopfermänner* would provide the ideal crews.

With the exact details of the missions remaining secret, it was the names of *Hauptsturmführer* Skorzeny and *Flugkapitän* Reitsch which attracted the first volunteers. Unaware of the intended suicide role, the pilots came forward in the belief that they were volunteering for a special mission similar to Skorzeny's daring rescue of *Il Duce*, Benito Mussolini, from his captivity at Gran Sasso in September 1943. Even with the *Reichenberg* aircraft incorporating a jettisonable canopy to allow its pilot to jump clear, it is doubtful whether the volunteer had much hope of surviving his first mission in a flying bomb complete with an explosive warhead of 1,874lb heading for its target at speed in excess of 490mph.

With the burden of responsibility now having passed to *Generalmajor* Walter Storp, it appeared as if he were actively collecting such plans. He issued a requirement that this initial group of volunteer pilots be extended to division strength. In a bid for secrecy indicative of the increasing paranoia of the time, the force were to wear Army uniforms to disguise their intended airborne role. It was also suggested that before being committed to action the group was to be eventually christened with the fanciful title 'Hermann Göring Fighter Division'. With the continued decline in the fortunes of the *Reichsmarschall*, it was perhaps an unfortunate choice of name.

Within the *Luftwaffe*, so many of the proposals being drafted met with hostility as a matter of course that when such extreme measures as the *Selbstopfermänner* and Reichenberg plans were circulated they met with even more vehement opposition. Elements did exist within the service which would have seized upon such plans as a possible means to achieve favour with Hitler. However, any hopes that by ignoring these proposals their demise could be assured were to be dashed when they came to the attention of both *Dr* Josef Goebbels, who expressed an interest in the propaganda value of such a sacrificial force, and *Reichsführer SS* Heinrich Himmler, always open to ideas which would promote his desire for the premier position alongside Hitler.

Initially willing to participate in any action that would achieve military success, the volunteers now found themselves caught within a labyrinth of plot and counterplot, plan and proposal, which had been built and was being extended by individuals intent upon gaining their chance for advancement by fulfilling the increasingly desperate wishes of the Reich leadership. It was to prove fortunate for the pilots and air crews that, for them, a guide existed, prepared to risk his own career, perhaps his own life, to lead them from the darker reaches to which they had become confined. *Generalmajor* Storp, serving as the Inspector of Bombers, passed the administrative requirements of establishing the force to *Oberst* Werner Baumbach, one of his most able officers. Testing of the *Reichenberg* aircraft had already fallen under the control of the experimental unit *KG 200*, where Baumbach and his experienced officers were horrified to learn of the intended use of the volunteer force. As well as fighting against the proposals with every official means at his disposal, he also set in motion the means to disperse the volunteers already assembled at the earliest opportunity. While attempting to ensure that reason prevailed during the numerous discussions, Baumbach personally took the decision to cripple the suicide force. This was a courageous act; indeed, as Baumbach himself was later to comment, 'My refusal to collaborate in such idiocy, and even command it, was within an inch of costing me and my officers our heads.'

As the talking and planning proceeded for the operational employment of the *Reichenberg*, it was to be *Oberst* Baumbach's friendship with Albert Speer which would prove to be decisive. Following a particularly forbidding conference, Baumbach approached Speer in the hope that the Armaments Minister's influence with Adolf Hitler could be used to halt the seemingly unavoidable outcome of these plans. Proving to be as horrified by such proposals as the *Luftwaffe* officer, Albert Speer rushed with him to a hastily organized personal audience with Hitler.

Despite being a supporter of many extreme proposals, when faced with the considered reason of these two men Hitler was to reinforce his opinion that the German soldier must always have a chance of survival, no matter how small such a chance should be. Quick to act upon such a pronouncement—it was not uncommon for Hitler to reverse his decisions—*Oberst* Baumbach informed his officers at *KG 200* that the *Selbstopfermänner* were to be disbanded, upon orders from the *Führer*. With the means already in place to ensure that the force was scattered to the four winds, the distribution was carried out rapidly. It was to prove a fortunate action, as within days a fresh order arrived on Baumbach's desk requesting that *Reichsführer* Himmler be given full control of the *Selbstopfermänner*—without any further reference to Hitler. Having already effectively destroyed the force by his pre-emptive action, Baumbach was left with no option but to meet Himmler and again argue in favour of a more reasoned approach using available resources. One is left to imagine the sigh of relief undoubtedly breathed by Baumbach as he left the headquarters of the *Reichsführer* with the latter's full agreement.

In the light of such proposals, those of *Oberst* Herrmann would offer the likes of Baumbach and Speer a viable alternative with which to counter the desperate suicide plans.

4. HANS-JOACHIM HERRMANN

By the close of 1944 many proposals were circulating within the remaining forces of the Third Reich. Intended to halt the seemingly unstoppable Allied tide, many were fanciful whilst others had been prepared by, or were supported by, experienced officers. Amongst those experienced officers who sought an effective use for the remaining *Luftwaffe* resources was *Oberst* Hajo Herrmann.

Born on 1 August 1913, Hans-Joachim ('Hajo') Herrmann, like so many of his generation, grew up in a Germany whose youth had a fascination with flying, and he was proud of his achievement of an 'A' grade gliding certificate. Whilst he was undergoing preparatory training for a possible Army career, a chance encounter with Hermann Göring allowed Herrmann enthusiastically to tell the First World War ace of his 31½ seconds' solo flying experience. This encounter with the second most powerful figure in the NSDAP and head of the still secret *Luftwaffe* was to be the foundation of a successful and varied career. The immediate result was that Herrmann joined the fledgeling *Luftwaffe* in August 1935, only five months after its existence had been finally revealed to the world. Herrmann would be able to claim membership of a very élite group, having received what was undoubtedly the best training in the world, consisting not only of the basic flying skills but also advanced navigation and instrument flying techniques. His membership of this select group was further enhanced when he served during the *Luftwaffe's* first testing period, in the skies over Spain.

With the launch of Hitler's campaign against Poland, Hajo Herrmann was to find himself in action on the first day flying a Heinkel He 111 as a *Leutnant* with *III. Gruppe* of *Kampfgeschwader 4 (III./KG 4)*. During this period of his career Herrmann quickly proved to be an outstanding pilot, and following a move to the Junkers Ju 88 and to *III./KG30* he became a formidable exponent of anti-shipping strikes whilst also showing himself to be a first class leader and tactician.

With operations now under way against England, one of Herrmann's memorable flights took place on the night of 22/23 July 1940. Flying his Ju 88 on an approach for a low-level mining operation against Plymouth, he found his aircraft in danger from the barrage balloons protecting the approaches to the port. Whilst attempting to avoid these balloons the Junkers lost airspeed and dropped on to one of them. As the balloon and its now captive aircraft began to fall, illuminated by what seemed to be every searchlight in

Plymouth, Herrmann found the sinking Junkers at last beginning to regain forward airspeed. Despite being now the target of the anti-aircraft guns of the area, the undamaged aircraft at last separated from the balloon with enough remaining altitude to allow Herrmann to manoeuvre at maximum speed away from danger. In what can be considered a typical example of Herrmann's courage, he then turned his aircraft back on to its original target and dropped his two mines in their designated positions. Such courage and successes led to the award of the *Ritterkreuz*, the Knight's Cross, to *Hauptmann* Herrmann on 13 October 1940.

By April 1941 Herrmann was leading *7. Staffel KG 30*, taking part in *Unternehmen 'Marita'* (Operation 'Marita'), the German invasion of Greece. In his first sortie on the night of 6 April, at the end of the first day of operations, Herrmann led a formation of Ju 88s in an attack on the Greek port of Piraeus, being used at the time to land British troops and supplies. As always leading by example, Herrmann singled out a freighter unloading in the harbour. By chance the target that his single SC250 bomb found was the *Clan Fraser*, still loaded with 250 tons of ammunition and explosives. The massive explosion from this direct hit ripped apart the night sky, not only completely destroying the freighter but sinking a further ten ships crowded into the busy harbour and causing such extensive damage to the facilities there that the port was unusable for several weeks. A further indication of the scale of this destruction can be gained from the fact that numerous windows were shattered in Athens, over seven miles away.

With a move from the warmth of the Mediterranean to the bleak airfields of northern Norway, the targets for *KG 30* became the Arctic convoys. Now leading *III. Gruppe*, Herrmann honed his skills during the hunt for the convoys sailing the inhospitable, freezing waters between Iceland and the Russian ports. After flying over 320 operational missions he then found himself summoned to join *Luftwaffe* Headquarters Staff in July 1942 as one of six experienced front-line officers required to contribute their knowledge to future planning and to the new equipment for the *Luftwaffe*.

In a period of a little over two years Hajo Herrmann had flown in the skies over much of Europe, including operations against targets in Poland, Norway, England and Greece. Having established himself as a specialist in anti-shipping operations, he could personally claim the destruction of twelve Allied ships, totalling over 60,000 tonnes. Despite having such an enviable background in bomber operations, his new position would require him to also to come into contact with all the various aspects of *Luftwaffe* operations. Serving on the staff of the *General der Kampfflieger*, the young officer attended never-ending meetings and conferences which brought him into contact not only with the leadership of the *Luftwaffe* but also with its rising stars, such as Adolf Galland and Werner Baumbach, together with aircraft and weapons designers and political figures like Armaments Minister Albert

Speer. With his proven experience and constant enthusiasm for his new role, Herrmann gained the confidence of his senior officers and soon discovered that his opinion had become valued.

By 1942 Hajo Herrmann found himself enmeshed in the increasingly bitter demands for more resources from within the various elements of the *Luftwaffe*. Although his position required him to plan for the continued development of the *Luftwaffe*'s bombers and their equipment, he become increasingly aware that the demands for ever more bombers, day fighters and night fighters could not be met by existing measures. The growing threat posed by the RAF bombers was seen by many, including Herrmann, as one of the greatest dangers facing the Reich. Based upon these factors, one of his earliest proposed solutions was radical.

Aware of the growing inability of the overstretched night fighter force to combat the nocturnal bombers, he called for a halting of the planned expansion of bomber production and the cutting of existing bomber formations. The surplus crews from thirty-five *Kampfgeschwader*, experienced in advanced navigation and blind-flying, could be formed into an estimated seventy-five *Jagdgeschwader*, this massive addition to the fighter force being further boosted by a further nine *Jagdgeschwader* formed by converting nine *Sturzkampfgeschwader*. The equipment for this force was to be multi-role, single-seat aircraft capable of employment as required as day fighters, night fighters or fighter-bombers.

In applying himself to the problems posed in the defence of the Reich, Herrmann had made the transition into the realms of the *Jagdwaffe*. As may have been expected, the proposals were rejected when put before the current experts. In an attempt to convince his bomber colleagues, now sceptical of such a change in attitude from a bomber pilot, Herrmann was obliged to explain his proposals for the bomber force. A multi-role fighter, employed in a fighter-bomber role, would be able to support ground forces as required whilst retaining the capability to be switched to defensive operations. In his plans the reduced *Kampfgeschwader* could be re-equipped with newer aircraft and improved weapons for any long-range offensive operations that might be required. The underlying desire in his plans was to create a strong defensive force not only capable of facing the existing threat but also capable of the growth necessary to combat the threat from a massive combined Allied air force which he foresaw in the future.

Failure to obtain official support for his plans led Hajo Herrmann to test some of his theories by unofficial means. As a trained bomber pilot he was convinced that similarly experienced pilots could make the conversion to nocturnal night fighters. He spent his nights flying any available fighters in the night skies around Berlin, and this experimentation gained him some support from *General* Adolf Galland, who was also committed to the requirements of defence. Galland was able to divert some valuable fighters to

Herrmann, to be used by the small group of pilots he had assembled who were willing to contribute their spare time to his trials. Still very much an addition to his existing workload, these trials helped him to refine his plans. By moving his force to the Ruhr in July 1943 and coordinating his operations with local flak units, his fighters were able at last to make their first successful interceptions of RAF bombers and claim their first kills. By demonstrating that single-engine fighters were indeed capable of carrying out night interceptions, Herrmann increased the capabilities of the night-fighter force without the increased demand upon production an expansion using existing aircraft types would have required.

Having proved his theories, Herrmann now found that his success brought official recognition. Summoned before *Reichsmarschall* Göring, he was tasked with establishing and leading the first *Jagdgeschwader* of the new '*Wilde Sau*'. By the middle of 1943 the *Wilde Sau* were expanded with the addition of a further two *Geschwader*. Under direct instructions from the *Reichsmarschall* himself, the 29-year-old Herrmann became *Kommandeur* of the newly created *30. Jagddivision* and received promotion to the rank of *Oberstleutnant*. Having proved to be both an imaginative planner and a capable leader, Herrmann found himself popular with Göring, at times being invited to Karinhall or to Obersalzburg for informal meetings.

By early 1944 the *Wilde Sau* force had established itself as a valuable part of the Reich defences. Once again leading his force by example, Herrmann was personally able to claim nine victories against Allied bombers. This success was to bring further promotion, to the rank of *Oberst*, followed on 23 January with his becoming the 43rd recipient of the Oakleaves and Swords to his Knight's Cross, presented personally by Hitler.

With Allied operations against the Reich now declining as the emphasis was switched to supporting ground forces in France, all available *Luftwaffe* fighters were allocated a new set of priorities. As the towns and cities of Germany received a much needed breathing space, the *Jagdwaffe* left these skies in search of new targets. Even with the decline in the number of Allied missions, fighter protection was still required for the heart of the Reich. It was therefore decided that the *Wilde Sau* force should be fully transferred to daylight operations. By the end of February 1944, after a period of brief but intensive training for their new role, *30. Jagddivision* was finally incorporated into *I. Jagdkorps*.

Thinking his time spent with the *Jagdwaffe* now ended, Hajo Herrmann returned full time to his previous duties. This was, however, to prove a short-lived reprieve. In March 1944 he was appointed to command *1. Jagddivision*, responsible for both day and night-fighter forces, defending an area which included Berlin. Because he had over 25,000 officers and men under his command, together with up to 10,000 ancillary personnel, many considered Herrmann unsuited to his new position. His youth and background combined to make his appointment unpopular with many of the established staff. Not only was he required to prove his abilities, he assumed command of *1. Jagddivision* at the time when the USAAF began to attack targets deeper inside the Reich. Having foreseen the threat such massed formations would pose as early as 1942, Herrmann was now frustrated by having under his command a force too small to cope effectively with the bombers.

During the summer of 1944 Herrmann attempted to apply himself to the problems now faced by his forces. Having flown the revolutionary Me 262 in July 1943, he, like so many others, was convinced that this was the fighter that could turn the tide against the Allied formations. What was demanded by circumstances was a breathing space in which the defences could retrain and re-equip themselves in order to face the Allies. With an estimated 20,000 young pilots undergoing training, he began to formulate a theory of using a force of 1,500 standard fighter aircraft in a single massive attack against the USAAF formations. By inflicting a mortal wound, it was hoped that the balance could at last be shifted in favour of the defenders. During his time with *1. Jagddivision* Herrmann continued to plan, to experiment and to lead by example, on occasion flying operationally himself. Such actions, finding favour with front-line officers but not more senior staff, were to lead to his being removed from command at *1.Jagddivision* in October 1944 and placed on the *'Führerreserve'* to await a suitable appointment.

With the men of the *Jagdwaffe* no longer in favour, *Reichsmarschall* Göring sought solutions from officers with a background in bomber operations. One of these officers was *Generalmajor* Dietrich Peltz, who found himself being tasked with arranging a conference, planned by Göring as a means of instigating a reform of the whole *Luftwaffe*. In November 1944 Hajo Herrmann was recalled from his isolation to assist Peltz in assembling the front-line officers for this meeting. The resulting conference was to be the famed 'Areopagus', a meeting which served only to add to the existing confusion. Bomber men and fighter men alike were dismayed by events: rather than listen to the various arguments and attempt to agree a common set of goals with his officers, the *Reichsmarschall* withdrew, together with his senior staff, to await the final transcript of the meeting. Both those elements in the *Luftwaffe* determined to continue the bomber offensive and those attempting to build the defensive force remained convinced that their own ideas offered the best hope for victory against the Allies.

Having assisted with the planning of this fated conference, Hajo Herrmann found himself now posted under *Generalmajor* Peltz at *II. Fliegerkorps*, where plans were being finalized for the *Luftwaffe's* support of the *Wehrmacht* winter offensive against the Allies in the Ardennes. Despite the fact that the operation employed both methods and tactics that Herrmann frowned upon, he carried out the duties required of him and even succeeded in flying an operational mission again. As always seeking the best employment of all available resources, he had suggested to Peltz that night fighters could be used to fly nocturnal ground-attack missions against Allied communication and transportation targets in Belgium and northern France. Returning once again to the controls of a Ju 88, Herrmann destroyed one of almost 150 locomotives which fell victim to the roving *Luftwaffe* night fighters during December 1944.

As the year drew to its close, the *Wehrmacht*'s desperate gamble in the West was being ground into failure by the Allies. Now Herrmann received yet another posting, this time to command *9. Fliegerdivision*, with its headquarters at Neubiburg near Munich. Once again his appointment coincided with a period of experimentation and re-equipment, the Me 262s beginning to reach bomber units under his command now being tasked with converting to fighter operations. With the units in his command attempting to train on the new jets and learn the tactics required against USAAF bomber formations, Herrmann found his airfields under seemingly ceaseless attacks from Allied aircraft:

> The Me 262 was our last hope, and mastery of the air was the key to our success. It must be obvious to anyone who had eyes to see and a brain to think . . . that we were lagging behind again and that the old propeller aircraft could not provide the cover beneath which the jets could multiply, one by one, in their tens, in their hundreds; that all the exhilarating numerical tables were being incinerated in their enemy's enterprise of fire; that they were wasting away in the mad rush to make good the inadequate training and shrivelling up in the lack of fuel.[1]

As with many such experienced men, by 1944 Herrmann had come to realize that the Reich was doomed. Numerical superiority and a massive production programme by the Allied powers was proving capable of wearing down all remaining resistance. What he and others now wished for was the opportunity to survive. Such survival required the fight to continue, until the Allies could be forced to offer acceptable terms. In another bold proposal, he resurrected his plan from the summer of 1944 which called for a massed formation of younger, inexperienced pilots to be employed in a decisive action against the USAAF. He considered the existing propeller-driven fighter aircraft now surplus to requirements: their crews would be more suitably employed in conversion to the jets. This force could be used in a final operation which would remove the USAAF bombers from the skies above the jet bases, allowing the force to be strengthened and fully trained. Herrmann's plan would, in effect, result in the last flight of the conventional *Luftwaffe*, which would then be allowed time to rebuild itself and emerge as a formidable jet force. Once again forced to seek official acceptance, he found that his proposals were supported by *Generalmajor* Peltz and a draft was forwarded to the *Reichsmarschall*:

---

[1] Herrmann, Hajo, *Eagle's Wings*, Airlife Publishing, p. 253.

The time until Me 262 operations can be expanded must be bridged; the time is also approaching by which the conventional fighter force, which, as is known, has only a slight prospect of success, will be completely exhausted and grounded. We need to achieve success of such numerical significance that the enemy will change both the frequency of his attacks and his methods. We need the consequences that only success can bring. The enemy's reserves of personnel and equipment are known. The enemy has fought for months and sustained few casualties. Therefore, the enemy is reluctant to take risks and would be hard hit by a heavy loss of blood. Our *Luftwaffe* men possess high operational motivation. No change can be expected or hoped for in the coming weeks using other means and methods.

Although not rejecting this proposal outright, the *Reichsmarschall* asked for further information and also time to consider fully the implications.

5. A REQUEST FOR VOLUNTEERS

With the hopes offered by *General* Galland's *Grosse Schlag* consigned to the increasing list of 'what might have been', and with the winter offensive in the West being ground into defeat before the Allies, the *Jagdwaffe* found itself again forced to continue its struggle in the battle of attrition in the air over the crumbling Reich.

It was at this time, when the fortunes of war had again turned against the *Luftwaffe*, that the latest plan from *Oberst* Herrmann finally reached the desk of *Reichsmarschall* Göring. The wording of this proposal struck a chord with the *Reichsmarschall*, his existing confidence in this experienced front-line officer undoubtedly aiding his acceptance of the plan. Retaining his access to Göring and having proved on previous occasions his ability to assemble workable solutions to military problems, Herrmann proceeded to explain at length his latest ideas.

Although his words, which he had so carefully prepared, began to convince his commanding officer of the plan's feasibility, he was well aware that by accepting the proposed mission the *Reichsmarschall* would be acknowledging the desperate nature of the Reich's defences. With the daily battles failing to achieve any measure of success against the Allied air forces, Göring was doubtful whether a suitable force of volunteers could be assembled to carry out a mission on the scale envisaged. Because of the requirement to protect the valuable *Jagdwaffe* pilots, Herrmann was calling for a group of young volunteers, by definition lacking experience in the brutal environment of aerial combat. Would such young pilots come forward, and could Göring ask them to risk their very lives in this mission? In answering these questions *Oberst* Herrmann replied with confidence. He was aware of the courage and determination of even the youngest *Luftwaffe* pilots. As with the vast majority of the German armed forces, they now accepted that they were fighting to protect their homes and their families. If such courageous men could be allowed the chance to contribute to a mission planned to remove the threat of the Allied bombers from the skies, Herrmann was confident that volunteers would come forward in large numbers.

Having carefully prepared his proposals and assembled the various facts and figures, Herrmann finally presented the draft of an appeal which would be issued in the *Reichsmarschall*'s name to request volunteers for the new mission. The details of the mission would remain secret, but both the danger and the promise of success on offer would be announced. Also to be in-

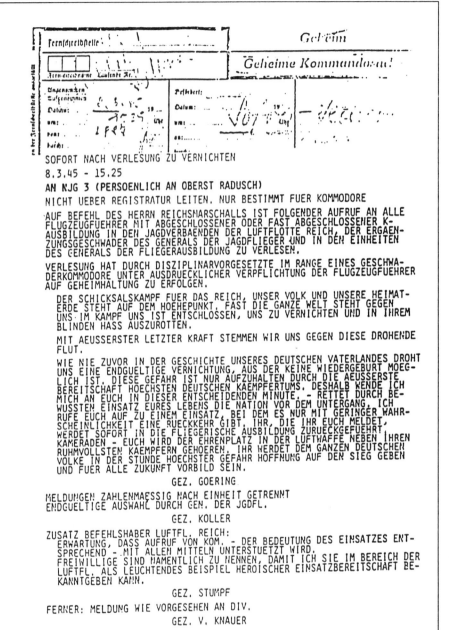

SOFORT NACH VERLESUNG ZU VERNICHTEN

8.3.45 - 15.25

AN NJG 3 (PERSOENLICH AN OBERST RADUSCH)

NICHT UEBER REGISTRATUR LEITEN. NUR BESTIMMT FUER KOMMODORE

AUF BEFEHL DES HERRN REICHSMARSCHALLS IST FOLGENDER AUFRUF AN ALLE FLUGZEUGFUEHRER MIT ABGESCHLOSSENER ODER FAST ABGESCHLOSSENER K-AUSBILDUNG IN DEN JAGDVERBAENDEN DER LUFTFLOTTE REICH, DER ERGAEN-ZUNGSGESCHWADER DES GENERALS DER JAGDFLIEGER UND IN DEN EINHEITEN DES GENERALS DER FLIEGERAUSBILDUNG ZU VERLESEN.

VERLESUNG HAT DURCH DISZIPLINARVORGESETZTE IM RANGE EINES GESCHWA-DERKOMMODORE UNTER AUSDRUECKLICHER VERPFLICHTUNG DER FLUGZEUGFUEHRER AUF GEHEIMHALTUNG ZU ERFOLGEN.

DER SCHICKSALSKAMPF FUER DAS REICH, UNSER VOLK UND UNSERE HEIMAT-ERDE STEHT AUF DEM HOEHEPUNKT. FAST DIE GANZE WELT STEHT GEGEN UNS IM KAMPF UNS IST ENTSCHLOSSEN, UNS ZU VERNICHTEN UND IN IHREM BLINDEN HASS AUSZUROTTEN.

MIT AEUSSERSTER LETZTER KRAFT STEMMEN WIR UNS GEGEN DIESE DROHENDE FLUT.

WIE NIE ZUVOR IN DER GESCHICHTE UNSERES DEUTSCHEN VATERLANDES DROHT UNS EINE ENDGUELTIGE VERNICHTUNG, AUS DER KEINE WIEDERGEBURT MOEG-LICH IST. DIESE GEFAHR IST NUR AUFZUHALTEN DURCH DIE AEUSSERSTE BEREITSCHAFT HOECHSTEN DEUTSCHEN KAEMPFERTUMS. DESHALB WENDE ICH MICH AN EUCH IN DIESER ENTSCHEIDENDEN MINUTE. - RETTET DURCH BE-WUSSTEN EINSATZ EURES LEBENS DIE NATION VOR DEM UNTERGANG. ICH RUFE EUCH AUF ZU EINEM EINSATZ, BEI DEM ES NUR MIT GERINGER WAHR-SCHEINLICHKEIT EINE RUECKKEHR GIBT. IHR, DIE IHR EUCH MELDET, WERDET SOFORT IN DIE FLIEGERISCHE AUSBILDUNG ZURUECKGEFUEHRT KAMERADEN - EUCH WIRD DER EHRENPLATZ IN DER LUFTWAFFE NEBEN IHREN RUHMVOLLSTEN KAEMPFERN GEHOEREN. IHR WERDET DEM GANZEN DEUTSCHEN VOLKE IN DER STUNDE HOECHSTER GEFAHR HOFFNUNG AUF DEN SIEG GEBEN UND FUER ALLE ZUKUNFT VORBILD SEIN.

GEZ. GOERING

MELDUNGEN ZAHLENMAESSIG NACH EINHEIT GETRENNT ENDGUELTIGE AUSWAHL DURCH GEN. DER JGDFL.

GEZ. KOLLER

ZUSATZ BEFEHLSHABER LUFTFL. REICH: ERWARTUNG, DASS AUFRUF VON KOM. - DER BEDEUTUNG DES EINSATZES ENT-SPRECHEND - MIT ALLEN MITTELN UNTERSTUETZT WIRD. FREIWILLIGE SIND NAMENTLICH ZU NENNEN, DAMIT ICH SIE IM BEREICH DER LUFTFL. ALS LEUCHTENDES BEISPIEL HEROISCHER EINSATZBEREITSCHAFT BE-KANNTGEBEN KANN.

GEZ. STUMPF

FERNER: MELDUNG WIE VORGESEHEN AN DIV.

GEZ. V. KNAUER

A copy of the original request for volunteers, issued on 8 March 1945.

cluded would be an announcement that *Reichsmarschall* Göring would personally visit the volunteers before their mission, to express his support and wish each pilot success. It was this final note alone with which Göring could not bring himself to agree. When *Oberst* Herrmann was dismissed from the meeting, the proposal and the draft still lay unsigned on the *Reichsmarschall*'s desk. As he returned to his quarters at Neubiburg he remained unsure whether his words had this time been enough.

The seemingly endless waiting, as hour by hour the war continued to follow its inevitable course, was at last broken as the teletype machine sprang to life, the message printed ending Herrmann's own doubts. Whilst agreeing to the proposals and allowing the draft appeal to be issued, the *Reichsmarschall* had made one deletion to the prepared text—the announcement that he would visit the airfield and meet the young pilots before their mission. When Herrmann later reflected upon the events of the time, he thought that Göring was unable to face the pilots because of the courage they were to display and because, if he did so, as leader of the *Luftwaffe* he would be finally conceding that the war was lost. With the accepted danger, inherent in such an operation, Herrmann believed that Göring was unable to recover from the feelings of guilt and remorse which he felt over the situation in which his once glorious *Luftwaffe* now found itself.

With the required agreement now received, the carefully prepared plans for the operation were now set in motion . The initial stage would be the issue of the request for volunteers, and, with his plans now revealed to the leaders of the *Luftwaffe*, Herrmann discovered that he had gained additional support. Before the appeal was issued it was endorsed with a brief note from *Generaloberst* Hans-Jürgen Stumpf, the well respected commanding officer of *Luftflotte Reich*. In confirming the value of the forthcoming mission, Stumpf said, 'Because of the importance of the mission, you can expect complete support by all means at our disposal.' In a comment directed to the various unit leaders who would receive the appeal, he continued: 'Please give me the names of all volunteers so that we may hold them up as shining examples of heroes of the operation.'

The appeal was transmitted at 3.25 on the afternoon of Thursday 8 March 1945 to all units of *Luftflotte Reich*. It was marked 'Secret' and 'Destroy after passing on message', but because of the administrative failings in the headquarters of *Nachtjagdgeschwader 3* (*NJG 3*), commanded by *Oberst* Günther Radusch, a copy of the appeal has survived:

The fateful battle for the Reich, our people and our Homeland has reached a critical stage. Almost the whole world is against us.

They have sworn to destroy us in battle and, in their blind hate, to wipe us out.

With one final effort we must stem this threatening wave.

As never before in the history of the Fatherland, we are facing a final destruction from which there can be no rebirth. This danger can only be averted by preparing to fight in the highest German tradition. I turn to you, therefore, in these deciding moments. I ask you to rescue, with one conscious effort, the life of your nation from a final downfall. I call you to an operation from which there is little possibility of returning. Those of you who are called will be sent immediately to flight training.

Comrades—a place of honour in the glorious history of the *Luftwaffe* will be yours. You will give the German people in this hour of grave danger a hope of victory and you will be an example for all time.

[Signed] Göring

The necessary security precautions prevented any details of the mission from being included at this stage. The commanders receiving the message were to read the appeal to their gathered men under strict instructions that even the appeal itself remain secret. Whist aimed at those who had just completed, or were in the process of completing, their fighter training, the appeal was also distributed to reserve units and to some front-line units, such as *NJG 3*.

Herrmann had from the outset been confident of a favourable response to this appeal from the young pilots of the *Luftwaffe*, but the reaction when it came was to shake him. When he later considered these events he was to state that he had never doubted that enough volunteers would come forward to make the mission viable. However, with over 2,000 pilots volunteering to this first appeal, he was forced to halt the issue of the request to further *Luftwaffe* units. This massive response indicates that the *Luftwaffe*'s fighting spirit had by no means diminished: as with so many young men throughout the centuries, when homes and families were under threat they were prepared to risk their lives.

From the very beginning, the pilots were told of the minimal hopes of survival. As the commanders ended their briefings they faced the young men in their charge and undoubtedly reflected upon events they themselves had experienced during five years of war. Having themselves fought in many bitter battles and lost many comrades, the older officers perhaps felt it necessary to add their own words. At Fürth the appeal was read to *II./JG 103* by *Oberst* Johannes Trautloft. With his vast experience of the course of the air war, Trautloft stated that he considered the hopes of survival to be perhaps less than 10 per cent. Despite such warnings, many pilots still wished to volunteer, and finally at least nine names were put forward from *II./JG 103* alone. In some cases entire units added their names to the growing lists. One such unit was that with which *Oberst* Herrmann already had a close association. Based at Mörtitz, near Leipzig, *I./JG 300* volunteered *en masse*. However, with the demands of front-line units remaining paramount, the list had to be reduced to ensure that such units could continue to contribute to the Reich's defensive requirements, and it is thought that only about five pilots were accepted from *I. Gruppe*. In another example, at least seven men from the Me 163-equipped *JG 400*, based at Brandis, volunteered. Again, these highly specialized pilots were considered more valuable to the continued operations of their existing unit and only two could be accepted.

At Haderslev in Denmark the appeal had been read to the pilots of *II./ EJG 1*. After hearing the request the pilots were told that they could consider it overnight and make their decisions the next day. As the young pilots talked amongst themselves two quickly reached their decision. Needing little time to consider their intentions, the friends, *Unteroffizier* Werner Zell and *Obergefreiter* Horst Siedel, would put their names forward at first light the next morning. The reasons given by these two young men were typical of the stories told by many of the volunteers. The last letter that *Obergefreiter* Siedel had received from his parents had been dated 12 February, and on the following evening the massed bombers of the RAF had arrived over their home, within the city of Dresden. Since receiving that letter Siedel had had no contact with his family: all that he knew about was the horrific destruction of his city, which even an American press report called an example of deliberate terror bombing. The only hope that he held on to was that his family could be amongst the refugee column rumoured to be leaving the area. As *Unteroffizier* Zell listened to his friend he reflected that, whilst his home may have escaped such bombing, his family were about to find themselves under Allied control. His home lay within Saarland, and the area was about to be captured by American forces.

In total six pilots would join from *II./EJG 1*. Many men volunteered in groups, bolstered by their friendships, excited by the opportunity at last to take part in combat, many hoping to be able to use one of the 'wonder weapons' which so many rumours suggested were on the verge of introduction. All were determined to play their part in the defence of their homeland. These men were not coerced into volunteering, and none appears to have been driven by any fervent Nazi fanaticism: they had all experienced the bitter consequences of warfare and as soldiers they intended to do what they considered their duty, by whatever means available.

With his vision at last beginning to take form, a vision of a formidable force of fighters cutting a swath through the massed ranks of the USAAF bombers, *Oberst* Herrmann could at last hope that his force would achieve the success so desperately needed. With in excess of 2,000 names already collected, even the most ambitious proposal appeared to be well within reach. Having received in advance an agreement that up to 1,500 fighter aircraft would be made available for his operation, he now had an ample supply from which to select his force. A suitable supply of aircraft was not to be a major factor influencing the size of the operation to be mounted: indeed, the German aviation industry continued to produce fighter aircraft despite the best efforts of the Allied bombers. However, the daily demands placed upon the *Luftwaffe* commanders required that their resources be stretched to cover every front, and with reserves of fuel insufficient for all of the necessary operations, *General der Flieger* Karl Koller and his staff were anxious that they be seen to offer continuing support to the *Wehrmacht* operations. Any favour granted to the *Luftwaffe* was determined by its ability to maintain support for the ground forces; any reduction in the availability of close-support aircraft was liable to incur the wrath of the *Führer*. By placing Hajo Herrmann's operation lower down their list of priorities it was consequently to receive a smaller allocation of fuel, and accordingly a reduced number of aircraft would be available for any operation.

Convinced of the vital importance of his planned mission, Herrmann now found himself being robbed of one of its vital ingredients. He had planned to decimate a raid of the hated *Viermöte*, but any reduction in the number of available fighters would in turn reduce the success they could achieve. Having already endured the process of promoting his plans, he was now required to barter for the necessary resources. With the planning about to be put into effect, *General* Koller now withdrew his initial promise of 1,500 fighters, suggesting instead that the operation could be mounted with a smaller number.

Herrmann, fearful for the future of his entire proposal, approached *General* Koller in an attempt to retain his support. The only concession that the *General* was able to offer was that if the proposed mission was successful on a reduced scale and thus proved the theory correct, resources would then be provided to reinforce Herrmann's cadre and enable a further decisive mission to be launched. With Koller insistent that *Luftwaffe* support for operations—especially in the East—remain a priority, Herrmann countered by suggesting that if the threat of USAAF raids were removed, industry would be better able to produce the essential weapons for front-line troops and their lines of supply and communication would be allowed to operate undisturbed. Koller was mindful of the demands of Hitler, however, and despite Göring having agreed to a minimum figure of 1,000 fighters the wishes of the *Führer* remained paramount. The negotiations resulted in the promise of 350 fighter aircraft, a figure which was to be reduced further when deliveries were finally completed.

Having assembled a sizable list of volunteers, Hajo Herrmann was understandably unwilling to now lose them. Hopeful that the promise of further support would materialize, *Oberst* Herrmann was able to arrange for a number of the now excess pilots to be transferred to his staff for use in other proposed missions, which included the large-scale follow-up to the attack upon the USAAF raid.

The reporting centre selected to assemble the volunteers was the air base at Stendal, where the pilots would be placed in the care of *Major* Otto Köhnke. Having served with Hajo Herrmann during his time in Berlin, Köhnke had a very similar background. As a *Leutnant* he had served with the Condor Legion in the skies over Spain during 1938. By 1941 he was flying Dornier

Do17s over England as a *Staffelkapitän* and he was badly wounded during an attack on Dover. With operations launched against Russia, *Hauptmann* Köhnke found himself amongst the forces assembled to defeat Stalin's armies, flying with *II./KG54*. During operations in the first half of 1942 his courage and skill resulted in the award of the *Ritterkreuz* on 1 August that year. Later his experience was to lead to an appointment to command the pilot school at Klagenfurt, and this in turn would lead to his becoming inspector of over twenty such training establishments. A capable leader, *Major* Köhnke was also outspoken and his criticism of senior staff is known to have offended some of his superiors. In one such outburst, the target being the *Luftwaffe* General Staff, his comments reached the ears of *General* Koller. In order to defend his friend from any serious recriminations, Hajo Herrmann informed the *General* that Köhnke's behaviour should be excused as he was a native of Friesland and also had a background which proved him to be 'congenitally impolite'! In contrast with such clashes with authority, when allowed to concentrate upon the important matters in hand such as the training of pilots and the planning of a vital mission, *Major* Köhnke proved himself to be a valuable member of *Oberst* Herrmann's team. More than one young pilot who joined the volunteers at Stendal remembers him as a capable leader and a 'cautious and paternal comrade'.

With the base of operations established, Köhnke organized the reception for the volunteers and also the necessary ancillary staff to support the project. One matter which remained outstanding was a suitable cover name for the plans. With so many of the pilots still in the process of completing their training, it was logical that the new operation would be called a training course, and with Stendal situated near the important defensive line of the Elbe river the logical cover-name was *Schulungslehrgang 'Elbe'* (Training Course 'Elbe').

As the request for volunteers produced the hoped-for reaction and the base at Stendal was prepared for the first pilots, the daily struggle for the survival of the Reich still continued. As 8 March was drawing to a close the struggle was directed to combat the advancing Soviet armour. The defence continued of the beleaguered fortified city of Breslau, surrounded by Soviet infantry. The encirclement was now reinforced by armoured units which included the 3rd Guards Tank Army. A German offensive had been launched during the night of 5/6 March around Lake Balaton in Hungary and fresh units had been committed by both sides in an attempt to decide the battle. On the 8th the 2nd SS Panzer Division was sent forward with over 250 tanks to join the already formidable armoured formations. In Pomerania the *Wehrmacht* reported heavy Soviet tank attacks aimed at Stettin (today Szczecin, Poland) on the River Oder, with a fresh advance from forces located in the area of Stargard. This battle was taking place less than 100km (70 miles) to the north-east of Berlin. The only major *Luftwaffe* operations of the day had been limited close-support actions in Pomerania in the face of very heavy Soviet air opposition, records indicating that only nine Russian aircraft could be claimed as destroyed. In the West, along the line of the Rhine, Allied troops were still pushing German forces back from positions between Cologne and Brühl. Strong Allied armour advanced to the east of Euskirchen, (towards Bonn), forward units reportedly reaching as far as Neuenahr. German reports indicate that the assumption was that this advance was aimed towards Koblenz.

The down-turn in the fortunes for the forces of the Third Reich can be judged by reports during 8 March that the strength of the Allied bridgehead on the right bank of the Rhine could not be confirmed because communications between Berlin and the West were simply 'not working'. In the face of continued USAAF daylight operations the *Luftwaffe* mounted only a small number of missions owing to the poor weather. The only sizable operations had been mounted by the *Nachtjagdverbände* during the hours of darkness, when 41 claims were made by the defenders. In his diary entry for the day, *Dr* Josef Goebbels responded to reports that Churchill had announced that he had no intention of recognizing any form of German government and that the defeated Germany was to be governed exclusively by its occupation forces. In recording his views Goebbels showed that the leadership of the Reich maintained their belief that the war would continue until the Continent had been reduced to rubble: '. . . a people of 80 million souls will never accept such a solution and Europe would prefer to go down in chaos, flame and smoke rather than submit to such a prescription for disintegration.'

As the circle of steel continued to close around the Reich the elements of the Elbe force began to form at Stendal. From their various units the volunteers arrived at the base on Saturday 24 March, their journeys via the scarred towns and countryside serving to reinforce the determination of the young men to defend their homes by whatever means available. Such determination is reflected by the story of six pilots from *JG 103*. As relatively experienced pilots the men had been based at Kastrup near Copenhagen, where they had flown Focke-Wulf Fw190s. Upon arrival at Stendal they were informed that, as the mission had been scaled down, only those with at least 50 hours on the Me 109 would be accepted. Dismayed by the possibility that their hopes of participating in the still secret operation could be dashed so early by their lack of experience, the pilots set about falsifying their papers, determined that they should be included. A large lecture theatre had been prepared, in which the pilots were greeted by a reception which included large quantities of wine, cognac, cigarettes and chocolate. With such precious supplies available on their first day, many of the men must have wondered about the mission ahead. They were allocated sleeping quarters and informed that they were to be addressed by *Oberst* Herrmann the following day when all were rested from their journeys.

Today we can only imagine the tense atmosphere in the lecture theatre that Sunday morning as Herrmann entered the room to outline his carefully prepared plans. Standing before the assembled young pilots and aware that so much depended upon their reaction, he was at last able to tell them the details of the mission for which they had volunteered. The details were basic. In a little over two weeks' time, using modified Bf 109s, the pilots were to cut down a formation of USAAF bombers and inflict such losses upon the Americans that they would be forced to abandon, a least for a period, their daylight missions over Germany. Because of the demands that existed within not only the *Jagdwaffe* but the entire *Luftwaffe*—indeed, the entire remaining formations of the German forces—their mission would be completed using a minimum of resources. Their fighters would be light in weight to escape the attentions of the escort fighters and would be unarmed, the bombers being destroyed by a determined ramming attack. As the details were considered by the assembled pilots, *Oberst* Herrmann concluded his briefing by announcing that, having now heard the details, any man present would be allowed time to reconsider his continued participation. It is evidence of the determination of these pilots, the latest members of the *Jagdwaffe*, that, even now, only one man left Stendal. For the others there was only one topic for discussion: how their mission could be carried forward. Nobody questioned the logic of the proposal and nobody considered the mission to be a suicidal act. Accepting instead that the impact of a Bf 109 and a USAAF *Viermot* would produce at best a disabled fighter, the men planned how they were to escape following the impact.

As 24 March drew to a close, elsewhere across Europe the war continued to reshape the battle lines. The *Wehrmacht* found itself involved in bitter struggles on its Eastern Front in Hungary, Silesia, both West and East Prussia, Slovakia and Courland. A particularly heavy Soviet attack was recorded in an area concentrated upon Danzig. On the Western Front a fresh Allied crossing of the Rhine at both Wesel and Oppenheim had been able to advance into an area to the north of Essen. Further to the south, despite opposition, the bridgehead at Linz remained intact, and at Mainz, 35km (22 miles) west of Frankfurt, the town was in the grip of fierce street fighting. By the evening the *Luftwaffe* had again recorded a day of large-scale operations by its enemies which it once more seemed powerless to stop. In the East, Soviet aircraft had taken to the air in large numbers in support of their ground forces. The now dreaded Ilyushin Il-2s, the 'Shturmoviks', seemed to fill the skies with the arrogance once reserved for *Luftwaffe* ground-attack aircraft. On this Saturday they had flown their typical low-level close-support missions over the heads of Soviet ground troops fighting for control of the towns of Eberswalde, north-east of Berlin and Bernau, little more than 15km (10 miles) from the very heart of the Reich. Against such opposition the *Luftwaffe* continued to offer its best defence, and in the frantic operations the German pilots had claimed 34 Soviet aircraft destroyed. Over the Western Front the skies had again been dominated by the swarms of Allied fighter-bombers which had made any military activity a great gamble. Launched to support Allied ground forces, the roving single- and twin-engine aircraft actively sought out their foe in any form and in every corner of the battle front. General Patton's latest crossing of the Rhine was identified by the *Wehrmacht* as being aimed towards Darmstadt. As for the *Viermöte*, their activities could only be listed by the names of the towns and cities which they bombed. From Italian bases, Vienna, Schwarzheide and Innsbruck received attention, while other formations delivered their bomb loads upon Bremen, Münster, Osnabrück, Bocholt, Rheine and towns throughout the Ruhr. Recording his thoughts on this day—thoughts that he would dare not reveal to his leader—Goebbels admitted that the time for advances was past and that survival depended upon defending what remained of the Reich. Viewing the situation in the West, he commented: 'Our ability to win even partially this decisive stage of the war in the West now depends on our soldiers' will to resist, and their morale, and the speed with which we can reinforce.' If *Oberst* Herrmann's plan succeeded, would it allow time for the defences to be strengthened? Could the Allied advances really be halted? Could the bombing be stopped? Only time would tell.

6. RAMMKOMMANDO!

In examining the Elbe mission and the plans of *Oberst* Hajo Herrmann, many post-war authors and historians have dismissed the operation as being, at best, a misguided suicide attack. This is to judge the events of early 1945 by modern-day standards, without due consideration of the facts. When a country is at risk from its enemies it should be expected that every effort be directed to its defence. When these same enemies are positioned with an aim of reaching to the very heartland and by their own admission intent upon destroying the country, the defence will inevitably become still more determined. Neither must the selection by the *Luftwaffe* of the means to destroy the USAAF bombers be judged by contemporary standards. All forms of air combat carry innumerable risks, and from the earliest beginnings of air warfare these risks have included that of collision. Whilst most may be considered to be a result of fatal errors of judgement during fierce dogfights, others were indeed intentional attempts by pilots to use every means available to defeat their enemy.

An early Hero of the Soviet Union had earned his position of honour during the bitter defence of Russia in 1941. Finding that their fighters were often unable to match the performance of the *Luftwaffe* opposition, Soviet pilots sometimes employed drastic measures in an attempt to even the odds. In October 1941, with Moscow under attack by *Luftwaffe* bombers, a young pilot, Viktor Talakhin, found himself amongst a formation of Heinkel He 111s. Having expended all his ammunition in a vain attempt to stop the bombers, he then deliberately rammed one of the aircraft. This victory by Talakhin was not considered a suicidal attack by his countrymen. His courage in a defensive action was praised, and the young pilot was compared to a Russian aviator of the First World War, Peter Nesterovs, who had also employed such tactics to defeat his opponents.

While the employment of such tactics may be dismissed as merely examples of fanaticism, it is also possible to find examples of such actions amongst the combat reports of the Western Allies, involving pilots not considered to be governed by political indoctrination. Two months after Talakhin had faced the *Luftwaffe* Heinkels over Moscow, US pilots, flying as part of the American Volunteer Group, were facing Japanese bombers on the other side of the world. On Christmas Day 1941 a group of P-40s belonging to the so-called 'Flying Tigers' were in action over Rangoon in Burma, assisting in support of the RAF operations in the area. Scrambled to intercept a large formation of Japanese bombers, protected by an escort of over twenty fighters, the AVG pilots flung themselves into a frantic battle to protect their own airfield. The resulting combat was to be a one-sided clash, the 'shark-nosed' P-40s claiming 28 kills for the loss of only two of their own aircraft and none of their pilots. In the midst of the combat one AVG pilot, Parker Dupouy, had been able to claim a kill not by his skill with the P-40's 0.303 machine guns but by the use of the fighter's wing. Attempting a series of diving attacks upon the Japanese bombers, Dupouy misjudged the distance between the aircraft and sliced into the Japanese bomber whilst trying to bring his guns to bear. The crippled bomber fell from the now fleeing formation and Dupouy was able to return to his base with a fighter missing four feet of wing-tip.

Another American pilot was to make his own daring kill in an arena closer to European skies. During 1943, from their base in Tunisia, Lockheed P-38 Lightnings of the 14th Fighter Group were tasked with offering protection to the many convoys suffering the attentions of *Luftwaffe* bombers. In one notable mission on 9 October 1943, three of the Group's P-38s, led by Colonel William Leverette, attacked a formation of Junkers Ju 87s. After shooting down six of the dive-bombers, Leverette found himself on the tail of another Stuka, only to discover that his guns were now empty. With his final burst having already silenced the enemy's rear gunner he decided that he should close with the Ju 87. As the gap between the aircraft shrank he then lined up his propeller with the Ju 87s rudder, and just as it bit into the rudder he cut his throttle and allowed the blades to slice large pieces from the unfortunate aircraft. As the Ju 87 lost control and spiralled into the sea, Leverette had accounted for his seventh victim of the day (his final score by the end of the war would eventually climb to 11). The American pilot had employed a tactic very similar to that later considered by *Oberst* Herrmann and his men.

It is also worth noting that American interest in the concept of ramming existed in official circles. Amongst the innovative aircraft produced in America by the designer Jack Northrop was the XP-79, an all-wing fighter design powered by one of the new jet engines. The aircraft featured heavy armour protection, intended to withstand the impact of ramming enemy bombers. Although development of this design was terminated in September 1945, it is interesting to consider how the design may have developed— or, indeed, how determined the USAAF defences would have been had America found herself in a position where massed formations of *Luftwaffe* or Japanese Air Force bombers were roaming at will above cities such as New York or Washington.

While information about Jack Northrop's designs of would have been inaccessible to Hajo Herrmann, details of combat operations involving the *Jagdwaffe Sturmjäger* were not. When the *Luftwaffe* had addressed the problem faced by its fighters in attempting to defeat the USAAF formations, one of the many possible solutions had been the development of heavily armoured Fw 190s of the *Sturmjäger*. In order to inflict the maximum damage upon the bombers, the *Sturmjäger* were expected to bring their formidable cannon to bear at shortest range possible, their defensive armour being intended to allow the fighter to withstand the punishment inflicted by the defensive fire of the massed bomber boxes. In pressing home such attacks these fighters often found themselves within the bomber formations but having exhausted their supply of ammunition. Many pilots then used their Focke-Wulfs as armoured rams, confident that the additional plating would enable their aircraft, and more importantly them, to withstand the collision. Even with their previously unheard-of level of protection, the *Sturmjäger* pilots who employed these aircraft were charged with a dangerous mission. Apart from the risks which still remained in such a hostile and closely confined combat arena, the performance of the Fw 190s was reduced by the weight of the additional armour. This weight penalty resulted in the aircraft becoming easier prey when caught by the USAAF escort fighters. It was therefore found necessary to provide a standard fighter escort for the more sluggish *Sturmjäger* fighters to deal with the threat posed by American fighters and allow the dedicated Fw 190s a clear run at the *Viermöte*.

As had become the case for the *Zerstörer* formations, additional fighters were now necessary to defend what had been intended to be special anti-bomber fighters. It seemed that every attempt to endow the *Jagdwaffe* with the ideal weapon to combat the USAAF formations was dogged by the same problem—how to mount an effective weapon in a fighter without reducing its combat capabilities. The testing of alternative weapons had been allocated to *Erprobungskommando 25*, formed during 1942. Amongst the systems the unit investigated was the *Wfr.Gr. 21cm* (21cm mortar), which for a time seemed to offer the ideal solution. Mounted singly or in pairs beneath the wings of aircraft, the mortars could be fired into a bomber formation to devastating effect. Not intended to result in any direct hits, the blast of the mortar shell literally blew apart the formation, resulting in damaged bombers which became easy pickings for the *Jagdwaffe*. First tested in combat by *II./JG26* during the summer of 1943, the mortars were a success; however, when mounted on single-engine fighters the weapons reduced performance and were quickly considered to be a dangerous addition posing a potentially lethal risk to the pilot. It was for these reasons that the 21cm mortars were passed to the larger *Zerstörer* aircraft, where as well as pairs of tubes underwing a possible installation of six tubes in a revolving mount in the nose of a Messerschmitt Bf 110 was considered. But the accuracy of this weapon remained a problem. Official records show that even during test conditions the mortar's accuracy at a distance of 1,000m (3,000ft) was limited due to a possible height deviation of ±7m (23ft) and a side deviation of 40m (130ft). At a greater stand-off range of 2,000m (6,500ft) the deviations grew to a height variance of 24m (80ft) and a sideways fan of up to 84m (275ft).

With conventional fighters either too lightly armed or armoured to deal with the bomber formations or too slow to avoid the escorting fighters, the only hope for the *Jagdwaffe* lay with the new jet and rocket fighters. Of the possible aircraft available, all sources seem to agree that the ideal fighter was the Me 262: it was capable of mounting very efficient weapons, even when limited to conventional cannon, and it possessed an undreamed-of performance. However, as has been seen, the aircraft would not be available in the numbers required in the necessary time. With such difficulties facing the *Luftwaffe*, Hermann's proposal of using his force of fighters was simple, but circumstances now demanded an unconventional approach.

The fighters which were to equip the force would be as fast and as manoeuvrable as possible to enable them to escape the attentions of the USAAF escorts, thereby avoiding the necessity of additional protection from other *Jagdwaffe* units. This increase in performance would not be achieved by any form of engine boosting, nor by jet or rocket power. Instead, the fighters were to be as light as possible in order to profit from every last ounce of existing power. To accomplish this, all excess weight would be stripped from the airframe; this would include the removal of the armour which had been gradually worked into fighter designs in order to offer pilots greater protection. Because the aircraft would be capable of avoiding the American fighters, any form of defensive armament was also to be considered dispensable. The removal of the weapons, moreover, allowed less experienced pilots—those recently converted to fighters or those perhaps yet to master the art of aerial gunnery—to be incorporated into the plans. If the objective for the fighters was for them to score their kills by ramming, they would certainly not require any weapons to do so.

By collecting the available material which documented cases where fighters had scored kills by the ramming of enemy aircraft, *Oberst* Herrmann learned of a number of successful methods. However, many of the tactics involved a level of risk that was quickly deemed too excessive. A head-on approach offered too small a target for the pilot and the closing speeds involved offered too brief a period to line up the fighter. If the pilot used his aircraft to slice into a bomber's wing he placed himself directly in the line of the heaviest defensive fire. He would also risk his aircraft becoming enmeshed with the torn metal of the crippled bomber as it began to fall from the formation, making any escape extremely difficult, or, worse, risked being caught in an explosion of fuel, bomb load and ammunition.

In his search for the most effective method of ramming *Oberst* Herrmann approached the *Luftwaffe* test centre at Rechlin and also interviewed many successful *Sturmjäger*. Now faced with the details of their mission and its demands, the pilots of *Schulungslehrgang 'Elbe'* also applied themselves to the required techniques. With the information at hand it was decided that the best option was in fact not to allow the fighter and its victim to collide.

Instead, the fighter should be positioned above and astern of the bomber, in a six o'clock high position, from where the greatest risk would be the defensive fire of the tail-gunner. Because of such a risk it was decided that the fighter would retain what was considered a minimal armament of a single MG 131 with 50 rounds of ammunition. Insufficient to destroy a bomber in itself or to deal with a prolonged duel with escorts, the weapon allowed a measure of self-protection and perhaps even a slight morale booster for the pilots. If necessary the 'Elbe' pilot could use this surviving weapon to dispatch any gunner considered too great a threat with a short burst. The fighter would then dive at its target, the aiming point being the trailing edge of the bomber's tail surfaces or the control surfaces of its wing. Rather than risk the aircraft becoming entangled, the propeller was to be used as a circular saw, which would rip apart these areas of the bomber.

In discussing these plans, the men also considered their method of escape, and here views differed as to how best to assure a jump to safety. The major obstacle which could make escape difficult was the canopy. Some pilots therefore decided that by jettisoning their canopy in the last seconds before their attack they could be guaranteed to fall free merely by unfastening their seat straps. Other pilots, perhaps wishing for the maximum protection until the last moment, opted to hold on to their canopy until after the attack. The selection of either of these methods was entirely a matter of personal choice. During the forthcoming operations both methods were to be employed, and in some cases, seeing the approach of a fighter without a canopy, American crews instantly considered the 'Elbe' attacks to be nothing more than aircraft out of control, unmanned or carrying dead pilots.

It must again be stressed that all involved in these preparations, both the young pilots and their commanders, were seeking a method of escaping the impact of fighter and bomber. Having accepted the task ahead and the importance of the mission to the *Jagdwaffe*, to the *Luftwaffe* and to Germany, each pilot had his own clear plan. At the given signal the pilots intended to launch their aircraft, reach the bombers whilst avoiding the USAAF escorts, claim their victim and then parachute to safety. Yes, their mission was dangerous, and yes, the costs would be high, but if they completed their task as expected they themselves would live to fight again, having proved their worth in combat. More importantly still, the USAAF would suffer a shock defeat sufficiently severe to halt its daylight operations for a desperately needed period.

7. PLANS AND PREPARATIONS

With *Oberst* Hajo Herrmann's plans finally revealed to the pilots of the newly christened *Schulungslehrgang 'Elbe'*, the time had come to hand over the volunteers to *Major* Otto Köhnke, who had the responsibility of preparing his latest charges for their moment of combat. The period of training for any special mission is vital to the success of the eventual combat operation. In the post-war literature that does make reference to *'Elbe'*, this period of training has become clouded by the passage of time and by many of the myths typical of the period.

The first such myth, often repeated, is that during the days before their operations the young pilots received training in the necessary tactics for their missions and in the handling of their lightweight Bf 109s. According to reports, this included flights at the high altitude at which the mission would begin. What actually occurred during the days prior to the mission was rather different, reflecting events at this late stage of the war in Europe. Any collection of fighters assembled on a *Luftwaffe* airfield would have received very unwelcome attention from Allied bombers and fighter-bombers. To avoid this the pilots were to receive their aircraft as near to the time of their mission as possible. Even more of a determining factor was the critical shortage of fuel. The mission itself had been allocated only the minimum of this precious resource: no excess was available for training flights, no matter how essential they may have been considered and no matter how high a level of support *Oberst* Herrmann had gained. Instead, the training which could be provided was limited to many hours of theory, the younger, less-experienced pilots listening with special attention to the words of their older, more experienced *Kameraden*.

It seems that all the authors who have made comment upon this mission have paid particular attention to the high proportion of 'political indoctrination' given to the recruits, intended to produce a frame of mind prepared for patriotic suicide. But are such claims a true picture of the events? Were these pilots indeed effectively brainwashed by a continuous bombardment of overwhelming, vehement Nazi propaganda? Was the mission to be guaranteed its success with the aid of the Ministry of Propaganda, controlled so skilfully by *Dr* Goebbels, or do such reports serve to further another myth which surrounds *Schulungslehrgang 'Elbe'*? Because the mission required the group of pilots be formed into an effective combat unit, it was essential that they should spend time together. As many were untried in combat, they were to be given as much of the required theory as possible. With the period before their actual operation being so brief, every minute was to be utilized. Moreover, facing as they were a particularly brutal form of combat, it would have been detrimental to group cohesion to allow the pilots to remain idle. It is not an accepted form of military practice to give combat troops, of whatever form, time in which they can dwell upon the task ahead. Therefore a series of discussions and lectures was arranged to occupy the assembled pilots. Attendance was, however, to remain voluntary: the entire planning for the mission depended upon willing participation, and at this stage *Oberst* Herrmann and his staff refused to desert this ideal.

In truth, the older pilots, having shared beforehand the common military situation of waiting for combat, welcomed the opportunity of occupying their minds. Once the group had been brought together, many of the younger pilots became well aware of the exploits of the more experienced men of *Schulungslehrgang 'Elbe'*—and, indeed, also of the exploits of the *Jagdwaffe* pilots they were to follow. Therefore they eagerly looked forward to learning whatever secrets they could. In particular they awaited a talk which was to be given by one of the experienced *Sturmjäger* pilots.

The *Sturmjäger* pilot selected to give this introduction to the requirements of achieving a kill by ramming was to be *Oberfeldwebel* Willi Maximowitz. All those present were aware of Maximowitz's success. A pilot who initially served with the *Sturmstaffel* of *Jagdgeschwader 1*, he had transferred in the summer of 1944 to *IV./JG 3 'Udet'*. During his career he had amassed a total of 25 victories, fifteen of which were four-engine bombers and seven of them *Viermot* kills made by ramming. Such a daring pilot, a man whose success and survival had earned him the right to wear the *Deutsches Kreuz* in Gold on his right breast, was to find himself before a very attentive audience. Unfortunately, as *Oberfeldwebel* Maximowitz addressed the *'Elbe'* pilots, it quickly became apparent that, whilst his experiences were indeed dramatic and his thoughts on combat informative, the assembled pilots were unable to find a direct comparison to their mission. Whilst the rugged Fw 190A-8/ R7 of the *Sturmjäger* protected its pilots behind the large frontal area of a bulky radial engine, encased him in armoured plate and armed him with a selection of cannon and machine guns, the *'Elbe'* pilots would be flying a lightweight, unarmoured, virtually unarmed Bf 109. Once the pilots had recognized these striking differences, their attention began to drift from the words of *Oberfeldwebel* Maximowitz to further thoughts of their task ahead. The risks involved in the form of combat that Maximowitz had adopted and which he had detailed to his silent audience at the end of March were finally to prove too great: on 20 April, at the age of 25, he was killed as he once again attempted to stop the USAAF bombers.

With a growing atmosphere of paranoia permeating all levels of the German armed forces it was certain that the *'Elbe'* volunteers would find themselves on the receiving end of more than their share of political rhetoric. It was the availability of suitable speakers, however, which restricted the impact of the chosen words. On 29 March *Professor* Karl Börger, who held the rank of *SS-Brigadeführer*, arrived at Stendal to give the first 'political lecture'. Those who chose to attend his talk found themselves listening not to carefully phrased words of propaganda but to a straightforward reading from Friedrich Nietzsche's book *Der Wille zur Macht* (*The Will to Power*). Despite suggested close links between Nietzsche's works and Nazi doctrine, it has also been said that even Hitler, who was liable to quote key words and phrases from Nietzsche, was not actually familiar with his works but simply attracted to the words themselves. Such dry words, written as they were in the late 1800s, may have been capable of creating epic images in the mind of the German leader, but they could exert little influence over, or inspire any bold gestures in, the assembled men. Once this preliminary exercise was over, *Professor* Börger seemed to consider his required duty to these uninspired young men to be over and proceeded to fill his remaining allotted time, which ran for several hours, with a wide-ranging lecture to his audience on topics such as the structure of the universe.

A more formidable speaker was later dispatched by the Ministry of Propaganda. With a more carefully prepared series of topics, *Professor* Hans proved very adept in his task. His words, however, contained nothing that the young men had not heard before. Indeed, the talk centred upon subjects familiar to both the military and civilians. These included the threat from the Red Army, growing internal disputes which threatened the continued survival of the Allies, the hopes offered by a range of new 'super-weapons', and the Morgenthau plan. All of these subjects had been well covered by the press and had become general knowledge.

It is interesting that, whilst the plan of Henry Morgenthau, Secretary of the US Treasury, had by March been dismissed by Joseph Goebbels, it remained a central theme of such talks. The plan had called for the industrial areas of Germany to be divided among its neighbours, leaving only areas of agricultural land to support the population. Adopted readily by President Roosevelt in the summer of 1944, it was said to have been instantly disliked by Churchill. It became the subject of a series of debates within the higher circles of the US Government, which resulted in Roosevelt's being persuaded to reject it in favour of more humane and realistic scheme. With access to Allied press reports, which indicated that the Morgenthau plan was now outdated, Goebbels had accepted that the Allies were determined that, even in defeat, the German people must be allowed certain standards of living. Such knowledge, however, would not create suitable fear in the minds of the German people, and the full impact of the original proposal remained a constant theme of the period. In his diary entry of 1 April Goebbels was to record his thoughts in vehement fashion:

The German people are being told that they face a period of starvation lasting for years ... the Morgenthau plan will be pursued, under which Germany is to be turned into a potato field, German youth of military age is to be compulsorily deported abroad as slave labour and reparations are to be paid—in short, anyone can see that it would be preferable to be slaughtered.

With the urging of Josef Goebbels his Ministry of Propaganda ensured that by 1945 such words had become widely known in Germany. The threat of the suffering which would be endured following an unconditional surrender was illustrated by the Morgenthau plan. To the German people dark memories were brought to mind of the period immediately before and after the end of the First World War when the population faced starvation and then the harsh restrictions imposed by the Treaty of Versailles. Since the outbreak of war in September 1939 Germany had been surviving under a programme of food rationing. The system had worked well, with the extended Reich easily able to provide the supplies required. But by the winter of 1944/45 the system began to falter, firstly as a result of a severe winter in 1941/42 which killed crops and destroyed stockpiles and then because of the steady shrinking of the country' borders and loss of productive land. By March 1945 food supplies had been reduced to what amounted to critical levels. It has been shown in post-war analysis that the average daily intake of food had fallen below the minimum levels essential for long-term survival, and the threat of starvation had suddenly became very real.

With their families and homes already suffering from the Allied advances, the pilots did not need to listen to lectures to convince them of the need to fight on. As *Professor* Hans concluded his lecture, American forces continued their advance on the Western Front as they captured Frankfurt. To the east Soviet troops had completed their advance through Hungary and by the end of 29 March they were less than 50 miles from Vienna. Such facts provided a stimulus many times greater than any officially approved words could create. As was the case for so many *Wehrmacht* ground troops, fighting for every inch of each town and city, each man present at Stendal had by now his own reason for volunteering and most already had personal experience of the impact of the war.

In the evenings the pilots were able to attend screenings of selected films. Had these films been selected with the intention of convincing the men of their duty, instilling a hatred of their enemy and boosting their will to fight? After the passing of so many years the selected films have been identified by the *Luftwaffe* men allowed to attend the showings. Three, *Jud Süss*, *Der Gross König* and *Kolberg*, all products of the director Veit Harlan, are illustrative of the German film industry of the period. The first film, *Jud Süss* (*Sweet Jew*), is clearly based upon all the elements of Nazi anti-Semitic hatred. It was later claimed that this film was produced and acted under duress, but today it is considered to reflect what is possible through the power of cinema. Set in 1733, the film shows the actions of young men inspired by patriotic rage against wrongs upon their Fatherland. It has been said that *Jud Süss* 'brilliantly orchestrates themes and archetypes of Nazi propaganda to stimulate righteous wrath in the audience', and in the history of film-making it is considered to have been 'never surpassed for sheer malignant expertise'. But this film was produced in 1940 and its impact would have been weakened by the fact that it would have certainly have been seen at least once by the assembled pilots. Indeed, upon its release *Jud Süss* had been pronounced by *Reichsführer* Himmler to be compulsory viewing for the armed forces, the police and his own SS.

The second selection, *Der Gross König* (*The Great King*), was also a well-circulated title. With Frederick the Great as its central figure, it contained the accepted historical comparison to Hitler. Released in 1942, it reflected the belief that the nation's leader, an isolated and lonely figure, knew what was best for his people and that even in the face of overwhelming odds victory could be achieved. This film, whilst more relevant to the current fate of Germany, was perhaps even better known to the audience. A survey during 1944 found it to be the most popular film amongst German youth.

Kolberg was the both the most recent film and the one which reflected the prevailing propaganda of the moment. It was intended to prepare the population for a last-ditch defence of their homeland. It was a personal project of *Reichspropagandaminister* Goebbels', who allocated it an estimated 8½ million Reichsmarks and valuable resources, including front-line troops, to ensure full dramatic effect. The two central themes of the film are, firstly, that every citizen must be prepared to contribute to a strong and successful defence, and secondly that soldiers must have the 'right heart' to succeed in battle against a superior enemy. Reinforcing the belief that no sacrifice was too great for the State, it closes with the lines: 'The people arise, the storm breaks loose. From the ashes and ruin a new *Volk* will arise like a phoenix— a new Reich.' *Kolberg* was only completed in 1945, and events would lead to the film receiving very few showings, the pilots of *Schulungslehrgang 'Elbe'* being amongst a very select group to have witnessed this last production of the Third Reich's film industry. On completion of this epic Goebbels is said to have remarked to those within his circle of friends that in 100 years' time a similar film would be made of their own desperate struggle through their darkest days.

It was undoubtedly the mission ahead of the pilots which led to *Kolberg* being shown. As their base also had the necessary facilities to show the film, to an almost captive audience, the Propaganda Ministry was provided with an ideal opportunity to display its masterpiece. There are two points which detract from the intended effect of *Kolberg*. The first is that it attempted to alter history for its purposes: the defences had failed and the town of Kolberg had in fact fallen during the war against France. Secondly, and more importantly to the pilots, despite some spectacular battle scenes it was a very slow-moving and boring film.

So it was that even the full might of the Nazi propaganda machine was unable to produce an intensive indoctrination programme for these young pilots. They were left with talks and films, attendance at which was entirely voluntary. With the exception of *Kolberg*, the films and the words were not new, so it was left to the pilots themselves to collect their thoughts and prepare themselves for their coming battle.

It should be remembered that the use of films to boost morale and maintain civilian support was not confined to Germany. The Allied film industry was itself making every effort to depict the war in a manner thought best to ensure that the population remained supportive of the war effort. In America even the might of Hollywood was monitored by the Office of War Information, which favoured patriotic themes and recommended approved subjects. The American film industry was not averse to depicting events in a way guaranteed to produce the best response from its audiences. Whilst the armed forces were often depicted as fully racially integrated (for example, in *Bataan*), in truth this never actually occurred, but the facts would not have made good propaganda material. Even the success of the segregated 332nd Fighter Group failed to gain the unit official acceptance or support. What *Dr* Goebbels had become aware of and had attempted to exploit with his control of the German film industry was the important entertainment value of film. As he himself said, the main goal of the German cinema was to keep the German people happy, because that in itself also had a vital strategic importance.

It is also a sobering thought that the German propaganda organization, well known for its own anti-Semitic work, was able to borrow existing material from one of its enemies. One of literature's most lasting characterizations of the evil Jew, who wields financial power, hates the Christian and indulges in bloody sacrifices, is to be found in Shylock, who appears in Shakespeare's *The Merchant of Venice*. Despite the specially prepared and powerful images of *Jud Süss*, this classic of the English language was staged to great popular acclaim and official approval in Germany during the 1940s.

One further myth surrounding the training phase of the *'Elbe'* pilots is that they were shown captured B-17s by *KG 200*, which were used to demonstrate the defensive weaknesses of the aircraft and allow them to practise their attacks. Whilst the existence of such captured aircraft and their operation by this *Luftwaffe* unit are now well documented, such a demonstration did not take place. As has been illustrated, desperate fuel shortages would certainly not have allowed any opportunity for the pilots to fly mock attacks upon these bombers.

At the airfield of Hildesheim, about 90 miles east of the assembly centre at Stendal, *I./KG 200* had established a base for its three B-17s and lone B-24.

By April 1945 the remaining operational capabilities of this unit had been greatly reduced. On 6 April, in an attempt to save its aircraft from the danger of advancing Allied forces, the four bombers were prepared for a flight to Bavaria. During this flight the inherent dangers involved in attempting to avoid Allied fighters and also friendly flak units whilst flying such 'unfriendly' aircraft was graphically illustrated: only a single B-17 survived the transfer. An attempt to use any of *KG 200*'s bombers as a teaching tool for the volunteer pilots would also have required a good deal of coordination and planning and a large amount of luck, three commodities in desperately short supply. Indeed, when asked about events during this stage of the *Schulungslehrgang 'Elbe'* operation, none of those involved could recall the use of captured aircraft or knew of any plans of this nature. The value of such a demonstration must also be questionable. As a former pilot remarked, what could have been gained, except perhaps forcing some of the pilots to the early conclusion that ramming a B-17 was not a sensible thing to do?

With only a matter of days before their mission, the pilots carried out tasks which would have been familiar to so many men, serving with all armed forces worldwide. Any personal belongings were collected and wrapped with care, and they were placed with the appropriate last letters home. The time available had allowed the men to concentrate upon such tasks, many of them deciding to include their last will in the bundles which were then stored in a cellar at Stendal for safekeeping.

As friends had volunteered together in self-supporting groups, it was friendship rather than military requirements which decided the eventual combat formation of *Schulungslehrgang 'Elbe'*. Following the initial formation and brief period of joint instruction, the pilots were split initially between Stendal and two bases near Prague, Klecan and Rucin. Whilst splitting the force was a means to safeguard a valuable commodity, it also positioned a part of the force on airfields from which it would be possible to attack USAAF raids mounted by the Fifteenth Air Force against the remaining southern areas of the Reich. In order to keep in touch with his units, *Oberst* Herrmann now spent much of his time at these sites. Despite the pressure of command, he always found time to spend in discussions with his pilots.

As the waiting continued, further depressing news from the Western Front reached the men on 1 April. The US Ninth Army, under the command of General Simpson, had at last linked with General Hodge's First Army, in the area of the Ruhr centred around Lippstadt. This manoeuvre had completed the trap which now held *Generalfeldmarschall* Model and his Army Group B, formed from the 5th and 15th Panzer Armies and consisting of almost 350,000 German troops.

As April arrived the leadership of the *Luftwaffe* once again attempted to interfere with the planning of the mission. In a further change of heart the

Reichsmarschall let it be known that any holders of the Knight's Cross would not be permitted to fly; a vague suggestion that they were to be included in a future mission was given as the reason for this decision. When informed of this latest announcement the *Schulungslehrgang 'Elbe'* pilots who held this award were quick to express their concern to *Oberst* Herrmann. As he was well aware of the effect such a decision would have on the morale of the remaining pilots, Herrmann was once again forced to argue his case with his senior officer. As in the past, his words had the desired effect and the *Reichsmarschall* agreed to withdraw his latest order.

The final act carried out whilst the pilots were collected together as a large group was that each man was requested to provide a photograph, new ones being taken for those without a suitable copy. Whatever the outcome of the battle ahead, the pilots of *Schulungslehrgang 'Elbe'* were to be remembered, and the propaganda machine would also demand faces to attach to the list of victorious pilots.

The news which continued to come from the remaining edges of the Reich did little to lighten the mood of the *'Elbe'* pilots or their commander. On Easter Monday, 2 April, services were held in Cologne cathedral by victorious US troops. The remaining German forces left behind in Holland by the Allied forces were finally being removed by a British and Canadian push aimed from Nijmegan, whilst the US Ninth Army continued to press forward, by-passing Münster on its way into Westphalia. To the east, massive concentrations of Soviet forces centred upon Cottbus were seen to pose a serious threat to Berlin. But as the maps were being redrawn on this Easter Monday the news which would have caused the most concern may have meant little either to civilians or to many of the *Luftwaffe* pilots. For the leadership of the armed forces, however, the news from Hungary would have struck a blow to their plans. A combined force of Soviet and Bulgarian troops had occupied the oilfields of Nagykanisza, which Hitler had ordered to be defended by any means available. These oil facilities had been Germany's last hope of maintaining adequate supplies to allow defence and resistance. The immediate impact caused by the loss of Nagykanisza became apparent to the Allies in 'Ultra' transmissions intercepted during the day. A planned German counter-attack to break free of the encirclement in the Ruhr was cancelled by *General* Kurt Student because of a lack of fuel. German resistance was being bled dry by its very attempts to defend the remains of the Reich. The fine balance which exists between military success and failure is illustrated by events in the Ruhr. Where only the day before plans had existed for a counter-attack, the failure of supplies resulted in collapse. By 3 April the defence by the trapped units had become almost total, US forces reporting that between 15,000 and 20,000 prisoners were being taken daily.

By 4 April the inability of German forces to defend themselves against Allied advances became inescapable. Although such truths would have been withheld from Hitler, his commanders had at last to accept the fact that no section of the front line could be defended against further Allied breakthroughs. Unknown to the Germans, their tactics suffered further because of the success of Allied signal interception. This resulted in each defensive move being anticipated. To the East the last German forces were pushed out of Hungary, allowing the Soviet forces to continue the expansion of their hold upon Europe, which was destined to endure longer than had Hitler's Third Reich. On the 4th the war ended for another of the *Luftwaffe's* top aces. Whilst flying as *Kommodore* of *JG 52* in the East, *Oberst* Hermann Graf was shot down and captured, his score standing at 212 victories which included at least ten four-engine bombers.

Whilst the *Luftwaffe* suffered yet another blow with the loss of *Oberst* Graf, all the planning and preparations for the youngest group of *Jagdwaffe* pilots also ended on 4 April. Their period of training, limited as it had been, was deemed complete and the pilots were further divided, into groups to be stationed at the selected operational bases. A group of 12–15 men remained at Stendal, where they would share their final preparations with pilots of *JG 3*. The base at Delitzsch was to be the final home of a group consisting mainly of pilots who had volunteered from *II./EJG 1*. Men from *JG 1*, *II./JG 102* and *II./JG 104* found themselves at Mörtitz, whilst pilots from *JG 300* and *IV./JG 102* were amongst the group to be based at Gardelegen. The fifth site for these groups was the airfield at Sachau, where the pilots included the men from *JG 400*. At these bases it was intended that the men would at last find themselves with their fighters in preparation for their mission. Events, however, would lead to a further delay in deliveries.

Because of the fear of Allied attack upon any airfield, it would be unwise to assemble fighters too far in advance. An attack on one of the bases would not only destroy the aircraft but could also possibly lead to the death of some of the pilots, and it would almost certainly render the airfield inoperable. Once again the restrictions upon fuel reserves would mean that any fighters that could be delivered could still be used only for ground-based familiarization. The Bf 109s themselves had to receive the attentions of the ever dependable ground crews (the *Schwarzmänner*), necessary in order to produce the specified modifications.

The planning had called for the force to be equipped with Messerschmitt Bf 109G-14 or K-4 models, deemed to have the required high-altitude performance. Once they reached the airfields the ground crews would go to work to modify the fighters. The first alteration would be to transform their fighting capability: instead of being fitted with their potent combination of twin machine guns and single centreline cannon the Messerschmitts would be virtually neutered, armament being reduced to only a single, cowling-mounted machine gun. Any effectiveness this weapon may have retained was further reduced by providing a supply of less than 60 rounds of ammunition, replacing the normal 300 rounds. It is likely that the now empty gun trough on the upper cowling would have been blanked-off in an attempt to improve aerodynamics.

As evasion was to be the best form of defence against American fighters, every effort would be taken to produce a lightweight fighter, better able to outrun the Mustangs and giving the Messerschmitts the ability to climb higher than their existing maximum altitude. The level of thoroughness with which this operation was carried out remains in doubt. There are reports that orders called for all additional armour protection to be stripped from the fighters, but the complexity of this task, especially in the time available, suggests that the level to which this was accomplished may have varied.

With the available fighters coming from the late G and K production batches, the simple 8mm plate which had formed the pilot's head armour in earlier G models had been replaced by the *Panzerglas* (armoured glass) and metal framework. This improved fit, introduced to offer greater rear visibility, would have been as quick and easy to remove as its predecessor. The armour which protected the fuel tanks would, however, have required a greater effort to remove. To gain access to this plating the canopy and pilot's seat would have had to be removed, followed by the fuel tank and tank bay lining. The final armour which could have been on the list for removal was that which served as the rear bulkhead behind the fuel tank. With only one of the MG 131s remaining in place, a few additional kilograms could have been gained by the removal of one of the twin oxygen bottles used for the guns and mounted in the rear fuselage. To what extent remaining equipment was stripped out is uncertain. The only other large piece of equipment upon which attention can focus was the radio, and this will be considered later as the mission itself unfolds.

The total weight saving which could be gained by fully stripping a Bf 109 could have been as much as 440lb (200kg), endowing the converted fighters with a maximum 24mph (39kph) additional airspeed at their operational altitude. Had sufficient time been made available, the performance of the fighters could have been improved by almost as much again through sealing joints and seams and applying a high-gloss paint finish, which is known to have been carried out on other front-line fighters to boost their performance (the phenomenal performance of the Messerschmitt Me 163 was assisted by a waxed and polished paint scheme).

With all the elements of the operation in place, *Oberst* Herrmann was able to inform his men on 6 April that their mission was to be mounted the next morning. But by 6 April many of the fighters were only just reaching their bases. The race was on to supply the required numbers within the remaining hours.

It was accepted that the modified *Schulungslehrgang 'Elbe'* fighters would be unable to defend themselves in the face of US escort fighters and Herr-

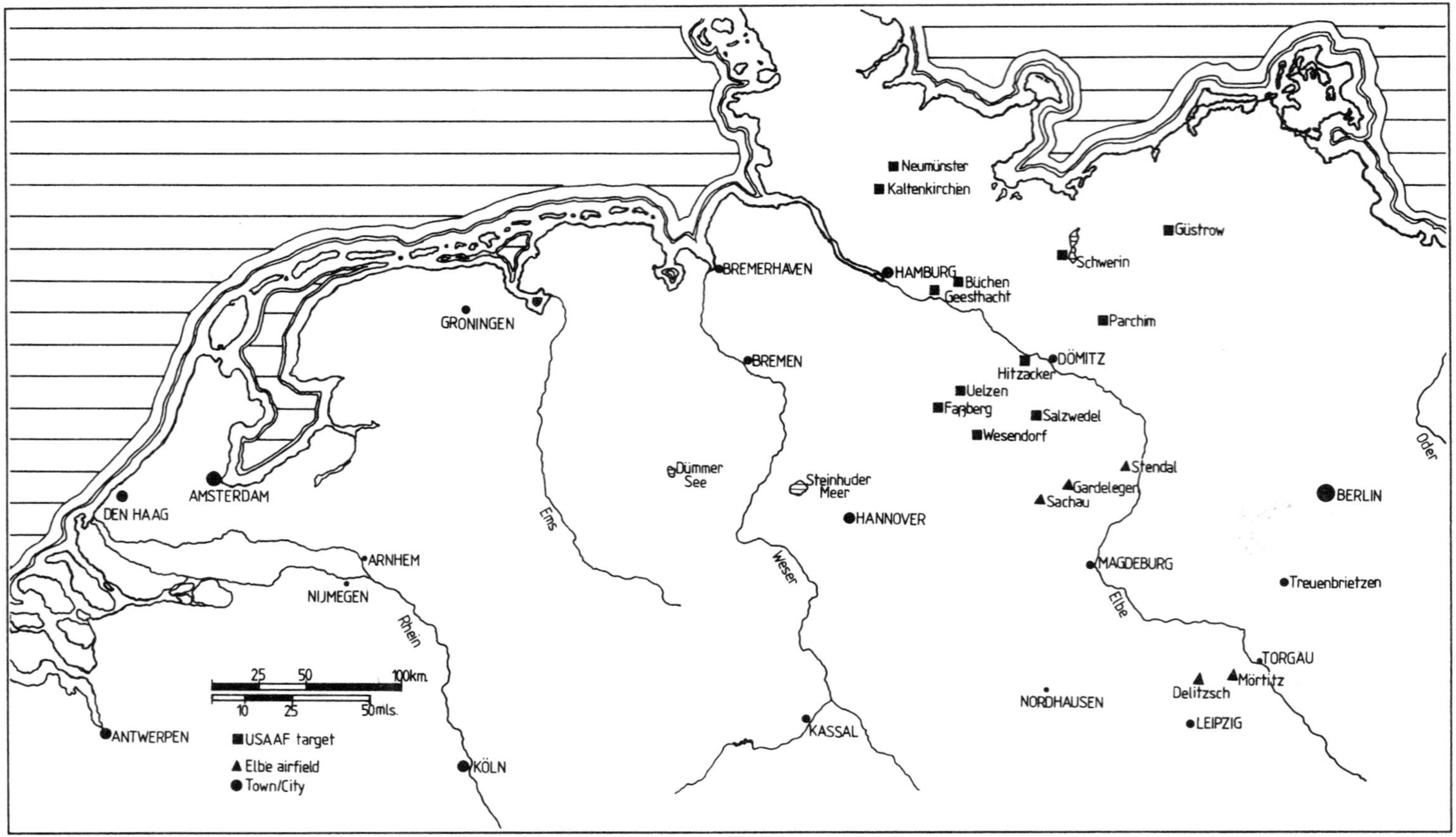

Map 1. Targets for USAAF raids of 7 April 1945.

mann's plans had accordingly been modified: the mission planned for 7 April would now be a large-scale operation with every available fighter in northern Germany joining the force. As *Luftwaffe* High Command issued the appropriate operational orders, it was something of an irony that a mission intended to allow a breathing space for the building of a large jet force would be allocated a protection force consisting mainly of Me 262s belonging to *JG 7* and *KG(J) 54*. To provide additional support to the *'Elbe'* force and to join their attack upon the American bombers, further conventional fighter units were included in the revised plans. It is also possible that these fighters were to provide protection to the jets during their take-off and landing manoeuvres. Reports suggest that the conventional fighters assigned to the *'Elbe'* operation were drawn from *JG 300* and *JG 301*, units whose origins lay with Herrmann's earlier plans. It has become clear that some reports which appear to suggest a large-scale involvement by *JG 300* and *JG 301* are incorrect. Both units had suffered extremely high losses and bore the scars which resulted from their involvement in defensive operations during the past months.

In correspondence with the author, *Generalleutnant* Günther Rall, at that time holding the rank of *Major* and appointed in March 1945 as *Kommodore* of *JG 300*, confirmed that he had found the *Geschwader* in chaos. His remaining command was constantly suffering as a result of repetitive transfers to new airfields. From Plattling in Bavaria *Major* Rall took his force further south to the outskirts of Munich, whilst at the same time two of the *Gruppen* were in the process of re-forming. By April 1945 Rall's force was subject to the disorder around it, organized missions had disappeared and the main concerns were now locating a supply of fuel to fly to the next airfield and enough food to survive until the next day. Now virtually cut off in the south of Germany, Rall continued to lead his command by his fine example during the closing stages of the war in Europe. It is interesting that, if *JG 300* had played such an important part in supporting *Schulungslehrgang 'Elbe'*, its *Kommodore* was never made aware of the planned operation. This would suggest that it was not *JG 300* itself but individual pilots from the *Geschwader* who had joined *Oberst* Herrmann's force as volunteers. It may also be possible that former *JG 300* pilots took with them their aircraft, but this has proved impossible to verify. The bulk of the conventional force would therefore come from *JG 301*, now a shadow of its former self following a period of extended combat operations. Despite the losses suffered by *Luftwaffe* fighter units, their identity remained a strong element in their continued existence, this identity being maintained even in *Gruppen* undergoing training, restocking and re-formation. With pilots from many units forming *Schulungslehrgang 'Elbe'*, those who found themselves with friends were proud of the former units in which they had served. It is this common identity and the links between *Oberst* Herrmann and *JG 300* that have added con-

COMBINED LOSSES, *JG 300/JG 301*

Date	*JG 300*	*JG301*	**Aircraft lost**
1 January	6 killed	3 killed	17
14 January	32 killed/missing	22 killed/missing	69
9 February	Combined 4 killed and 2 wounded		11
14 February	Combined 10 killed and 1 wounded		20
25 February	–	3 killed	3
2 March	6 killed/missing	17 killed/missing	30
24 March	6 killed/missing	–	18
	Combined total 112 pilots killed/missing		**168**

Source: Gerbig, *Six Months to Oblivion*, 1975

fusion to the composition of the additional forces supporting *Schulungslehr-gang 'Elbe'*. Although the more experienced pilots employed to support the operation were being drawn from a front-line and in theory combat-ready *Gruppe*, quite possibly they had only slightly more experience than the volunteers themselves.

The standard *Jagdwaffe* units received their instructions for the following day and noted a major change to the usual standing orders. To support the *'Elbe'* fighters the jet aircraft of *JG 7* and *KG(J) 54* were to ignore their usual targets, the USAAF bombers, and instead concentrate their attentions upon the escorts. By this change in operations it was hoped that the American escorts would become enmeshed in a battle with the jets and ignore the *'Elbe'* fighters as they climbed into their attack positions.

Having received their orders, the German pilots now tried to spend their time resting. For the ever-dependable ground crews the hours of darkness were again a time to complete urgent repairs: tomorrow was to see an all-out effort. The amount of time available and the number of ground crews at each airfield would result in a far from uniform force of modified fighters. It is certain that whilst many aircraft received conversions carried out to the letter, others may quite possibly have remained unmodified. The ground crews were experts at their tasks and the stripping of guns and cockpit armour could have been achieved in a short space of time. Pride in their work may even have meant that some of the fighters received a special polish for their missions the next morning. The ground crews knew something of the mission for which these fighters were being prepared. All those collected on the airfields, whatever their role, knew that for the young men of *Schulungs-lehrgang 'Elbe'* the next morning would bring their meeting with the enemy.

8. USAAF FIELD ORDER 1914A

The USAAF mission of 7 April 1945, Field Order 1914A, was officially the 931st raid by crews of the Eighth Air Force. This mission was to be the target for the pilots of *Schulungslehrgang 'Elbe'*. An examination of the list of targets selected by Eighth Air Force commanders finds a typical mission for this late-war period. Targets had been selected from the high-priority list and concentrated upon ordnance depots and jet airfields.

The 1st Air Division was allocated as its primary targets petrol and oil facilities at Hitzacker, together with the airfields of Kohlenbissen and Wesendorf, with a secondary target at Lüneburg. Consolidated B-24s belonging to the 2nd Air Division were provided with primary targets near Hamburg at the Krümmel and Düneburg explosive plants; their secondary target would be at Neumünster. The longest list of targets was allocated to the largest contributing force, the 3rd Air Division. This Division found that their daily listing included as primaries Kaltenkirchen and Parchim airfields, the Büchen oil storage facilities and the Güstrow ordnance depot. Sites at Schwerin and Neumünster were selected as secondary targets for the 3rd AD, Neumünster being the single duplication in the target list of 7 April. Even in this, the final full month of the European conflict, the routes selected were carefully chosen to avoid areas in which a strong flak defence was known to exist.

The Targets

To gain some understanding of the reasons such targets were being selected, the intelligence reports prepared for 7 April should be examined. The following extract has been taken from the 3rd AD's 'Intelligence Annex' to its field orders and lists the reasons for the selection of the primary targets:

GN-3773 (Güstrow):
This ordnance depot has shown marked activity on recent (photographic) cover and is the most important depot of its kind in this portion of Germany. It is sufficiently close to the Eastern front for the Russians to be well aware of its importance. A successful attack will not only be a tactical aid to the ground troops, but will also strengthen the diplomatic ties between the Allies.

GU-3910 (Parchim):
This is an operational field for both jet aircraft and conventional single-engined fighters. Recent cover has shown between 75 and 100 aircraft on this field, including both

Me 262s and Ar 234s. About two weeks ago P-51s were able to confirm the operational use of GU-3910 by jet aircraft when they trailed three Me 262s, which had been attacking 8th Air Force bombers in the Hamburg area, back to this field and destroyed them as they were landing. [This actually seems to refer to 25 March, when P-47s of the 63rd FS, 56th FG, chased six or seven Me 262s which had attacked a 2nd AD formation. The victims on this occasion were Me 262A-1bs belonging to *JG 7*. One of the successful American pilots was Captain George E. Bostwick, who would also be actively involved in the mission of 7 April.]

GU-4277 (Kaltenkirchen):
This Me 262 operational base was being used by a Gruppe of Jagdgeschwader 7 at last report. Recent cover has shown both Me 262s and a moderate number of other types of aircraft on this field.

GQ-2038 (Büchen):
Despite 2nd Air Division's attack of March 25th, the majority of storage tanks remain intact. Photographic coverage shows two of the nine tanks in the central section severely damaged, and another probably damaged. The southern and central tank areas have not yet been covered over with a protective cover of earth and concrete as has the northern tank area. This accounts for the MPIs being placed upon the two most vulnerable tank areas. [In fact the raid of 25 March mentioned above had been something of a disaster, bad weather causing the 1st and 3rd ADs to be recalled, leaving the 2nd AD alone to attack the oil facilities at Ehmen, Hitzacker and Büchen. Only 57 bombers had actually attacked Büchen.]

GH-5556 (Neumünster):
This marshalling yard has been assigned as the secondary priority target for all of the 2nd Air Division's 32 squadrons as well as 6 Groups of this Division. Operations Officers should brief Lead crews concerned of this fact. [Whilst every effort was being made to destroy the factories, industrial plants and workshops, the bombers still had to ensure that any material produced by surviving facilities could not be moved by rail.]

Based upon the weather forecast, the mission had been planned with a time over target of 1100hrs. The 3rd AD would lead the raid as the 'First Force', and the bombers were routed to cross the coast north of Amsterdam and on through the Dummer lake area to their targets. The mission plans state that the targets had no heavy flak defences and the sun would be behind the bombers at the time they appeared overhead. Those units attacking Kaltenkirchen were to withdraw north-west, crossing the coast north of the Elbe estuary and heading back across the North Sea. Other elements of the 3rd AD would have to fly further east to their targets. The withdrawal route for this force would follow the same general route as their outward journey as far as Osnabrück. From here the Fortresses would head west-south-west before crossing the coast near Ostend. An alternative route had originally been planned, but it was decided that with Western Europe now in Allied hands a journey back over friendly territory was a better option than a long overwater flight across the North Sea.

The Liberators of the 2nd AD were to fly a route similar to those elements of the 3rd AD who had targets around the city of Hamburg. They would cross into Europe near Harlingen after flying over Texel island. From here their route, until the time they returned to their bases, would be almost parallel to that of the 3rd AD. The routes had been planned to allow enough airspace between these two Divisions so that they could be dispatched simultaneously to their various targets.

The most southerly flight path was selected for the 1st AD. These boxes of B-17s would cross into Holland over the group of islands to the south of The Hague. From here their almost straight route would take them near to Hildesheim, south of Hanover, before a sharp turn to the north would lead them towards their targets. After hitting their targets the units of the 1st AD would complete a turn to allow them to re-join their outward path southeast of Münster. The formations would eventually cross out again over the North Sea at almost the same point as they had entered.

To achieve the planned time over target the zero hour for this operation was originally set at 0730hrs. However, once again nature altered the plans of man as an unexpected dense fog covered the Eighth Air Force bases. With weather conditions over Europe not expected to alter from original reports during the day, the mission would remain unchanged. Zero hour was, however, moved to 1030hrs to allow time for the fog over England to lift. A further last-minute change was made to the take-off time for the 1st AD. In order to allow the 3rd AD bombers sufficient time to clear their targets, a further 40 minutes was added to their zero hour: the 1st AD would now take off at 1110.

Amongst the crews preparing for their mission were men from the 100th Bomb Group at their base at Thorpe Abbotts. The crews had been woken just before 0200 to find an airfield blanketed by ground fog, with visibility reduced to only twenty yards. Whilst the bleary-eyed men huddled together in loose groups attempting to eat their early breakfast, one of many topics of conversation was the weather: would the mission still go ahead? By the time of their briefing, 0255, the crews found that the initial postponement of thirty minutes had been changed again. The new orders which reached the Group from their headquarters at High Wycombe informed them of the rescheduled zero hour: take-off would now be at 1030. Upon hearing the revised take-off time many men complained about the now unnecessary early start to the day. In quite a few of the post-mission reports a common complaint amongst Eighth Air Force crews was that no extra provision had been made to feed the crews again before their mission began—a long wait for bored and hungry young men.

For the third day in a row the crews had waited for the curtain to be drawn back from the map in the briefing room to reveal their target. On 5 April they had flown to Nuremberg (Nürnberg), and the 6th found them flying to

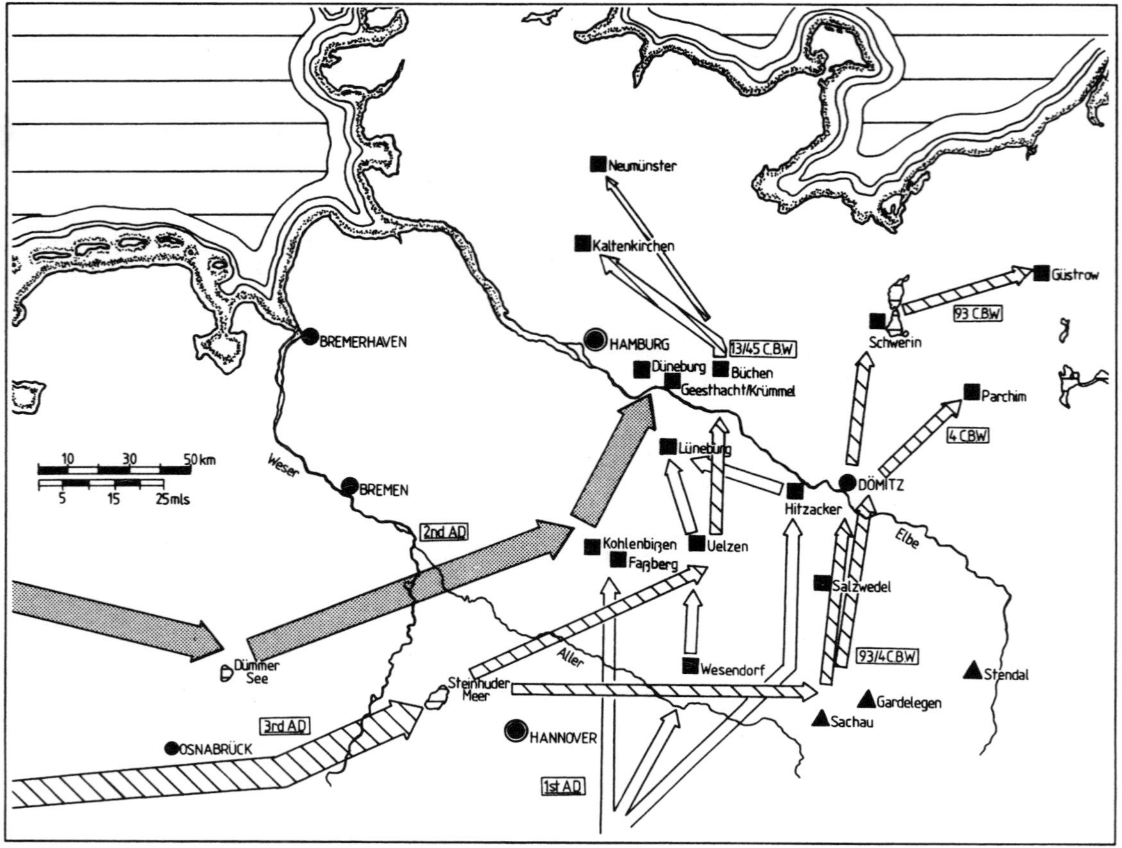

Map 2. Routes to targets, 7 April 1945.

Leipzig. Both involved long flights, and returning crews were exhausted, relieved to get back to their bunks. These two flights had marked the return to combat operations for Lieutenant William Howard and his crew. Having flown 22 missions, the crew had been allowed a rest period, nicknamed by the bomber units 'flak leave'. Once the enjoyable break was over they had returned to Thorpe Abbotts to complete their tour. Finding themselves required to fly these two missions immediately after their return, the crew could have been forgiven for believing that someone was determined to ensure that the rest of their tour was long and tiring.

When, finally, the curtain was drawn back the crews packed into the briefing room took one look at the map and began to cheer and applaud. Compared to the previous missions the coloured wool used to mark the route today appeared to have been halved in length. The most distant point of the route appeared to be Hamburg, but the line did not stretch into the city nor into its defensive belt of flak. Although any mission had its dangers, this particular one was quickly becoming a 'milk run'—and, as every crewman knew, every mission made the end of their tour and a return 'Stateside' that much nearer. As the assembled crews again settled to listen to the intelligence reports, it was confirmed that their targets were not protected by flak and that the *Luftwaffe* no longer seemed capable of posing a serious threat to their mission. The crews of the 100th BG found that they had been allocated as a target the underground oil depot at Büchen, about 30 miles from Hamburg. Their briefing officers informed them that the lack of defences resulted from the Germans' belief that these camouflaged facilities had remained secret. The fact that their target had already been selected for an earlier raid appears to have escaped the officer giving this briefing. The final 'icing in the cake' was the required bombing altitude, only 15,000ft; in his previous 22 missions Lieutenant Howard had not flown below 23,000ft. Today there would be no need for all of the cumbersome heavy fleece-lined jackets and trousers, and in addition the slightly warmer lower altitude would mean that there would be less time to spend wearing face masks and breathing oxygen.

The feelings of the 100th's crews as they left the briefing room that morning are reflected by William Howard: 'All in all, things sounded great and we were anxious to get going and get this one in and then have a day or two off before flying the next mission.' The only change in Lieutenant Howard's normal nine-man crew was for the ball turret position: today it would be occupied by Sergeant Lehrman, replacing the usual fresh-faced ball turret gunner 'Junior' Truitt, who was too sick to fly. Any frustration that this young gunner felt in missing today's 'milk run' was, however, destined not to last until the end of the day.

The declining numbers of *Luftwaffe* fighters being encountered by the bombers of the Eighth Air Force in the previous weeks had led to a growing belief that the enemy were becoming a spent force. Indeed, the bombers had not faced any conventional fighters from *Luftflotte Reich* since 2 March. Despite continued attention from the feared Me 262s, the reduction in the number of operations even by these jets seemed to confirm some intelligence reports which suggested that the remaining *Luftwaffe* fighter force was being diverted to face the danger on the Eastern Front. With a previous break in operations having being used to build the force eventually allocated to 'Bodenplatte', it was being suggested that this current lull in single-engine operations signified the building of a new ground-attack strength intended to support the increasingly desperate attempts to stem the flood of Red Army armour and troops.

The Eighth Air Force field orders for 7 April indicate that the *Luftwaffe* jets were expected again to make an appearance. The clear weather forecast over the target areas and the *Jagdwaffe* airfields would allow the jets to reach the bombers despite possibly being delayed by lingering patches of weather on take-off. Intelligence reports suggested that a jet force estimated to be around 50 aircraft could be brought to bear. Interestingly, the orders suggested that it would be the B-24 Liberators of the 2nd Air Division which would receive the most concentrated attacks by the defending fighters. This resulted from the forecast improvement in weather conditions as the day progressed which would coincide with the Liberators' attacks. With such a threat being posed by the strong formations, all the escort fighters on this day were forbidden to attempt freelance patrols and strafing attacks and were instead told to ensure that close support was provided for the bombers. Again, an examination of the Intelligence Annex to the 3rd AD's field orders illustrates the expected dangers:

Enemy Air Opposition.
All forces will be crossing the area where approximately 200 tactical fighters are located. These are not expected to react, but are capable of opposing the bombers anywhere east of eight degrees. There are approximately 250 fighters located in the area south of Bremen. Most of these aircraft are thought to be non-operational. Forces on GU-3910 and GN-3773 (Parchim and Güstrow) are reminded that 2nd Air Division was attacked by 30–35 Me 262s in target area on 4th April. Also near target area are six operational jet fields, each of which has ten or less Me 262s.
Weather is against take-off and assembly of large numbers of enemy aircraft.

It will be seen, as the events of 7 April unfold, that the weather forecasters of 1945 often had the same problems as their modern counterparts in being unable to predict conditions accurately. The actual conditions encountered over Germany were to have a dramatic effect upon both defenders and attackers.

The stillness and quiet of the English countryside was finally shattered as one by one the massive collection of 1,200hp Wright Cyclone engines first coughed and then roared into life. In a space of only a few minutes what could, by the dim light of this early spring morning, still be mistaken for farmland had once again become the front-line of a new type of war. Where once horses ploughed the field, in a scene unchanged for decades, now plane after plane prepared to carry its load of 4,000lb of explosive into the heart of the enemy homeland.

As the bombers of the Eighth Air Force gradually rose from their airfields, they began the time-consuming process of assembling in the skies above south-east England. The massive formations which filled the sky would today be led by 529 B-17s of the 3rd AD, supported by an escort of 338 P-51 Mustangs. Following this leading formation would be the 2nd AD, 340 B-24s with their mixed escort of 55 P-47 Thunderbolts and 229 P-51s. Trailing behind this already formidable force would be a further 442 B-17s and 222 Mustangs of the 1st AD.

Over 1,300 bombers and almost 850 fighters were launched by the USAAF for this mission, and their presence was reported quickly, via the remaining communication links, to the headquarters of *IX Fliegerkorps* at Treuenbrietzen. The assembly of the force would not have been the first sign of an imminent attack. Throughout the morning the *Luftwaffe* would have been intercepting both the signals of the Eighth Air Force units in England and also the reports from the weather and route scouts already airborne in advance of the main force. Although the targets could not yet be forecast with any accuracy, these initial warnings were common indicators of large formations, indicators which the *Luftwaffe* had a great deal of experience in interpreting. This activity was enough to persuade *Oberst* Hajo Herrmann to issue an order which placed the *Schulungslehrgang 'Elbe'* force on standby.

At the many airfields occupied by the Eighth Air Force fighter units, the morning began later than it had on the bomber airfields. As the fighter pilots began their morning routines they were able to benefit from a few precious hours' extra sleep. Without the fear of attacks from *Luftwaffe* fighter-bombers their aircraft had been checked and prepared by their assigned team of ground crew the night before; only a few last-minute checks were necessary before a pilot could be strapped into his cockpit to begin a mission which could last for anything up to seven hours.

Amongst the pilots receiving their final briefing was the 434th FS officer who today would lead the 434th Fighter Group. Major Robin Olds had already reached ace status flying the P-38, having become the leading Eighth Air Force Lightning ace with nine confirmed kills. After his group converted to the P-51 Major Olds was quick to adapt to his new mount and was able to exploit its numerous virtues. He would add a further three victories to his total whilst flying a series of Mustangs which carried the name *Scat*, ending the war with thirteen kills. Having proved himself to be an both an outstanding pilot and an outstanding leader of men over Europe, Robin Olds would continue to serve the Air Force and rise to a higher command. He was later called upon to repeat his role as a fighter pilot over the very different countryside of Vietnam. As commanding officer of the 8th TFW he was to create the most successful MiG-killing Wing to see combat in South-East Asia. Once again seeming to become at one with his fighter, Colonel Olds set a formidable example to his 'Wolfpack'. Having already seen more than a lifetime's share of combat, he achieved four kills while flying the McDonnell Douglas F-4 Phantom, an aircraft which symbolized American air power in this new war as much as the Mustang did during its service between 1943 and 1945.

As these men at their bases in England prepared themselves for their missions, some of their fellow pilots from units based in Europe had today already tasted combat. Two reconnaissance pilots belonging to the 160th RCN squadron had flown a mission which carried them close to Hildesheim and to the area to be overflown later in the morning by the 1st AD bombers. Their early morning flight had led to a combat with a *Rotte* of Fw 190s which resulted in the American pilots being able to claim one kill each. A larger clash began at 1030hrs and involved a formation of Mustangs from the 356th FS, 354th FG. By April many of these pilots had themselves become convinced that the *Luftwaffe* had only a few days of operations left. When they did still encounter their opponents it was in small numbers. The 354th FG had seemed to follow the advancing Allied armies into Europe: they were now actually based within Germany, flying from an airfield at Ober Ulm which lay to the west of Mainz. Here the crews had been at last able to benefit from accommodation built for the *Luftwaffe* and to a much higher standard than their previous temporary bases in France, and even better than many of the quarters in England. Their mission today was a typical one—a patrol forward of their own troops with orders to attack any enemy vehicles on the roads or positions in the area ahead. Leading the two flights was Captain Richard Asbury, now flying his second tour with the 354th FG having previously flown with the 363rd FS, when he had claimed two kills.

Having reached the area to the north of the Thüringer Wald, the reconnaissance pilots' uneventful flight suddenly ended as enemy fighters were spotted ahead. After many days of only occasional contact, the sight of a mixed formation of ten to fifteen Bf 109s and Fw 190s was something of a surprise. In contrast to their previous encounters, this group did not appear to have been involved in a ground attack operation. But Captain Asbury wasted no further time considering their destination; instead he ordered his fighters to attack. As the Mustangs of the 356th FS fell upon them, the *Luftwaffe* pilots scattered. But their attempts to escape were not completely successful as Asbury quickly opened the score by downing a long-nosed Fw 190 after a brief chase. This kill was quickly followed by victories by other pilots, who destroyed three Bf 109s and a single radial-engine Fw 190. These five *Luftwaffe* fighters fell only 70 miles south-west of the airfield of Delitzsch, on which at that moment part of the *'Elbe'* force sat in readiness—and this raises the possibility that they had been on their way there to join in the planned operation. Thoughts that the fighters could have been flown by inexperienced pilots had not entered the minds of the 356th pilots. When asked about this encounter, Asbury commented that by that stage in the war the standard of enemy pilots did vary, but that in each encounter one dare not judge one's opponent too soon—'you prepared as if he was the best.' This attitude obviously served Richard Asbury well, as he ended his second tour having achieved ace status with five confirmed kills. He returned to the Air Force in 1950 and after a successful career ended his service in 1972 with the rank of Lieutenant-Colonel. The 356th had not yet ended its day's hunting with these fighters as its pilots also dispatched a pair of Do 217s, although one of these, claimed by 2nd Lieutenant Green, could not be confirmed. After six confirmed kills by his fighters, Captain Asbury had reason to be satisfied with the morning's work. Even if the ownership and the destination of the *Luftwaffe* fighters remains unknown, the encounter set the scene for 7 April: the *Jagdwaffe* had started the day by making an appearance in force.

With the Eighth Air Force formations assembled and now on the first leg of their journey, their approach was monitored by the remaining elements of the *Luftwaffe*'s early warning systems. With their foe approaching, the time had come for the young *Luftwaffe* pilots of *Schulungslehrgang 'Elbe'* to climb into their fighters. Special attention had been given to the collection of parachutes: unlike normal operations, if these pilots succeeded they would be returning to their airfields after having used their parachutes. The pack containing the carefully folded silk was today a very important piece of equipment. All of those men collected on the airfields occupied by the *Schulungslehrgang 'Elbe'* fighters, whatever their role, knew what lay ahead. After all the planning and preparation, for the young men in the cockpits the time to do battle had arrived.

As the first bomber formations reached the Dutch coast the escorting fighters, their 'Little Friends', positioned themselves to defend their flock. By 1100hrs the leading groups were over Holland itself and this now enabled an estimated plot to be calculated by the staff at Treuenbrietzen. The bombers seemed to be heading for the area between Hanover and Bremen, and in about an hour they could become the targets for the *'Elbe'* pilots. *Oberst* Herrmann committed his force.

The final briefing for the pilots had told them that they were to assemble over two selected points. Part of the force would be positioned over Magdeburg on the southern edge of the expected route and others over Domitz, thought to be on the northern edge. However, today the route which the bombers were following would swing to the north and those fighters over Domitz would find themselves in the middle of the target area.

The first *Schulungslehrgang 'Elbe'* fighters to take off were to be the formations at Stendal, Gardelegen, Sachau, Delitzsch and Morlitz. Despite the planning, events taking place on these airfields are indicative of the constant state of confusion which seemed to hamper every aspect of German military operations at this late stage of the war in Europe.

Despite the promised supply of fighters, on the morning of 7 April the pilots at Stendal were still awaiting their aircraft. Whilst sixteen Bf 109s, which appear to have been prepared in advance but held at an alternative location, were finally rushed to the airfield a further 40 pilots were left with no suitable aircraft. Even the promise of a number of unmodified Fw 190s could not be met. At Delitsch the Bf 109s were ready, although ground crews were only now completing the refuelling process and only a limited number of suitable drop tanks could be found. These difficulties, added to the expected mechanical problems, reduced the number of fighters which could respond to the order to take-off. Again, at Morlitz a series of mechanical problems which could not be resolved in time resulted directly from the late delivery of aircraft. With a shortage of spares and a shortage of fuel, it had proved impossible to test the fighters thoroughly, and only a reduced force to 24 aircraft was available. In addition, only twenty of the fighters assembled at Gardelegen could be made ready; a further twenty pilots stood by in disbelief as they were told that repairs were still being carried out in an attempt to make ready more aircraft and that replacement fighters were also expected.

As the selection of pilots was made at Gardelegen it forced two friends from school to say their goodbyes. The young pilots *Oberfähnriche* Fritz Marketscheffel and Armin Thiel had been friends for years, and together they had volunteered for *Schulungslehrgang 'Elbe'*. Now they were to be unable to carry out their mission together: Thiel had been allocated a fighter but Marketscheffel had not. With the ground crew helping to strap his friend into the cramped cockpit of his Bf 109, *Oberfähnrich* Marketscheffel struggled to think of suitable words to wish him good luck. Although Marketscheffel survived the day and was to survive the remaining weeks of war, he was never to see his friend again—and the tale was to be repeated many times this day.

Only at Sachau were the required number of aircraft ready. From this airfield thirty of the stripped Bf 109s leapt from the ground even as the green flare still appeared to hang in the air, their take-off run reduced because of the unusually light weight of the fighters. Once airborne and gaining height, the fighters were pointed towards their enemy.

On these airfields the ground crews, those involved in the training and the pilots without aircraft of their own had watched as the young men walked to their Messerschmitts, each pilot from the various *Rotten* pausing only briefly to shake hands with his comrade. Aware of the mission ahead of these pilots, aware of the dangers they faced and fully recognising their chances of survival, those watching saluted the taxying fighters and the men in them. As had become more and more widespread as the war approached its inevitable end, these salutes were not simply Nazi salutes, demanded throughout both the armed forces and much of civilian life, but the more traditional military salutes, given in defiance and as a tribute to the pilots.

With its short take-off run, each fighter was seemingly keen to join the others in its mission. The *Schulungslehrgang 'Elbe'* operation was at last under way. In a matter of hours, when all the reports were in, *Oberst* Herrmann would discover if his plans had succeeded. At the five airfields nearest to the incoming bombers, a total of 120 Messerschmitts had been launched. The time was just after 1115. On take-off the resounding notes of martial music were broadcast over their headphones to the pilots; as the pilots climbed to gain altitude and their mission began in earnest, this music was replaced by a woman's voice reminding them of the dead of Dresden and of the hopes of their family and friends

Having split his force during the previous days, both to cover all of the expected bomber routes and to protect his valuable aircraft, *Oberst* Herrmann now found that part of it was badly positioned to reach today's raid. Having a further 60 fighters spread between the airfields of Klecan and Rucin, on the outskirts of Prague, he had placed all the fighters on alert together with the main force. With the targets for the bombers still unclear, this force was also given the signal to take off: the aircraft could be aimed towards the Americans as the raid progressed.

At this point it is perhaps worth examining the radio messages reaching the ears of the German pilots and also being recorded by the Allied listening stations. It had become standard practice in both daylight and nocturnal *Luftwaffe* operations for a running commentary to be given to guide fighter pilots to their quarry. On 7 April this commentary was again quickly noted by Allied listening posts: a defensive operation was under way. What distinguished today's broadcasts was the inclusion of the patriotic slogans and various appeals to the pilots. Obviously lacking in navigation skills, the *Schulungslehrgang 'Elbe'* pilots required a commentary which attempted to place the fighters in the correct airspace. The other sections of the transmissions were attempts to reinforce the commitment of the pilots to their task. Although something of a melodramatic touch—after all, the pilots had already decided their reasons for taking part—the commentary did serve to concentrate the minds of many. To this day, even after the passage of so many years, many of the *Schulungslehrgang 'Elbe'* survivors clearly remember the voice of the woman who seemed to be speaking directly to them, reminding them of the destruction wrought upon their homes by the hated bombers they were about to face. The other unusual aspect of that day's radio transmissions was that they were one-sided: the Allied monitoring services failed to record any messages from the *'Elbe'* fighters themselves. Former pilots from *Schulungslehrgang 'Elbe'* confirm that they were unable to speak either to each other or to their commanders.

Two possibilities exist for this. The first is that, in order to save weight, the fighters had been stripped of their radio transmission capability, though any weight gain from this would be minimal. It would also be impossible for all of the fighters to have been fitted with revised radio equipment. A light-weight radio had been designed to be carried by reconnaissance fighters, but it is very doubtful if a supply of such sets could have been made available for the *'Elbe'* force. However, even these sets retained a transmission capability.

The second possibility is that the standard sets remained in place but had been set only to receive messages. This is similar to the 'Y-system' which had been used successfully by the *Luftwaffe* on many occasions before. In the battle for control of the night sky the *Luftwaffe* had used the 'Y-system' to broadcast a running commentary, on the *Reichjägerfrequenz*, to guide a single night fighter towards its target. This fighter would then be used to pass the information to other fighters not equipped to receive the commentary. It will be noted that in this type of operation the pilot retained the ability to switch frequencies and talk to other fighters in the air. If this was the method employed to guide *Schulungslehrgang 'Elbe'*, quite why their fighters remained 'dumb' is unclear. It is true that the Allied monitoring services failed to pick up the fighters themselves, noting instead only their instructions from the ground. But once the *Luftwaffe* formations reached altitude they became visible to Allied radar. Bearing in mind that the pilots were by and large inexperienced, an ability to gain assistance from those around them could have been beneficial. If, on the other hand, it was an attempt to isolate the pilots from any uncertainty that their comrades may have displayed, it was to have a detrimental effect on the mission as a whole. The ability of this group of *Luftwaffe* pilots to talk to each other, offering words of support and allowing words of warnings to be given, would be missing from the clashes which followed.

With the German fighters beginning to climb to the relative safety of their operational altitude, further problems began to appear. The inexperienced young pilots found that it was more difficult than expected to maintain even the loose formations adopted by *Schulungslehrgang 'Elbe'*. Weather conditions were far from ideal: the cloud reduced visibility and the freezing air contributed further difficulties. Whilst ground temperatures were hovering between 8° and 10°C as the aircraft climbed, the fall in temperatures became dramatic. At 10,000ft –12° was recorded; by 15,000ft it was down to around –20°. Still the fighters climbed and still the air became colder. By 20,000ft it had become –29°, and it fell a further 10 degrees in 5,000ft so that at around 30,000ft it was estimated to be approximately –48°. In addition, the strain involved in flying the fighters also began to tell. It requires a great deal of effort for even an experienced pilot to control a fighting aircraft. Struggling with his still unfamiliar mount, each pilot was well aware that there was now the constant threat of danger from roving enemy fighters.

The main force of fighters was now airborne and attempting to reach to specified altitude of 10,000m (32,800ft). With two distinct American formations now being traced by *Oberst* Herrmann's headquarters, it was decided to spilt those fighters nearest to the bombers. Those from Sachau, Delitzsch and Mortitz were instructed to head towards Magdeburg, which was expected to be on the southern edge of the approaching *Viermöte*. To block the northern edge, the smaller force of 36 fighters from Stendal and Gardelegen was directed over 120km (75 miles) further north, to a position over Domitz on the River Elbe. It had been intended that the 84 fighters of the larger formation would reach their position above Magdeburg by 1140hrs, but these young pilots, many on their first combat mission, were still encountering problems.

As 1140 arrived many of the scattered *Rotten* were still on their way to Magdeburg, several fighters having developed mechanical problems, forcing the nervous pilots either to return to their airfields or, worse, in desperation to abandon their aircraft. Despite the early USAAF forecast, the skies over Europe this Saturday were in some places filled with clouds. Many of the German pilots found themselves enveloped by a freezing blanket, immediately cutting them off from their fellow pilots. In such conditions, and with their minimal instrument flying training, several quickly became disoriented, in some cases turning their aircraft through 180 degrees. Fighters from Sachau turned north-west, in the direction of Hamburg, instead of south-east towards Magdeburg.

By midday only about 70 of the *Schulungslehrgang 'Elbe'* fighters, led by those from Sachau who had remained on course, had assembled in a loose formation over the Magdeburg. With the force being reduced by the minute, a decision was made which was to have a dramatic effect upon the day's mission. Having arranged for the positioning of the larger force over Magdeburg, Herrmann had to decide what to do with the 60 fighters still approaching from Prague. Dogged by delays, this group was not yet in a position to join even the most southerly formation. To play a role in the forthcoming combat, the Prague-based aircraft would have to be committed almost immediately to combat: they had little in the way of fuel reserves and any further delays would undoubtedly scatter the formation even more. Faced with this choice and with all reports indicating that the course set by the USAAF formations was beginning to veer further north, Herrmann decided to order the 60 fighters from Prague to return to their airfields. The music and demands for retribution being broadcast to these pilots were replaced by the message to return to base. Less than 25 minutes into their flight, before they had even reached the Leipzig area, the fighters which had launched from Prague received their recall signal. At a stroke the *Schulungslehrgang 'Elbe'* force, at one stage approaching 200 aircraft, had been reduced to less than 120. It was now even below the minimum strength of a standard *Jagdgeschwader*. The 60 aircraft returning to their bases would have to be used another day. Having seen his plans frustrated at every turn, Herrmann now had a force below what he had considered to be the minimum required. At this point he may have considered recalling the remaining force, but the operation had required so much preparation and his pilots seemed so committed that he allowed it to continue. He also knew that it was unlikely that sufficient fuel supplies to mount another attack would appear for a number of days, especially after having abandoned the first mission. The major question now was whether the remaining fighters could inflict the required losses upon the bombers. The reduced force of *Schulungslehrgang 'Elbe'* fighters was directed north-west, to begin their hunt for the approaching American formations.

Had the Eighth Air Force bombers turned south, instead of north, it is possible that the full force of defending fighters could have been employed. However, even had the delayed 1st Air Division flown its route according to the original schedule, this force would still have escaped the attention of the Prague-based *Schulungslehrgang 'Elbe'* fighters, which had only become airborne at about the same time as the rest of the force. That these fighters had proved incapable of joining the other *'Elbe'* aircraft adds further support to the idea that they had been placed by *Oberst* Herrmann in a location that would suit their employment against other raids, perhaps those flown by the Fifteenth Air Force bombers who operated from more southerly bases than the Eighth.

At about midday the USAAF formations began the turn on to the leg of their journey which would carry them towards their target areas. Near to Lübeck the leading bomber crews prepared themselves for the hardest part of their flight. As well as facing any danger from flak above their targets, they were now approaching the areas where the *Jagdwaffe* was known still to hunt. Despite the reduced danger now posed by the depleted enemy force, each gunner, in each bomber, began to search his section of sky for any warning of the approach of an unfriendly fighter.

9. 1155: THE FIRST COMBATS

Ahead of the massive formation of bombers which steadily droned towards its targets, the leading American escorts suddenly spied their foe. The B-24s of the 2nd Air Division had as a part of their escort the 56th Fighter Group from Boxted. This group was unique amongst the Eighth Air Force fighter units: the first group to convert to the P-47, it would retain the bulky Republic fighter as its preferred equipment throughout the battles over Europe. In contrast to the gleaming silver P-51s, so representative of Allied air superiority, the 56th still painted their 'Jugs' in more traditional disruptive camouflage colours. It was one of these fighters, its rudder painted in the blue of the 63rd Fighter Squadron, that claimed the first Bf 109s from *Schulungslehrgang 'Elbe'*.

To the north of Celle, at the southern edge of the 2nd AD's route, the leading P-47s from the 63rd FS, call-sign 'Household White', crossed the path of a single *Rotte* aiming for the bomber formation at about 30,000ft. Startled by the formidable ranks of American fighters, the two *Luftwaffe* pilots, finding themselves hopelessly outnumbered, reacted by instantly forgetting the rules of air combat and separating, one disappearing into the sun, the other finding himself with a pair of P-47s on his tail and with no support from a *Katchmarek*, his wingman. The leading Thunderbolt was flown by 2nd Lieutenant Charles McBath, who gradually pulled back on the stick to keep the *Luftwaffe* fighter in sight. As the Messerschmitt attempted to out-turn McBath's fighter it flew directly into his sights. Pressing his thumb to release the firepower of his battery of 0.5in machine guns, the American could see debris fly from the right wing of the Bf 109. With the damaged fighter seeming to slide across the sky in front of his P-47, he was able to cut through its contrail and centre his sights upon the cockpit. Under a further concentrated burst the *Luftwaffe* fighter almost seemed to disintegrate, a cloud of metal, shattered parts and fuel erupting in front of McBath, forcing him to take rapid evasive action. Streaming a trail of smoke and coolant, the mortally wounded fighter began an almost vertical dive, the dead or dying pilot trapped within the remains of the latest comet to streak from these skies. It was 1155. The day's battle had yet to begin.

Fifteen minutes later, as the 2nd AD continued towards its targets, a single Bf 109 was spotted north-east of Düneburg by the red-nosed P-51s belonging to the 334th FS, 4th FG. As the Bf 109 flew between the various formations of the 334th it was the trailing 'Cobweb Blue' Flight which dispatched fighters to deal with this solitary attacker. The two Mustangs which gave chase were flown by 1st Lieutenant James W. Ayers and his wingman 2nd Lieutenant John R. Mummert. In a further very brief encounter Ayers was able rapidly to climb and close to within 400yds of the enemy fighter. Under a concentrated burst which hit the cockpit area, the *Luftwaffe* pilot had no hope of escape, a lethal hail shattering canopy, instruments and flesh alike. Although the pilot was able to jettison his canopy and unbuckle his seat belt he was too badly injured to jump. As Ayers flew past his victim he was followed by Mummert, who was able to look into the Bf 109 cockpit and see a slumped figure at the controls. Without the necessary control the damaged fighter suddenly rolled, throwing its pilot free, but his injuries were such that he plunged to earth. It was now 1215.

These initial, very one-sided encounters were reported to the other fighter and bomber groups. But, for the pilots and air crews, a far greater danger had already been spotted. The larger formation of *Schulungslehrgang 'Elbe'*, directed from Magdeburg towards the American formations, had been seen by Allied radar as it approached Hanover at 1213. As the advancing Allied armies pushed back the German early warning defences, so their own mobile MEW (Microwave Early Warning) network could advance to offer warning of the approach of *Luftwaffe* formations. Such warnings were now broadcast throughout the bomber formations, and the crews braced themselves for the attacks.

The parallel flight paths for the 3rd and 2nd Air Divisions had spread their bombers between Hamburg and Hanover, an area over 90km (56 miles) wide, and with the *'Elbe'* fighters now also spread over a wide area attempting to reach the American formations, both Air Divisions were to find themselves simultaneously under attack during the next hour. With the main battle only a matter of minutes away, *Oberst* Herrmann unleashed the units intended to support the *'Elbe'* pilots. The Me 262s of *JG 7* and *KG(J) 54* turned west and headed for the area about to be occupied by the 2nd AD. Added to this formidable force were the mixed formations consisting of long- and short-nosed Focke-Wulfs, the Ds and As from *JG 301*.

With the warnings and sightings from fellow pilots now coming over the radio, the pilots of the 351st FS, 353rd FG, caught their own glimpses of the approaching enemy fighters. The boldly coloured formation of Mustangs with yellow and black chequerboard noses were slightly to the east of Steinhuder lake when three contrails were sighted approaching their bombers from 3 o'clock at about 30,000ft. Blue Flight reacted by dispatching fighters to carry out the interception. The leading fighters, 'Lawyer Blue One' flown by Captain Charles L. McGraw and 'Lawyer Blue Two' flown by 2nd Lieutenant Robert F. Hahn, had to climb to meet the *Luftwaffe* fighters. They had been able to gain 6,000ft when suddenly one of the Bf 109s flashed over the Mustangs, making a diving attack upon the B-17s positioned behind the screen of fighters. In a stomach-churning manoeuvre, McGraw and his wingman jettisoned their drop tanks and hauled their fighters around to give chase. Having two determined pilots sitting on his tail had a detrimental effect upon the concentration of the *Jagdwaffe* pilot. Faced with the option of following through his attack or evading the Mustangs, he opted for the latter, flipping the Bf 109 on to its port wing tip and heading for the possible safety of the cloud cover which lay over 10,000ft below. Keeping the diving Bf 109 in his sights, McGraw was able to close to within 600yds before they reached the clouds. The first shots from the Mustang split the air about the fleeing fighter. Desperate to shake free from this attack, the Bf 109 pilot began to pull his fighter into a climb, at the same time sliding from right to left in front of the Mustang. But this only placed the fighter directly into the line of fire from McGraw's twelve machine guns, strikes being visible on the fuselage and wing root. Another Mustang from his Flight dived past Captain McGraw, forcing him to lift his thumb from the control column. As he again lined up the Bf 109 it began to roll under the renewed hail of fire. Before his eyes the entire tail section suddenly broke free from the Messerschmitt, the doomed fighter instantly spinning, trapping its pilot as it hurtled to earth.

Climbing back to continue their escort duty, Captain McGraw and Lieutenant Hahn found themselves separated from the other two P-51s of their Flight. Before the pair could re-join the bombers they spotted another single Bf 109 heading for the bombers. Aiming at putting themselves between the fighter and the bombers, the Mustangs succeeded in a near perfect interception, dead astern of the *Luftwaffe* fighter. Before any action could be taken by the Bf 109 pilot his aircraft shuddered from strikes from McGraw which punctured the wings and ignited fuel. Having lost any chance of surviving this assault, the German pilot needed no further prompting before jumping free from his aircraft, being able to parachute clear. Within the space of fifteen minutes McGraw had been able to claim two kills. Before the day had ended he would increase his score further.

As the radio began to report the growing contacts and sightings, the American pilots found themselves in an action of a scale not seen for some time. It could no longer be assumed that the approaching dark shape would turn out to be a friendly fighter. Any aircraft, especially any approaching the massed ranks of bombers, was carefully followed by many watchful eyes. With so many aircraft now becoming concentrated within a relatively small area of sky, the number of encounters increased—as did the confusion.

The Thunderbolts of the 56th FG spotted some of the Me 262 force as they approached their flock of bombers near Nienburg. Their immediate reaction was to turn towards the menacing jets. This was exactly the response the German pilots had hoped for, the escort force being drawn away from the bombers. In one of the P-47s of the 63rd FS Captain George Bostwick found himself giving chase to a swiftly departing Me 262. His attempts to hit the jet seemed futile and it became clear that it did not intend to turn back into the bomber formation. Thinking that the screen of escorts was having the desired effect, Bostwick was startled by the calls from the pilots who had remained to cover the bombers. Further contrails had been spotted above the bombers. Quickly realizing that these aircraft posed a greater threat than the jets he was chasing, Bostwick turned and put his P-47 in a steep climb to intercept them. At about 30,000ft he was able to catch one of the aircraft and position himself astern. In his combat report completed after this encounter, Captain Bostwick was to identify his quarry by its fixed tail wheel, and with the information available to him at the time he associated this feature with the 'Me 109E'. Judging the distance to be about 300yds between himself and what was in fact a later model of the Messerschmitt fighter, the American pilot opened fire. The burst of bullets which ripped into the German aircraft were enough to inflict crippling damage. As the Thunderbolt passed below its victim, Bostwick noted a stream of coolant and briefly glimpsed the German pilot as he leapt from his stricken mount. Having passed this Messerschmitt at the very second the pilot had jumped clear, Bostwick failed to see him slam against the tail. He was, however, spotted by Bostwick's wingman, 1st Lieutenant Andermatt, who was later to confirm that the *Luftwaffe* pilot had no chance of surviving the impact; indeed, the parachute never opened as the body continued to fall. These may have been the final moments of *Fahnenjunker-Feldwebel* Gerhard Bohnke, whose body was found south-east of Verden.

With this first victim dealt with, the American pilot searched for his next target. He spotted another single contrail and gave chase. As the gap narrowed he saw that this fighter was a P-51 and he followed the unknown pilot, finding himself being led directly to a flight of five Bf 109s. Selecting one of the enemy fighters, Bostwick found his intended victim more alert than his first. The Bf 109 'split-S'd from about 30,000ft', catching the Thunderbolt pilot by surprise and forcing him to give chase without firing. Finding his target in a high-speed dive, Bostwick followed by instinct, the two fighters flashing earthwards at increasing speed. After plunging almost 20,000ft Bostwick spotted a dark object, which the thought may have been the pilot, separate from the German fighter, which continued its dive and crashed into a small area of water to the north of Hamburg. Having seen the fate of the *Luftwaffe* aircraft, Bostwick judged that the time had arrived for him to pull out of this dangerous manoeuvre, and he activated his flaps to recover from the dive. Although this did abruptly halt his dive, the intensity of the recovery caused the pilot to black out for a few seconds. As he regained his sight and control of his fighter Bostwick was able to climb back to altitude and continue his protection duties. However, he found himself in the midst of a fast-moving battle between *Luftwaffe* fighters and a formation of P-51s.

Attempting to assist the Mustangs, he found his P-47 becoming the target of their attentions. He was lucky to escape their fire on a number of occasions, and it can only be assumed that his aircraft being a different shape from the P-51 was enough to make him identifiable as hostile. These errors of identification would not be the only ones on this day.

The B-24s of the 2nd AD and their escorts continued to record the first clashes as they moved across the skies towards their targets. Positioned second in the 2nd AD formation was the 20th CBW, which consisted of the 93rd, 446th and 448th BGs, the twin tails of their Liberators decorated with bold yellow and black markings. Today the Wing had as their assigned escorts the Mustangs of the 479th FG. In contrast to the bold colours of the bombers and also in contrast to so many other P-51s in the sky today, these examples of the sparkling silver North American fighters bore little in the way of individual identification markings. For the 479th FG fighters there were no chequerboard noses, nor were there any bright splashes of red, blue or yellow streaming back along their forward fuselage. Instead the Group had chosen the least decorative of the myriad schemes to be found within the Eighth Air Force. Only the rudders of their fighters received any extra colour: for the 434th FS they were painted red and for the 435th FS yellow. The 479th FG had assumed the title 'Riddle's Raiders' in honour of their commander, Colonel Kyle L. Riddle, who had led the Group from December 1943 but had been shot down during combat on 10 August 1944. Any period of grieving for their commander was, however, cut short when he was returned to the unit at the beginning of November.

As with Captain Bostwick's combat, it was the approach of Me 262s which signalled the start of today's action for the 479th FG as their bombers flew towards their target at Düneburg. Although Major Olds was responsible for leading the pilots of the 479th FG, he was flying as leader of the 434th FG, in position as a part of 'Newcross White'. A similar role was being carried out by Captain Verne E. Hooker, who was leading the 435th FS. Both Olds and Hooker were concentrating upon the type of mission which had already honed their skills and were about to meet again the foe against which these skills were tested.

Flying to the north of the leading bombers, as they began to approach the Weser south of Bremen, it was the pilots under Major Olds who spotted the first tell-tale contrails of approaching Me 262s. It was now approximately 1220. The airwaves began to fill with reports of the jets. They were flying at about 30,000ft and were now clearly heading for the Liberators. Leaving the other two squadrons to offer close protection to the bombers, Olds led the 434th FG towards the jets. In what seemed a matter of only a split second, the Mustangs had dropped their tanks and were heading towards the jets, only to find themselves facing twelve of the twin-engine Messerschmitts in an almost perfect formation, already beginning their dive towards the bombers. The jets increased their speed as they passed the American escorts, and Olds was left to push his squadron through a series of tight turns to place them on to the tails of the German aircraft. Hearing the calls of approaching enemy fighters, followed by instructions to drop tanks and give chase, one of the 435th FS pilots searched the sky around him for signs of contrails. Already feeling alone, 1st Lieutenant Richard G. Candelaria had lost contact with the rest of his Flight and on reaching the rendezvous with the bombers had decided to attach himself to the Low Squadron of Liberators. Finding no sign of the German fighters, Candelaria held his position and held on to his tanks. Little did he know that he was about to experience a day to remember.

Amongst the 434th FG pilots, 'Newcross Yellow' Flight now found themselves giving chase to this formation of jets which had flown under them. Flying 'Yellow Leader', 1st Lieutenant Gail E. Jacobson and his wingman, 2nd Lieutenant Robert L. Munson in 'Yellow 2', seemed to think it was their presence which forced the jets away from their quarry. Although attempting to chase, Munson admits that his progress was rather sluggish because of a slight problem which had caused his right drop tank to hang up. Having little hope of catching the twin-engine fighters, the 479 FG pilots were able only to fire a few bursts as their quarry continued to pull away.

Positioned towards the rear of the bomber stream, Captain Hooker and the other pilots of the 435th FS quickly spotted the danger of approaching enemy aircraft. Turning towards a pair of jets, Hooker opened fire at long range on the leading aircraft in an attempt to divert the pilot from his selected targets. Even such a brief and spontaneous burst succeeded in finding its target, the left wing of the approaching jet receiving a number of hits. The strikes appeared to have the desired effect as the jet turned away from the bombers and their screen of escorts, but Hooker was unable to pursue his target as a second *Rotte* of Me 262s had been spotted heading in his direction. Turning to face this further threat, Captain Hooker missed the pilot of the damaged Me 262 jettison his canopy and leave his fighter to crash to earth. A number of Me 262s had remained near to the trailing bombers, and in order to protect these more vulnerable B-24s Hooker attempted to position his force to deter further attacks.

From his position alongside the lower bombers, Lieutenant Candelaria was at last alerted to the presence of the jets when the bombers began to fire flares as a general warning to the rest of the group. Spotting a pair of Me 262s which had started to climb back towards the bombers, he turned towards the jets, facing the leading aircraft head-on. Hoping to divert the jets from their direct approach, Candelaria must have begun to have doubts as to the wisdom of this move as the *Rotte* made no attempt to alter its course. With only fractions of a second separating the fighters from a collision, the Me 262 pilot pushed his aircraft into a shallow dive beneath the Mustang. In a very unusual move, Lieutenant Candelaria tried to drop his tanks on to the jet below him, then half-rolled his fighter into a position on its tail just as the German pilot opened fire on the bombers. With his drop tanks tactic having no effect, Candelaria opted for his more conventional armament and let loose a burst which scored direct hits on both fuselage and wings. With the fighter still in his sights, his concentration was broken by the sight of streams of red and white tracer 'the size of golf balls' flashing past him. Glancing in his rear-view mirror, he saw the second jet, which he had ignored for only a brief moment, hugging his tail, its nose ablaze as the battery of four 30mm cannon fired—described by an RAF pilot as a sight similar to a gas ring. Candelaria was in grave danger: a direct hit from even one of the 30mm rounds was capable of literally blowing a target apart. Before he could break away from this new danger the Me 262 scored hits on the Mustang's right wing, the shots somehow passing through without inflicting a mortal wound. At the same instant the leading jet broke to the left and entered a half-roll which became a steep dive with smoke trailing behind. Hoping to catch the second jet, Candelaria attempted to haul his fighter into a turn, but the jet was diving at high speed, perhaps in an attempt to assist his crippled *Kamerad*.

In his combat report of this incident, Major Olds confirms the thoughts of fellow pilots by describing how the jets had flashed through the bomber stream without firing; as they circled back, seemingly intent upon preparing for a fresh pass, they were driven off by the sight of the approaching Mustangs. A more likely interpretation is that the Me 262s were being flown according to the orders of the day, attempting to draw away the escorts without engaging the bombers, leaving these targets unprotected for the following conventional fighters. This interpretation seems quite accurate as the P-51s were led further and further from the bombers. By the time they broke contact they had been led down to 15,000ft into the area around Bremen.

This would appear to be confirmed as the 434th FG pilots broke contact with the departing jets and turned back to re-join the bombers. In the minutes that they had pursued the jets the bombers were very vulnerable. As they once more approached the boxes they heard the desperate cries for assistance from a pilot who had spotted a formation of up to fifteen Bf 109s heading his way. As the more distant American fighters did their best to increase their speed in order to assist the bombers, the lone pilot who had given the warnings prepared himself as best he could.

Having stuck closer to his charges than his colleagues, it was Lieutenant Candelaria who had spotted the new contrails approaching from a higher altitude. The formation appeared to consist of a loose collection of three *Schwärme*, each with a more experienced leader. With only a matter of seconds to make his decision, Candelaria opted to select the nearest 'leader' but found himself flying against a very competent *Luftwaffe* pilot. All

Candelaria's best efforts failed to place him any firing position, and he trailed after the Bf 109 as it led a *Schwarm* against the bombers. The young American pilot noted that none of the *Schwarm* attempted to fire upon him or even the bombers but simply followed their leader as he made several passes which succeeded in downing one of the bombers. It must be assumed that the *Schwärme*, at least, were formed from *Schulungslehrgang 'Elbe'* pilots but it remains unclear if their leaders were pilots from *JG 300* or *JG 301*. The fighter being followed by Lieutenant Candelaria obviously had enough ammunition to carry out a conventional attack and would appear to have been flown by a very skilled pilot. Whilst obviously aware of the P-51 trailing in his wake, the German pilot seemed to be revelling in his combat, making inverted firing passes and even shooting at the bombers while rolling his fighter. With mounting frustration Candelaria chased after the Bf 109 and for a split second found it in his sights. The luck of the *Luftwaffe* pilot had finally run out: the brief burst of fire struck his fighter. Perhaps in order to escape the confines of the bomber stream to concentrate on the annoying American, the Bf 109 broke away from the B-24s with his formation remaining in close contact. None of the other Bf 109s made any attempt to intercept the P-51, which reinforces the belief that they were very inexperienced in the techniques of aerial combat. The leading Bf 109, now aware that the Mustang on his tail was out for blood, would have to fend for himself and eliminate the danger by his own skills. However, with a number of aircraft in close proximity he selected the wrong direction to attempt a roll and the battery of Browning machine guns being aimed at him unleashed a burst of hot metal which ripped into the Messerschmitt.

With a trail of smoke and coolant erupting from the Bf 109, panic erupted amongst the now leaderless *Schwarm*. Breaking their formation, they belatedly attempted to discourage Lieutenant Candelaria but the damage had already been done and the leading Bf 109 continued to lose altitude until the pilot jumped free at about 2,000ft. The *Schwarm*, now in disarray, had no success in either hitting the P-51 or in chasing it away and a second *Schwarm* leader arrived to assist. In his eagerness this new *Luftwaffe* pilot misjudged his speed and overshot the Mustang, which placed him directly in the centre of the K-14 gun sight. Needing no second chance, Candelaria immediately hit the firing button. He was only able to manage a brief burst before the German pilot cut his throttle and the two fighters found themselves flying side by side. To his surprise, as Candelaria glanced across at his enemy he saw the pilot free himself from his seat straps, open the canopy and bale out.

With two *Schwärme* now leaderless, the confusion around the Mustang multiplied as any attempt at coordinated action by the *Luftwaffe* fighters evaporated. Finding himself the subject of the attentions of several Bf 109s, Lieutenant Candelaria continued to fight his way free. Able to out-turn his pursuers, he again opened fire and almost instantly a third Bf 109 levelled out and the pilot jumped free. A fourth Bf 109 followed only seconds later as the pilot lost control of his fighter attempting to follow the Mustang. This *Luftwaffe* pilot was trapped in his wildly spinning machine as it crashed to earth. As Candelaria claimed this fourth Bf 109, his fifth victim of the day, help finally arrived as other P-51s reached the bombers. The first pilots to arrive included 1st Lieutenants Charles Heathman and William Barksky, who were both in position to observe the final moments of Candelaria's combat and confirm the burning wreckage of four Bf 109s, all within a radius of less than five miles. Not wishing to tempt fate further that day, Lieutenant Candelaria stayed with this group of pilots for the remainder of his mission. In his post-action report Candelaria wrote that he thought the arrival of these Mustangs saved him from the remaining Bf 109s, but on such a day it is doubtful if anything could have proved a danger: surely his guardian angel must have been sitting in his cockpit throughout his flight.

Not having flown as far from the bomber stream as many other pilots, Captain Hooker was near enough to spot the approaching Bf 109s. Deciding that these conventional fighters now represented a greater danger than the remaining jets, the Mustangs turned their attentions towards the individual Bf 109s. With the pilots of the Messerschmitts concentrating upon the bombers ahead of them, searching for a suitable target, they failed to spot the Mustang intent upon closing the gap between them. It proved relatively easy for Captain Hooker to select a lone Bf 109 and open fire, flying his Mustang to within 50ft of the now doomed fighter. As the *Luftwaffe* fighter began to trail smoke, Hooker broke to the right and had to glance over his shoulder to see the young *Luftwaffe* pilot leap free from his now burning aircraft.

As his formation finally neared the boxes of B-24s, Major Olds spotted a lone Bf 109 which had already commenced a dive towards a selected target. Locking himself on to this new foe, Olds quickly realized that he would be unable to fire: the *Luftwaffe* pilot was leading him between the individual bombers within one of the tight combat boxes, and he was still too distant to guarantee that his shots would only find their intended target. Forced to trail the Bf 109, he was powerless as the German pilot opened fire on one of the B-24s, instantly scoring hits that Olds could clearly see as he desperately pushed his fighter closer. At last he was free from the bombers and he was able to open fire. There was no possibility that he would allow this Bf 109 to escape: having been unable to offer the bomber protection, he was now about to exact his revenge.

As his first burst struck the Messerschmitt, its pilot attempted to escape by rolling, but Major Olds was perfectly placed to follow and continued to score direct hits as both aircraft rolled together. Having no hope of avoiding these shots, the *Luftwaffe* pilot leapt from his mount whilst still in his roll. As Olds levelled out he saw the Bf 109 dive straight towards the ground.

Another kill had been added to a score which was to continue to climb for many years to come. This chase was not without a small cost to Olds. During the dive he had lost a wheel fairing, which proved troublesome for the rest of his mission—the Mustang was unable to reach its expected speed and was sluggish in a climb. With a fighter now unable to give the expected 100 per cent, its very frustrated pilot was unable to reach other Bf 109s and on one occasion was overtaken by another P-51, which proceeded to dispatch the *Luftwaffe* fighter which Olds had singled out. After a combat cut short due to mechanical problems, Olds wrote in his report, 'After another futile attempt to get to a high gaggle of 109s, I headed for home'—not the sort of decision likely to please this ace. Throughout his brief combat Major Olds had only used 377 rounds of his 0.50-calibre ammunition.

Amongst the formation arriving with Major Olds were Lieutenant Jacobson, now finally free of his troublesome drop tank, and Lieutenant Munson. Sticking close together, both pilots spotted a further group of *Luftwaffe* fighters. Estimating this force to be ten to fifteen strong, Jacobson thought that a number of Fw 190s appeared to be leading a formation of Bf 109s flying behind and above them, at approximately 32,000ft. This was the same formation that Lieutenant Candelaria was doing his best to destroy single-handed. The 'Yellow Flight' pilots had to gain altitude to give them any hope of dealing with this threat. However, the advantage lay with the German fighters and the two pilots were forced to tag on to what they assumed to be the trailing Bf 109. Just as Jacobson thought he was in an ideal firing position, Munson called out over the radio: glancing in his mirror, he found he had a Bf 109 sitting on his tail. In a coordinated move, both men hauled their fighters to the right. The intention had been that the Bf 109 would follow Munson in his turn and that Jacobson would then be able follow both fighters and deal with the Messerschmitt. In fact what happened was that Munson entered a very tight turn which the German aircraft had little hope of matching. With his Mustang still completing his 360-degree turn and his fighter in a 40-degree bank, he found that he had outmanoeuvred his opponent. A final glimpse through his K-14 gun sight confirmed his success and he opened fire. Without releasing the pressure upon the firing button, Lieutenant Munson virtually flew the rounds into the doomed enemy fighter. Both American pilots could see the damage being done by this assault as the canopy shattered and the wings shed chunks of ripped metal. As the Bf 109 snapped into a vertical dive trailing coolant and flames, the *Luftwaffe* pilot was somehow able to bale out from his fighter, which had suffered from the impact of almost 1,000 rounds from Munson's P-51.

As this combat ended it was the turn of Lieutenant Jacobson to look into his rear-view mirror and feel the grip of approaching danger: a Bf 109 was now sitting on his tail. Luckily for Jacobson this *Luftwaffe* pilot was in no hurry to test his ability against a P-51: it was quite probably one of the

Schulungslehrgang 'Elbe' pilots, perhaps even more scared than the American at the prospect of entering what would have most probably have been his first dogfight. After only one turn to the right the danger was gone and Jacobson was free to seek a new target. With so many aircraft in the area a further Bf 109 was quickly singled out, and after pulling their aircraft through 360 degrees the two 'Newcross Yellow' Mustangs gave chase. Almost instantly the Bf 109 was in Jacobson's sights, and at 200yds he let loose a two- or three-second burst, which was enough to damage the Daimler Benz engine. Although the aircraft was less severely damaged than Lieutenant Munson's victim, this fighter was also seen to enter a dive and the pilot was seen to jump free. These two combats had led the American pilots south-east, back across the bomber stream they were protecting, and both of their victims were recorded as having fallen near Celle. However, some doubt must surround this position and it is perhaps more likely that the combats occurred between Soltau and Hermannsburg. In giving chase to the Me 262s and the standard *Luftwaffe* fighters, elements of the 479th FG had now become scattered over a sizable area. Whilst many had maintained contact with their allocated wingmen and remained in their combat formations, others, like Lieutenant Candelaria, found themselves seemingly alone in a hostile sky.

In his Mustang 2nd Lieutenant Milton O. Thompson had given up the fruitless chase of the jets and turned back in the general direction of the bombers. As he scanned the sky around him for further enemy aircraft he realized that he had lost contact with his fellow pilots. He now knew that the *Luftwaffe* was active in the area, and his reaction was to try to make contact with any friendly fighters. Flying at an altitude of 26,000ft and hoping to spot his squadron returning to cover the bombers, he sighted a single Me 262 about 2,000ft above him. This jet appeared to be in no hurry, the pilot in the process of a gentle climbing turn. Having found one of the jets at last not using its great speed advantage, Thompson decided to give chase again. Pulling his fighter into a climb, he followed the Me 262 to 31,000ft , cutting inside the jet's turning circle. As his climb had enabled him to remain hidden from the German pilot until the last minute, he was able to close to within 800yds before opening fire. Now alerted to the danger, the German pilot attempted to take avoiding action, pulling the Me 262 into a tighter turn. However, the damage had already been done: the first shots from Thompson had found their mark in one of the extremely sensitive Jumo turbojet engines. As the turn became a roll and then a dive, the Mustang continued to pour fire into the *Luftwaffe* fighter, now hitting the cockpit area. By this time Lieutenant Thompson was in a high-speed dive following his quarry, and at about 15,000ft large pieces of the jet began to break loose. With his target critically damaged and the speed of his own fighter causing some concern, Thompson decided to pull out of the dive. In doing this he lost sight of the Me 262 and remained in ignorance of its fate until the debriefing session at Wattisham later in the day. Although he was unaware of the approach of friendly fighters, as he began his attack a formation of P-51s had spotted this lone Me 262 and had been following the chase with interest. One of the aircraft was being flown by 1st Lieutenant Robert I. Browmschwig, a fellow 434th FG pilot. Just as the Mustang broke contact and began to level out, Browmschwig saw the German pilot leap free and his parachute open as the jet continued its dive to earth.

The preceding battles had seen many of the individual pairs of *'Elbe'* fighters under attack before they had the opportunity of approaching their prey. In many cases both fighters which formed the *Rotte* were lost only minutes or even seconds apart. This was to be the fate of *Fahnenjunker-Feldwebel* Karl-Heinz Schrader, who had taken off with Gerhard Bohnke. It appears that both pilots may have fallen before the guns of the 56th FG. At 34 years of age Schrader was one of the oldest *'Elbe'* pilots, but he had travelled from *II./EJG 1* in Denmark filled with a similar excitement to many of the younger men: here at last was the chance to contribute to the defence of his country. His flight today finally allowed him to fly in defence of his own home town of Braunschweig. But, as with so many soldiers and airmen who had gone before, fighting over familiar ground was no guarantee of survival. Schrader's wrecked Messerschmitt was eventually found after the war, the body of the pilot still firmly strapped to his seat.

Although the 479th FG performed their protection duties well, the 20th CBW did not completely escape the attentions of the *Luftwaffe* fighters. Throughout the Wing crews would later to report the 'very bold' attacks upon the formation. The Group which bore the brunt of the attacks was the leading 93rd BG, the 'Travelling Circus', which could claim to be the oldest B-24 unit in the Eighth Air Force. The Germans almost seemed to single out the squadron wearing the most conspicuous markings, for the bulk of attacks fell upon the 330th BS. This Squadron had the noses of several bombers decorated with fearsome dragon markings, but today these proved unable to ward off completely the attacking fighters. Whilst the 479th FG continued to add to their scores, several lone fighters broke through to dive upon the B-24s. However, only one attack resulted in a successful ramming, this being upon the B-24 coded 'J'. As the gunners fired upon the diving fighter, it veered off its selected course at the last instant and smashed into the left wing of the bomber. The *'Elbe'* pilots had decided before the mission that any attempt to ram a bomber's wing would be very dangerous because of the position of the fuel tanks—no one wished to be engulfed by an inferno of burning fuel. Only a matter of feet had separated the point of impact from the tanks of this bomber. The top-turret gunner had the best view of the damage and reported that the fighter had removed over two feet of the wing tip and that the outer engine appeared damaged. Having survived the ramming, the crew of the B-24 soon found themselves flying on three engines as the

Above left: *Oberst* Hajo Herrmann believed that his plans could remove the threat of USAAF bombers long enough to allow the *Jagdwaffe* time to re-equip. He saw a jet fighter force as the only hope of protecting Germany. (Zell)

Above right: *Generalmajor* Adolf Galland, one of the outstanding pilots and leaders of men, photographed when he held the post of *General der Jagdflieger*. After his own High Command wrecked his plans in January 1945, Galland spent the remaining months of the war doing what he did best—leading his men and flying the ultimate fighter of the period. (IWM MH6038)

Left: By the winter of 1944/45 *Reichsmarschall* Göring, once the second most powerful figure in Germany, maintained his position in name only. As Speer noted, 'Göring had relapsed into his lethargy, and for good.' (IWM MH6041)

Above: Albert Speer (on the left), already appearing to distance himself from *Grossadmiral* Dönitz and *Generaloberst* Jodl. It was Speer's personal influence with Hitler which halted the *Selbstopfermänner* plans. (IWM BU6173)

Below: *Obergefreiter* Horst Seidel (left) and his friend *Unteroffizier* Werner Zell (right). They volunteeered to join the new unit together. (Zell)

Above left: *Fähnrich* Franz Winter, an *'Elbe'* volunteer who later joined Bienenstock. (Zell)

Above right: *Leutnant* Franz Zens, a *II./EJG 1* pilot who volunteered for *'Elbe'*. (Zell)

Below left: A poor photograph but an interesting subject: *Unteroffizier* Klaus Molly, who also volunteered, was a nephew of *Reichsmarschall* Göring. (Zell)

Below right: *Obergefreiter* Henfried Breinl. (Zell)

Above left: *Leutnant* Hans Bott. (Zell)

Above right: *Oberfähnrich* Otto Stumpf. (Zell)

Below left: *Feldwebel* Hans Fussinger. (Zell)

Below right: *Major* Kohnke's adjutant, *Leutnant* Karl-Heinz Anton, joined him at *Schulungslehrgang 'Elbe'*. (Zell)

Above left: *Gefreiter* Ernst Tetzel. (Zell)

Above right: *Unterfeldwebel* Manfred Wienkotter-Wolf. (Zell)

Below left: *Oberfeldwebel* Ernst Rummel. (Zell)

Below right: *Obergefreiter* Hans-Dieter Eitle. (Zell)

Above left: *Feldwebel* Mathias Kruchem. (Zell)

Above right: *Obergefreiter* Hugo Harms. (Zell)

Below left: Often outspoken, *Major* Otto Kohnke proved to be an ideal choice to build the *Schulungslehrgang 'Elbe'* force. (Zell)

Below right: The *Kommodore* of *JG 300* on 7 April 1945 was *Major* Günther Rall, destined to become the third-ranking ace in history. In 1956 he returned to the military to assist in the rebuilding of the post-war *Luftwaffe*, which he was to lead from 1970 to 1974. In 1976 *Generalleutnant* Rall retired from a senior position at NATO headquarters. (IWM MH6079)

Above and below: Two stills from *Kolberg*, one of the final products of the Reich film industry. One scene depicts the townspeople joining the soldiers to protect their homes in a last-ditch defence so appropriate to March 1945. (British Film Institute)

Above: According to USAAF records, this photograph of crews receiving their briefing was taken at Little Walden as the 493rd BG prepared for their mission on 7 April 1945. (USAF via NASM)

Left: Major Robin Olds of the 434th FS in front of his P-51D, named *Scat #5*. After scoring thirteen aerial victories over Europe as a Colonel, Olds led the 8th TFW by example over Vietnam, scoring four kills flying an F-4C. (American Fighter Aces' Association)

Above: One of the first clashes over Germany on 7 April involved two Flights of P-51s from the 456th FS, led by Captain Richard W. Asbury. (Asbury)

Below left: 1st Lieutenant Richard G. Candelaria of the 435th FS. After an eventful mission on 7 April he was able to claim four confirmed Bf 109s and a probable Me 262. (American Fighter Aces' Association)

Below right: With a final wave to his friend, Zell aimed at the American formation. He was never to see his friend again. (Zell)

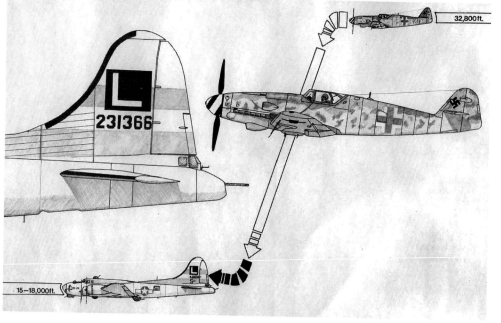

Left, upper: Through seemingly peaceful skies, a mixed 487th/486th BG formation leads the 4th CBW to its targets at Parchim airfield. (USAF via NASM)

Left, lower: The task of locating the 3rd AD bombers was made more difficult because of the unexpectedly low altitude on 7 April. When the 'Elbe' pilots finally found their quarry they were to perform a steep dive, intended to push their Bf 109s past any USAAF escorts and carry them on to the tail of the chosen B-17.

Above: Photographed in November 1944 before leaving for Europe are the crew who would fly B-17 44-8334 for the 100th Bomb Group on 7 April 1945. Left to right: (back) Lt Sandford (who remained in the US), Lt Howard, Lt Delgano and Lt Jones; (front) Sgt Hall, Sgt Truitt, Sgt Thomas, Sgt Lunsford and Sgt Maty. By the end of that day Maty, Thomas and Truitt's last-minute replacement Sgt Lehrman were

dead and the rest of the crew prisoners. (Howard)

Below: With the aircraft safely back at Thorpe Abbotts, the damage to the tail of *E-Z Goin* could be examined. For the purposes of the photograph, the panel bearing the code '38514' has been pinned back in place.

Above left: *Leutnant* Armin Thiel. (Zell)

Above right: *Oberfähnrich* Fritz Marktscheffel was never again to see his friend Armin Thiel after the latter's take-off from Gardelegen. (Zell)

Below left: *Leutnant* Dietrich Schulz-Sembten was able to complete his mission and return to Stendal by the end of the day. (Zell)

Below right: Alone in the freezing sky, *Unteroffizier* Klaus Hahn found the USAAF bombers. A brief but brutal combat left his body battered and would cost him an arm—but he lived to tell the tale. (Zell)

Above left: After his successful ramming attack the first thought for *Hauptmann* Roman Pesch was to ensure that his last letter home was not posted. (Zell)

Below left: Knight's Cross holder *Hauptmann* Ernst Sorge found that even his experience did not bring him success. (Zell)

Above right: Twenty-eight-year-old *Leutnant* Hans Nagel died doing what he had pledged to do—defend his home and family from the *Viermöte*. (Zell)

Below right: Although able to escape from his damaged Bf 109 when attacked by Mustangs, *Unteroffizier* Jakob Zapp died as he drifted beneath his parachute. (Zell)

Above left: A keen volunteer for the mission of 7 April, *Fahnenjunker-Oberfeldwebel* Karl-Heinz Schrader died with his fighter. (Zell)

Above right: *Oberleutnant* Olaf Hansen, classified as missing in action since 7 April 1945. (Zell)

Below left: Even an experienced pilot like *Oberfeldwebel* Heinz Müller, who had five

confirmed kills from his time with *III./JG 300*, was lucky to survive the battles of 7 April. (Zell)

Below right: Although taking off from Sachau with other *'Elbe'* pilots, *Leutnant* Hans-Ludwig Loscher was forced to land early with engine problems. (Zell)

Above left: After being accepted because of a forged log book, *Fähnrich* Franz-Josef Schmidt made a false start to his mission but even a second Bf 109 could bring no better luck. (Zell)

Above right: *Fähnrich* Eberhard Prock appears to have scored a victory against the bombers of the 45th Combat Wing, but he paid the ultimate price. (Zell)

Below: A pair of smoke markers point the way for the B-17s of the 1st AD, but a pall of smoke from the burning depot at Hitzacker shows that some crews have already found their target. (USAF via NASM)

Above: A column of smoke marks the target of the 'Flying Eightballs'. The target is Krummel, and this B-24 belongs to the 67th BS/44th BG. Its crew can now begin their flight home to Shipdam. (USAF via NASM)

Left: The memorial at Celle.

damaged Pratt & Whitney finally failed. The lame bomber turned for home, the first of three 330th BS Liberators to set an early course for their airfield at Hardwick. The bomber coded 'M' followed closely behind, also flying on three engines. Within twenty minutes another attack resulted in B-24 'F' turning back with two wounded crewmen. Each of the bombers contacted the air/sea rescue organization on the 'B' channel to report its problems. Because of the damage to the first B-24 a pair of 'razorback' P-47s from the 5th Emergency Rescue Squadron and a lone PBY rendezvoused 50 miles out over the North Sea in case the crew were forced to ditch. But, as would be the case for the rest of the day, the supporting ASR aircraft had only to perform some precautionary escort duties: none of the damaged Eighth Air Force bombers would require their full services.

The trailing formation of the 2nd AD was the 96th CBW, consisting of the Liberators of the 458th, 467th and 466th Bomb Groups. The tails of these bombers, each painted a bold red with an identifying white stripe, made ideal targets for the *'Elbe'* pilots. Although few of the fighters actually reached this formation of bombers, when one did the pilot needed no second chance to select his victim. The German pilot made a diving attack upon tail of his selected B-24, the Messerschmitt slamming into the right-hand vertical stabilizer of a 467th BG aircraft. The speed of the dive pushed the fighter past its target but it carried with it the severed fin and rudder of the bomber. The crew of this B-24 opted to nurse their damaged charge home and began a careful turn which carried them away from the formation. The damage to the B-24 appears to have made manoeuvring difficult as the course set by the crew took them through a dangerous piece of sky across the routes of both the 3rd AD task forces. This lone bomber would have made an ideal target for any *Luftwaffe* fighter hunting in this area, but its luck appeared to be holding. As it crossed the route of the 4th/93rd CBW, P-51s from the 357th FG peeled off from their B-17s to accompany the injured Liberator. As the aircraft headed for the safety of home the Mustang pilots inspected the damage to the tail of the bomber—or, more accurately, inspected what remained of the right side of the tail. To a fighter pilot the damage looked horrific: a piece of tail which seemed bigger than their own wing was missing, only a jumble of twisted metal marking where it had been attached. But as the Liberator passed Hanover with all engines working well, its crew decided that the danger from prowling fighters was over and that they could safely reach an airfield in France. With a final salute the P-51s left the bomber to seek more gainful employment. However, the bomber crew appear to have been too confident about the ruggedness of their aircraft, for not long after it crossed the Weser they were forced to abandon ship.

10. THE TURN

As the battle began to rage in the skies above Lüneburg Heath the USAAF crews realized that they were experiencing an attack of a scale not matched for some time. Both the number of *Luftwaffe* fighters in the air today and the tactics being employed marked 7 April as unusual. Until now each day's mission had been recorded in a diary, reflecting the steady decline in the defensive operations mounted by German aircraft.

Regardless of the unexpected ferocity of the attacks upon them, the bomber crews were attempting to keep to their timetable. The planned left turn by the B-24s of the 2nd AD towards their targets near the River Elbe was a little ahead of schedule and in the circumstances perhaps a little ragged. But by 1230hrs the trailing bombers had completed their manoeuvre and the entire formation was on its new heading.

Supporting the rear of this formation, and apparently caught somewhat off-guard, several of the escorting fighters found themselves between two vast masses of bombers. The B-17s of the 3rd AD had been following behind the 2nd, and as the leading division executed its turn the Fortresses were able to close the gap. The 3rd AD crews not only found themselves flying into contested airspace, their radios having alerted them well in advance of the danger, but they also now had a stronger protective force as many fighters lingered as a result of their encounters.

As the *Luftwaffe* pilots turned their attention to the next stream of bombers, they at times found double the expected concentration of defending fighters. Red-nosed P-51s of the 334th FS, 4th FG, were amongst the American fighters who now had B-17s to protect instead of B-24s. One of the 334th FS pilots, now in a position to watch the initial attacks upon the B-17s, was 1st Lieutenant Ralph H. Buchanan, leading 'Cobweb Purple' section. The nearest Bf 109 to Buchanan was being chased through the bombers by a P-51 from another Group when suddenly the defensive fire from the bombers hit the Mustangs, forcing the pilot to break off from his pursuit. Seeing this, Lieutenant Buchanan followed the German pilot, who was undoubtedly thanking God for his narrow escape. Unaware of the fresh danger now facing him, the *Luftwaffe* pilot was levelling off after breaking through the cloud cover at about 10,000ft as Buchanan burst from the clouds behind him, closely followed by Lieutenant Farington in 'Cobweb Purple 3'. Caught by the P-51s, the Bf 109 pilot had no time to react before a rapid burst of fire from the first Mustang ripped into his aircraft. The Messerschmitt shuddered in the air as the bullets hit and again as the right wheel began to fall into the slip-stream. With a wounded target now in his sights, Lieutenant Buchanan closed and continued to fire. The damage to the Bf 109 was sufficient to convince the young German pilot that delaying his escape a moment longer could cost him his life. Very rapidly the canopy was unlocked and pushed clear, and he got out.

Having left their base at Martlesham Heath with a mission to escort the 1st AD, the fighters of the 356th FG had been ordered to reposition themselves to provide additional support to the 2nd AD. At the moment the B-24s made their turn, the 359th FS, 356th FG, were about to investigate a call which warned of further 'bogeys' east of Steinhuder lake. Before he could turn his aircraft to investigate, 1st Lieutenant Jack B. Cornett spotted a lone con-trail above him heading towards the B-17 formation to the south. Deciding this likely target worthy of his attention, Cornett opted to ignore the earlier calls and deal with this fighter which he identified as an Fw 190. In doing this he was now attempting to offer protection to the 3rd AD!

Flying on Lieutenant Cornett's wing was 1st Lieutenant John Meade, who had started the day as the Flight's spare aircraft. By this time he had at-tached himself to Cornett and together they jettisoned their tanks and be-gan a steep climb towards the Focke-Wulf. As the two Mustangs neared the enemy fighter it began to dive upon the B-17 formation. Still closing, Cor-nett opened fire and was instantly rewarded by seeing a number of strikes hit home. At the same moment Meade found his engine suddenly cutting out and his fighter falling behind in the chase. Calling out a warning to his leader, Meade was able only to level out and watch as the two fighters ahead flew ever closer to the bombers, the *Luftwaffe* aircraft already leaving a thin trail of coolant in its wake.

Once again the approach of two fighters caused the gunners in the For-tresses to open fire. On this occasion, well aware of the danger to himself in a close pursuit, Lieutenant Cornett decided to break off and fly around the bombers to catch the Focke-Wulf as it broke through on the other side of the formation. As the *Luftwaffe* fighter emerged its pilot began a left turn, per-haps now conscious of the damage to his aircraft. Grasping this opportu-nity, the young American pulled his fighter into a sharp left turn and again lined up his target. At the very point Cornett began to depress his firing button he saw the canopy of the Focke-Wulf being jettisoned and an object he took to be a cushion fall away. Of course, as in his own fighter, a seat cushion was a luxury item that *Luftwaffe* pilots lacked: what he most prob-ably saw was the bundled figure of the pilot attempting to make himself the smallest possible target whilst escaping from his aircraft. Having released his firing button, Cornett waited in vain for the German pilot to make an appearance. Instead the *Luftwaffe* fighter began a series of erratic manoeu-vres, now trailing in its wake a dense cloud of burning fuel. Believing he was watching the death throes of his target and now without a wingman to confirm his victory, Lieutenant Cornett fired two further bursts to record its last moments in support of his claim. With the enemy fighter slipping and rolling before his eyes, its propeller now virtually still, the continuing battle above again beckoned. Leaving the Focke-Wulf during its dying moments Cornett re-joined the aircraft above. The last sight he had of the fighter was as it disappeared out of control into the clouds below, heading towards earth with its pale underbelly pointing to the heavens.

The 354th FS, 355th FG, were sticking close to their herd of lumbering B-24s as they made their turn towards the first of their targets. A mixture of *Luftwaffe* fighters appeared around them, intent upon the destruction or mortal wounding of their opponents. In the clear sky the approach of these new enemy fighters was relatively easy to follow. As a single Me 262 made the first pass at the leading box, 'Falcon Blue' Flight attempted an interception from its position 5,000ft above the bombers. Once again the jet was not about to linger: after one firing pass the pilot continued through the formation and headed towards a fresh target.

Having seemingly discouraged this adversary, 'Blue' Flight, led by 1st Lieutenant Joseph E. Mellen, was quickly made aware of the approach of more conventional *Luftwaffe* fighters. Turning back towards the bombers, Mellen and his wingman spotted a Focke-Wulf 190D on course for the bombers from 6 o'clock low. Diving on to the long-nosed fighter, the Steeple Morden-based P-51 unleashed a three-second burst which tore through the cockpit and fuselage, visibly knocking the *Luftwaffe* aircraft off course. As the fighters passed, Mellen decided not to follow the 'Dora', which seemed to be trailing smoke and flames, instead seeking out a fresh target. Although Lieutenant Mellen was credited with the destruction of this Focke-Wulf, it met other fighters from the 354th FG before the destruction was complete.

Having chased a damaged Bf 109 which flew in front of the B-24 formation, two pilots from 'Falcon Green' Flight had caught and dispatched it with little effort. Now, as 1st Lieutenant Paul W. Vineyard and 2nd Lieutenant Glenn D. Beeler sought new targets, a long-nosed Focke-Wulf appeared above, at their 10 o'clock. Calling for his leader to attempt the interception, Beeler quickly saw that Vineyard was too close to complete his turn on to the diving fighter. From his slightly higher position it was easier for Beeler to line up the Fw 190 and he took the lead, placing the fighter in the centre of his K-14 but certain that this target required none of the gun sight's technical wonders. Again with a damaged fighter before them, this time Beeler and Vineyard had selected an even easier victim. Before a shot could be fired the *Luftwaffe* pilot jettisoned his canopy and jumped from his aircraft. In a somewhat bold encounter report, Lieutenant Beeler claimed the destruction of the fighter and promptly received confirmation of the award. Having in their own minds at least removed two enemy fighters with little effort, the two P-

51 pilots returned to their bombers as a new wave of Me 262s was reported in the area.

So much devastation having been wrought upon the *Luftwaffe* force, especially upon the *'Elbe'* force of Bf 109s, it is would be easy to believe that the escorts were successful in their protection duties. However, the determination of the young *'Elbe'* pilots and the sheer numbers of fighters approaching the bombers ensured that today the *Viermöte* would not pass unmolested. At the head of the 2nd Air Division's four combat wings was the 2nd CBW, and leading this formation were the B-24s of the 389th BG. The 'Sky Scorpions' were being led by their group commanding officer, Colonel John B. Herboth Jr. Finding his force on the receiving end of so much unwanted attention, Herboth would have wished to get his crews to their targets and then on to their route home as soon as possible. With his attention focused upon his unenviable task, he was undoubtedly unaware of the approach of a Bf 109, piloted by a young German on his first combat mission. This *'Elbe'* pilot was *Unteroffizier* Heinrich Rosner, who had volunteered for the operation soon after he had qualified as a pilot with *III./JG 102*. Somehow he had avoided the escorts and, now in the air to the west of Soltau, had found the hated bombers. He required no further bidding, knowing he had been fortunate to get this close to his target. Pushing his Messerschmitt into a dive, he had selected as his quarry the Liberators leading the formation before him.

The last seconds before Rosner's fighter impacted with Herboth's B-24 are understandably confused. The propeller of the *'Elbe'* fighter ripped into the huge four-engine bomber before the crew could react. The extent of the damage this caused is difficult to judge. Whether it was enough to bring the bomber down instantly or whether Colonel Herboth was at the time attempting to haul his aircraft away from the enemy attack, the result was horrific. Although the Messerschmitt and the Liberator appeared to part company, the bomber then swung wildly from its position at the head of the formation and was brutally thrown on to its nearest neighbour. Both of the bombers were unable to survive such a collision, indeed it is amazing that both were not instantly engulfed in a fireball. In the second B-24 Lieutenant-Colonel Kunkel, the Deputy Leader of the Group, miraculously regained control of his bomber, but only for a brief moment. He hoped that he could provide his crew with the seconds they needed to escape, but his efforts were frustrated as the dying bomber began to break apart around him. As the first B-24 fell to earth the second was following close behind. The 389th BG and so the 2nd Air Division had in a matter of seconds been robbed of their leaders. In his first combat mission, and before he had perfected the usual skills required in air combat, *Unteroffizier* Rosner had achieved a double kill. Whether he was in any position to savour such a success is questionable, for at that moment he was attempting to preserve his own life and escape from his crippled fighter. In a state of panic he was able to disengage the canopy of his fighter and jump free. These were to be his last conscious thoughts for a number of hours: although he somehow released his parachute, he blacked out as he fell.

Hours after the battles above ended *Unteroffizier* Rosner awoke to find himself amongst some farm buildings and in much pain. His very rough, uncontrolled landing had inflicted a broken collarbone and concussion. After receiving rudimentary medical attention Rosner was to return to Stendal, one of only a small group of *'Elbe'* pilots who did so after the day's combat. Even had the battered and bruised pilot been better placed to enjoy his double victory, he would perhaps have hoped that he had wrought greater havoc amongst the bombers. Although the loss of its two senior crews had shocked the 389th BG, the latter still had a mission to fly and, like the mythical hydra, the bomber formation quickly sprouted a new head as the remaining crews reorganized themselves.

Further back along the bomber stream, Thunderbolts of the 56th FG spotted above their positions contrails marking the path of *Luftwaffe* fighters piloted by the young *'Elbemänner'*. One of the first USAAF pilots to react was 1st Lieutenant Frank Ogden III, who was leading a formation of four 63rd FS aircraft in an orbit to one side of the bombers. As one of the German fighters headed for the B-24s it crossed above the P-47s, which allowed Ogden to pull into a tighter turn and place himself directly on the tail of what he identified as a Bf 109. At less than 700yds, and with his target taking no evasive action, the American pilot opened fire, ripping pieces from the wing roots and tail assembly of the Messerschmitt. As Lieutenant Ogden continued to pour bullets into the *Luftwaffe* pilot, the latter, unwilling to be deterred from his task, pulled his fighter into a turn to correct his course towards the bombers. This caused the big P-47 close on his tail to overtake, placing it on a direct path towards the bombers. With no intention of getting any closer to the gunners who were already firing in his direction, Ogden was forced to change direction sharply and lost sight of the Bf 109. It was left to the other P-47s of the Flight to report that the Messerschmitt had in fact exploded just as Ogden passed by. His violent evasive action before the guns of the bombers had probably saved his aircraft from the cloud of vicious shrapnel and flying debris. As the Flight re-formed and re-joined the formations above, the remains of the Bf 109 fell away below.

It was now approaching 1245 and the attacks upon the B-24s of the 2nd AD were beginning to diminish as the B-17s of the 3rd AD flew in turn across the River Weser into the designated hunting ground of the *'Elbe'* fighters. One of the final encounters by the escort fighters of the 2nd AD took place five minutes later. Trailing above their bombers at 25,000ft, the P-47s of 'Platform Blue' Flight, 62nd FS, remained wary of the *Luftwaffe* fighters they knew to be in their area. Expecting the approach of a large formation or a high-speed dash by the feared jets, the sight of a single contrail below them did not unduly concern the Flight Leader, Captain Robert E. Winters. Telling his Flight to keep an eye on the lone fighter, Winters continued his patrol, searching for a more dangerous foe. Suddenly a call from 'Blue 2', 2nd Lieutenant Dennis A. Carroll, informed the Flight that the contrail was definitely now on a heading for the bombers and entering a dive. Part of the *'Elbe'* force that had gathered in numbers around Hanover, this pilot had, like so many of his *Kameraden*, become separated but intended to continue his mission alone. Whether or not he spotted the bulky shapes of the P-47s which began to dive upon him is uncertain, but the pilot was not about to be diverted from his target. Leading his Flight, Captain Winters had pushed his fighter into a high-speed dive. After 3,000ft he caught the enemy fighter, which he was able to identify as a Bf 109. Opening fire from less than 400yds, he was angry to see his shots miss his target. Not about to repeat such an error, Winters reset his K-14 gun sight to 35ft and opened fire again, now less than 300yds astern. The new burst appeared to light up the Messerschmitt as it struck fuselage and wing roots. Holding down his firing button, Winters continued to rip apart the enemy fighter as he flew closer and closer. The damage inflicted by this assault is in no doubt. The report reads: 'I continued firing to zero range, but could not see any more strikes as coolant and smoke were so thick I could hardly make out the outline of the aircraft.' To Lieutenant Carroll, both the fighters ahead of him had almost disappeared within this dense trail.

As the leading Thunderbolt overshot the Messerschmitt, Captain Winters began to pull up, dipping his wing to get at glimpse of the damage he had inflicted. But both the fighters had continued upon a course which had taken them directly toward the bombers. This resulted in Winters' finding himself on the receiving end of a very unfriendly stream of fire. As the cockpit of the big P-47 reverberated with the sound of bullets hitting the tail, Winters decided, swiftly, that further evasive action was called for and he hauled his fighter away from danger. Sticking as close as possible to his leader, Lieutenant Carroll also pulled his Thunderbolt up and away from the bombers, this move causing both pilots to lose sight of the damaged *Luftwaffe* fighter. In order to confirm the demise of the Messerschmitt, the pair turned back when safely outside the range of the gunners and spotted the Bf 109 spinning away down below them. They followed it down until it eventually struck the ground. Captain Winters then shot up the wreckage to gain photographic proof which would confirm his kill.

With their assigned bombers now on course for their targets, the fighters allocated to protect the 2nd AD followed. Gradually the American fighter pilots began to realize that there were fewer enemy fighters around their flock and they began to return to their duties. As the formations flew on, the contrails which marked the frantic combats of the past minutes began to be left behind. Throughout the squadrons, adrenalin levels slowly dropped, breathing slowed and pilots could try to make sense of what had just occurred. Had this marked the return of the *Jagdwaffe*'s standard fighter force? More importantly, would they return again to the bombers as they neared their targets?

Whilst the answer to the first question could not have been known at the time, that to the second was revealed very quickly. The airwaves were now filled with bursts of instructions and snippets of excited conversation as the B-17s of the 3rd AD began to suffer the attentions of *Luftwaffe* fighters. Having done their best to protect their charges, the pilots who had just experienced combat now listened as their fellow pilots began their own series of combats. The sky around the Fortresses of the 3rd AD was to be the new battleground.

11. FOCUS ON THE 3rd AD

Trailing in the numerous wakes and fading contrails of the leading formations, the crews of the B-17s belonging to the 3rd AD were well aware of the danger into which they were flying. Around these tight ranks of bombers the pilots in the escort fighters also knew of the task which awaited them. The *Luftwaffe* had chosen today to re-launch its attacks upon the Eighth Air Force and its pilots were about to be asked, once again, to stop their enemy from succeeding.

By now the *'Elbe'* fighters had reached the formations of bombers in larger numbers and reports of conventional enemy fighters were replacing earlier warnings of the jets. Reaching the north-eastern corner of their hunting ground, over Celle, the Bf 109s were spotted by the escorting fighters of the 339th FG. This Group was positioned above the 388th and 452nd BGs at the head of the bomber stream. The danger to the *'Elbe'* fighters was now increased because of the presence of the escorts. Whilst planning had called for the Me 262s and more experienced conventional fighters of *JG 300* and *JG 301* to disperse the escorts, the *'Elbe'* fighters had reached their targets to find the escorting Mustangs still in position. They were faced with making a decision: attack now, with luck before the escorts could react, or wait for their own 'escort' formations. Determined to carry out their mission, and well aware that every minute they remained near to the bombers increased their chance of being intercepted, one by one the pilots made their decisions.

Further to the west, the Duxford-based 78th FG had made its rendezvous with the 13th CBW just after 1215. The pilots of the P-51s quickly found their bombers under attack from high-flying fighters. They were forced to climb to meet these enemy aircraft, and it was immediately clear that the *Luftwaffe* fighters were not making the usual approach but instead individual diving attacks. Once again the speed of the attacking fighters allowed them to reach their targets before the P-51s could put themselves between the *Luftwaffe* aircraft and the bomber formation. One of the first of the 78th FG fighters on the scene was an 83rd FS P-51 bearing the Group's bold black and white checked nose markings, a white rudder with red trim and the nickname *The Green Hornet*. The aircraft was flown by the experienced Captain Robert T. Green, but even this proven combination of man and machine was at first powerless to stop the attacks. Picking out a Bf 109, Green broke contact when the wall of defensive fire from the B-17s cut down the *'Elbe'* fighter. A second Bf 109 appeared in front of Green, but again the pilot watched as the gunners appeared to find their mark. Still trailing this second fighter, Captain Green intended to complete the kill as the enemy aircraft flew beyond the bombers. Instead he watched as the Bf 109 crashed into the nearest B-17. Shocked by the sight of the collision, Green was then forced to push his P-51 through a rapid series of manoeuvres to avoid the lethal cloud of debris thrown out by the two crippled aircraft. Once he was safely free from this danger, he singled out a third 'Elbe' fighter which he found was attempting a different approach. Perhaps seeing the defensive fire being thrown from the bombers, or perhaps shaken by the sight of the collision, this pilot had decided upon an approach from below. As the Bf 109 was pushed into a dive a safe distance from the massed guns of the bomber formation, it was followed by Green's fighter, but the distance between the two aircraft, and the speed advantage of the diving Bf 109, would make an interception difficult. Beginning his turn towards the bombers, the young 'Elbe' pilot then made a fatal mistake. As with so many of the actions of 7 April, it was his lack of combat experience together with the lone approach which had been adopted and the large number of Eighth Air Force escorts still around the bombers which combined to make the Bf 109 very vulnerable. Having quickly completed his turn, the *Luftwaffe* pilot straightened out, almost directly before the guns of the P-51 following behind. Startled by this unexpected end to his chase, Captain Green was forced to chop his throttle or risk over-running his target. With both of his hands back on the control column he opened fire, two short bursts being enough to rip into almost the entire length of the Bf 109. So close were the two aircraft that the P-51 was surrounded by fragments torn free, and coolant from its target covered the windscreen. As his vision cleared Green found that he was less than 200yds from his target, and to avoid a collision he pulled his aircraft up sharply. The damage to the Bf 109 proved fatal. As Green glanced back he saw it nose over and slowly spin down to earth. The pilot was not seen leave the cockpit.

Not far from the encounter of Captain Green, other 83rd FS pilots were having their own successes against the 'Elbe' force. Flying at 19,000ft, 'Blue' Flight, led by 1st Lieutenant Francis E. Harrington in his P-51D *Boston Bean*, spotted contrails above him heading for 'their' bombers. As the Flight climbed to meet the danger they singled out the nearest Bf 109, which had levelled out at about 23,000ft. Again the 'Elbe' pilot displayed a level of inexperience. Although spotting the approaching hungry Mustangs, the pilot entered a tight circle as a defensive measure but he failed to jettison his drop tank. Any advantage the German pilot had hoped for was lost as the tank added drag and cost him speed. Opting for a change in tactics, the 'Elbe' pilot cut his speed, hoping to force the Mustangs to overshoot. The move almost worked, as 'Blue 3', which had been lining up for a shot, flew past. Unfortunately, Lieutenant Harrington found himself perfectly placed to take over the lead and he 'dropped into place about 150 yards astern'. Sitting on the tail of the Bf 109, Harrington now had a relatively easy shot and poured fire into his target. Another *'Elbe'* fighter met its end.

During this brief encounter 'Blue' Flight had become split. Spotting contrails above him, Harrington decided to investigate, taking with him 2nd Lieutenant Richard E. Phaneuf, who had become his wingman after the first action. This time the contrails were grouped together in twos and threes, and the pair of P-51s found themselves facing a more dangerous and experienced foe. Reaching 29,000ft, they met an Fw 190 leading a pair of Bf 109s. The Focke-Wulf pilot seemed intent upon removing the threat posed by the Mustangs. Later Harrington said that because of the aggressiveness of the Focke-Wulf he decided to make this his first priority. It would be perhaps more accurate to say that the choice had already been made for him. Very quickly the two Mustangs and the Fw 190 were in a tight Lufberry turn. With two keen pilots against him, the Focke-Wulf pilot received a few hits, most likely from Lieutenant Harrington. To avoid further damage and in an attempt to gain some advantage, the *Luftwaffe* pilot flipped his fighter on to its back and began a series of wide barrel rolls whilst diving. Attempting to follow, the Mustang pilots found that their opponent had a wide repertoire, suddenly cutting his speed, forcing Harrington to use 40 degrees of flaps to stay with him. The German was unable to shake off the pair of Mustangs with these moves, and they were repeated a number of times as the Focke-Wulf lost altitude. Clearly a more experienced opponent, the pilot of the Fw 190 was nevertheless unable to escape the occasional burst of fire. The damage inflicted was not serious as for several minutes the three aircraft continued to twist, turn and dive towards the clouds below. The first of the cloud layer was reached at about 7,000ft and now the hunt became more difficult. The lower the aircraft flew the thicker the clouds around them became. Now trailing his leader, Lieutenant Phaneuf was forced to break contact when another Bf 109 appeared on his tail.

Entering the thicker cloud, now alone in his pursuit, Lieutenant Harrington burst through into clear sky to find himself flying alongside the Focke-Wulf, seemingly in formation. Before the American pilot had any opportunity to react the *Luftwaffe* fighter rolled away, once again in an attempt to reverse the chase. However, despite his undoubted flying skills, the pilot had focused his attention too closely upon his enemy. Misjudging his altitude and with no hope of making a recovery, the fighter struck the ground and was enveloped by a large explosion.

Originally flying below and on the left of 'Blue' Flight, the 83rd 'White' Flight also found itself near enemy fighters. A solitary Bf 109 crossed ahead of the Flight and immediately became the target of 1st Lieutenant Richard I. Kuehl in his borrowed P-51D *The Horrible Hoosier III* (the assigned aircraft of Captain Robert Wise). Closely followed by his wingman, 2nd Lieutenant Earle W. Strobel, Kuehl began to follow the Bf 109 and was able to open fire

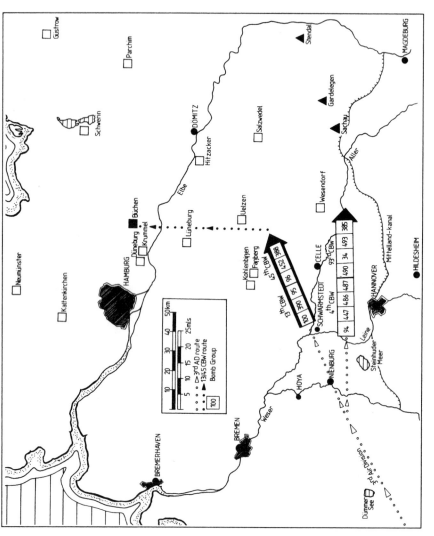

Map 3. Route taken by 13th/45th CBW during 'Elbe' attacks.

whilst still making a left turn. These first short bursts caused visible damage to the fuselage of the Bf 109, which executed a sharp wing-over to avoid further strikes. However, after only a couple of rolls the German pilot levelled out, still within the sights of the Mustang. A further brief burst of fire once again caused a number of strikes and inflicted enough damage to the Messerschmitt to convince the pilot that he should abandon his aircraft. Both Kuehl and Strobel watched as the canopy fell free from the Bf 109 and the pilot jumped clear.

As the leading 3rd AD formations, the bombers of the 45th CBW, flew between Steinhuder lake and Hanover, they crossed the area which was the planned assembly point for part of *Schulungslehrgang 'Elbe'*. Fresh contrails were spotted above the last 45th formation, B-17s of the 96th BG, just after 1230 by the fighters of the 351st FS, 353rd FG, who had first reached the area over twenty minutes earlier. Again the enemy fighters, some approaching from well over 30,000ft, turned on to the tail-end of the formation and made their dives alone. Yet again the close escort being flown by the 351st FG Mustangs offered only a slim chance of success and very quickly fresh victims fell from the sky. In less than ten minutes two Bf 109s had been damaged by Captain Gene E. Markham and another had spun to the ground, shedding a wing as a result of an attack by 2nd Lieutenant Robert F. Hahn. A further success was to be the third victim to fall this day to the Mustang flown by Captain Charles McGraw. In an almost text-book encounter, McGraw and his wingman Lieutenant Hahn had climbed together on to the tails of two Bf 109s. Without breaking their formation, both pilots dispatched their selected targets with little difficulty. In the case of Robert Hahn his encounter had required only 167 rounds to be fired. The escorts succeeded in protecting their charges: no bombers from the 96th BG were lost on this mission.

Just over twenty miles north-east of this one-sided clash, near Celle, the largest battle of the day was about to take place. As their watches ticked past 1245 the Mustang pilots of the 339th FG had already reached this area, all the pilots now alert for any signs of the approaching *Jagdwaffe*. It was not long before their vigilance was rewarded by the first sightings. Almost simultaneously the airwaves were filled by the numerous warnings of enemy fighters being spotted. To add to the instant confusion the pilots found themselves attempting to scan all the sky around them as the warnings reported the enemy approaching from every side. The scattered *Schulungslehrgang 'Elbe'* force was closing at the same time as its more potent escort. The jets would have little time to draw off the USAAF fighters, and again the planned attack began to break down into a series of brutal and confused clashes.

Having remained close to their bombers, the Fowlmere-based 503rd and 504th Squadrons of the 339th FG reacted at the same time. Spotting his first contrails above the bombers, Captain Frank D. Guernsey of the 504th was about to decide upon the best course of action when a glance behind showed another pair of contrails already closer to their targets. Turning his P-51 to face this pair, he watched as the leading fighter rolled on to its back and made a diving attack upon the leading B-17. Pulling out after causing little visible damage to the bomber, the fighter was heading directly for Guernsey. As the fighter approached above the P-51 Guernsey identified it as an Fw 190. At the same moment the *Luftwaffe* pilot spotted the Mustang and attempted to lower the nose of the Focke-Wulf on to this new target. As the two fighters closed at almost 800mph Guernsey did his best to ensure that the enemy fighter could not get into a good firing position. Realizing that he could not achieve a good shot on this head-on approach, the *Luftwaffe* pilot levelled out before he overshot the Mustang. In the few seconds before the two planes crossed Captain Guernsey saw an opportunity to hit the undersides of the Focke-Wulf. Even with the shadow of the Fw 190 about to cover his fighter, he was able to pour fire into its belly. As both fighters crossed, a tongue of fire was already trailing from the German aircraft. Before the P-51 could be turned back towards its target the Focke-Wulf erupted in a fireball and the other pilots of the 504th suddenly found debris falling past their aircraft. Certainly having attempted to protect some of the virtually defenceless '*Elbe*' fighters, the Focke-Wulf pilot had met his match and more of the Bf 109 force were now unprotected amidst a dangerous foe.

As Captain Guernsey and his wingman Captain Kire B. Everson looked for further targets they quickly spotted one of the lone Bf 109s heading for the bombers and climbed on to its tail. Leading the pair of Mustangs in towards their prey, Guernsey opened fire at about 150yds and hit the right wing of the Messerschmitt. Flying closer to the Bf 109, Guernsey was badly positioned to react when his target seemed to stall in front of him. Finding himself drawing level to the cockpit and catching a glimpse of his opponent, he spared no thought for his enemy, calling Everson to follow up the attack. Needing no further bidding, the second Mustang unleashed three sustained bursts into the Bf 109. In his post-combat report Everson described how this assault had the effect of 'knocking off large chunks of metal. He went into a vertical dive streaming coolant and oil.' Following the stricken fighter lower, he found it levelling out in a shallow dive. Keen that his quarry should not escape, Everson made three further firing passes, and with the Messerschmitt making no attempt at evasion he assumed that the pilot was already dead at the controls. After his final pass the Bf 109 crashed to the frozen ground and hit a stand of trees which ripped the damaged wings from the fuselage, completing the destruction.

Having received their P-51s only after they arrived in Britain, the pilots of the 339th FG had been forced to learn their craft quickly. By April 1945 the Group had been in action for a full year and had shown themselves to be an extremely capable fighting force and very quick learners. By the end of hostilities the Group's total for air-to-air victories would stand at $239^1/_2$, placing it almost on a par with Groups that had twice the amount of combat experience. On this day the Mustangs, with their red and white-banded spinners and red and white checked noses, would again prove their hard-earned skills, providing an escort to the leading 3rd AD formation, the bombers of the 388th and 452nd Bomb Groups.

With so many aircraft now in the same part of the sky, the level of skirmishes intensified. Leading 'Blue' Section of the 503rd FS, 1st Lieutenant Phillip E. Petitt was one of the pilots who found the sky suddenly full of potential targets. His first choice was one of the single Bf 109s attempting a climb towards a box of Fortresses. However, the appearance of six Me 262s heading in his direction from his seven o'clock altered his priorities. Breaking into the fast-approaching jets, Petitt had little time to react. As he repositioned his P-51 he found that the jets were already pulling away. In this case the jets had opened up too quickly for 'Blue' Section to give chase, and Petitt decided to stick more closely to the bombers and look for other targets.

The initial encounters had happened so quickly that when a *Luftwaffe* fighter was spotted, about to complete a pass on the nearest bombers, Lieutenant Petitt had to drop his tanks before he chased after it. With the distance between the fighters decreasing by the second, the American pilot was able to identify his prey as an Fw 190. The *Luftwaffe* pilot was making no attempt to turn back towards the bombers and Petitt realized the he had made a perfect approach: he was now sitting in the blind spot of the Focke-Wulf. Relieved that this opponent would offer little resistance, the Mustang pilot flew to within 150yds of the rudder and slightly above before he pressed the firing button. At such a distance the streams of fire were deadly, each bullet finding its mark. As a large piece of engine cowling flew free, the BMW engine burst into flames. The next identifiable item amongst a cloud of fragments falling away was the canopy, and Petitt had to break away to avoid damaging his P-51. With the victim heading to earth, Petitt and his wingman looked on as the *Luftwaffe* pilot abandoned his fighter.

With so many enemy fighters making attacks upon the bombers, the American escort flights began to break up as the pilots selected their targets. 'Red' Flight of the 503rd FS had being flying above the leading bombers of the 45th CBW at about 22,000ft when one of the lone Bf 109s attempted a climbing attack into a position on the tail of a B-17. Leading the Flight was 1st Lieutenant Lawrence Poutre, who immediately pushed his Mustang into a dive on to the enemy fighter. After a short burst from 400yds he flew closer and completed the destruction of the damaged Messerschmitt. Another Bf 109 which fell to the 503rd was claimed by 1st Lieutenant Richard E. Krauss, who had been forced to chase the fighter down to 15,000ft before inflicting the fatal damage.

The 504th FS was also having further successes. Both 1st Lieutenant Raymond Creswell and 1st Lieutenant Lyle Carter were able to score victories against Bf 109s as the latter attempted passes at the formation of bombers. As Creswell was trying to catch a second Bf 109, which eventually escaped only to be pursued by another flight of P-51s, Carter was firing on an Me 262 which had crossed his path. This encounter also ended in frustration, Carter's gun camera footage showing the jet 'going like a bat out of hell'.

By now the area of the combat had expanded as the bombers continued to fly towards their targets. At 1255hrs 1st Lieutenant Clair M. Mason found himself closer to the leading bombers, near to Uelzen, when an Me 262 made a single pass at the Fortresses. As was so often the case, the pilot of the Me 262 chose not to tangle with the P-51 which dived after him. Simply by opening the throttles of the twin Jumo engines the *Luftwaffe* pilot was able easily to outpace his pursuer. Five minutes later other 339th FG Mustangs also reached the area around Uelzen. This time a more dangerous foe was sighted attacking the bombers. Having found no suitable targets since his first encounter, Lieutenant Poutre, together with his wingman 1st Lieutenant John Potthof, suddenly spotted the distinctive shape of an Fw 190D diving towards the bombers. Too far away to reach the *JG 301* fighter before it completed a pass, the two American pilots watched helplessly as cannon fire from the 'Dora' shredded the tail of a B-17 flying as a part of the High Squadron. Determined to stop a follow-up attack, the P-51s swooped upon the Focke-Wulf as the pilot straightened up. The *Luftwaffe* fighter had also been spotted by 1st Lieutenant Raymond Johnson, who joined the two fighters of 'Red' Flight in the chase. Reaching the long-nosed Fw190 before the pilot was able to complete his turn, Poutre was close enough to open fire first. The closing speed of the first pair of Mustangs proved to be too great and both fighters were pushed past the Focke-Wulf before either was able to score further hits. It was left to Johnson to make good the attack and he fired two long bursts into the already smoking enemy aircraft. All three fighters were then forced to pull away as they approached the bombers, but the pilots watched as the Focke-Wulf seemed to disintegrate as a result of their gunfire. It is quite probable that this critically damaged Focke-Wulf was the same fighter which then appeared before Captain J. Brooks Bline of the 505th FS.

Before Captain Bline could close with this 'Dora', the *Luftwaffe* pilot baled out at about 15,000ft. Still closing fast with the now abandoned fighter, Bline decided that the opportunity was too good to miss and flew a long burst into the fighter 'just for the hell of it'. Backed up by a report from 1st Lieutenant James Wooley, this Fw 190D was actually credited to Bline.

The 505th FS had been alerted to the threat of enemy aircraft since crossing Steinhuder lake some twenty minutes earlier. Several sightings were reported of jets flying at about 30,000ft, almost 10,000ft above the P-51s and their bombers, the 452nd BG flying second in the 45th CBW. With the expected attack not materializing until 1300hrs, many of the 505th pilots, like Captain Bline, were eager to exploit any possible encounters. A second pair of 505th P-51s, flown by Lieutenant-Colonel Joseph L. Thury and 1st Lieutenant Oscar K. Biggs, were also watching for any enemy aircraft closing with their bombers. They began a turn to the left, and their vigilance was rewarded when they spotted a *Rotte* of Bf 109s passing unimpeded through a 351st Flight, at that moment flying over the space which separated the Fortresses of the 452nd and 96th BGs. The pair of Messerschmitts, doubtless thankful for their luck in avoiding the eight Mustangs, opened fire as they neared the bombers. But their good fortune was short-lived as the leading fighter fell before guns of the bombers and the second fighter was then bounced by Thury and Biggs. The bombers seem to have also damaged the second Bf 109, as before either of the two American pilots could open fire the pilot baled out. Without a shot being fired, the 505th pilots were allowed to share the victory.

Although the 351st FS would appear to have been negligent in allowing the two Bf 109s to pass by them, it is more likely that their attention lay elsewhere. 'Yellow' Flight, led by 1st Lieutenant Harold W. Chase, had spotted contrails above its position and had already begun to climb to investigate. With the enemy aircraft scattered and making no attempt to maintain a supporting formation, selecting a target proved difficult. As a Bf 109 dived to make an attack at the rear bomber, almost in front of his flight, Lieutenant Chase had a decision made for him. As the Messerschmitt broke first to the right and then to the left to pass under the bomber, Chase closed at high speed, his airspeed indicator pushing 450mph. He opened fire at 400yds, the speed of the P-51 and the turning circle of the Bf 109 allowing him only a four-second burst. Once again the K-14 gun sight proved its worth. Chase had fired fewer than 500 rounds, but it appeared that every one had struck home. The port wing of the Bf 109 began to disintegrate, 2nd Lieutenant Thomas Pryor having swiftly to avoid what appeared to be an aileron flying past his Mustang. As the rest of the flight gained on the Messerschmitt they caught sight of the ripped fuselage, smoking engine and shattered cockpit. As he pulled level, Pryor saw the *Luftwaffe* pilot struggling to free himself before his fighter suddenly snap-rolled on to its back then began to spin into the clouds below.

12. AT THE HEAD OF THE 45th CBW

Although the score of the 339th FG was rising, the leading elements of the 45th CBW did not escape the attentions of the *Luftwaffe* pilots. Well aware of the battle erupting around them, the crews of the 45th were undoubtedly growing uncomfortable knowing that they were the targets of the *Luftwaffe* attacks. Even the strong escort force was unable to stop every enemy fighter from breaking through the protective cover.

The leading 45th CBW B-17 boxes belonged to the 388th BG. For these bombers, especially the formation leaders with no other bombers in front of them, the empty sky ahead made their position very lonely. Listening to the now constant commentary of warnings and reports, the crews waited. Would today be their turn?

At 1230 the airwaves were filled with the feared news: elements of the formation were already under attack. The air around the 96th BG, at the rear of the 45th CBW, had seemingly filled with the dark shapes of both *Luftwaffe* jets and conventional single-engine aircraft. For the 96th BG, the escort of Mustangs was having greater success than its attackers, but such details offered little comfort to the bomber crews flying ahead, unable to watch these initial encounters.

The 388th BG had to wait less than two minutes before the enemy materialized. Suddenly the shapes of Me 262s streaked past the B-17s, overtaking the formation at high speed. The twin-engine jets made only brief attacks, which were not driven home with the expected ferocity. To the crews of the bombers it appeared as if the jets intended to unsettle them and possibly loosen the formation, in order to assist the conventional fighters now approaching. These fighters made their attacks from positions ranging from 3 o'clock to 9 o'clock, and these varied from diving attacks from high positions to climbs from beneath the formation. With gunners calling out the warnings of these attacks, the chaos mounted, crew members even within the same bomber attempting to concentrate their fire upon different fighters. As the individual Fortresses within the formation began to shift uncomfortably under these attacks, the tight spacing between the bombers became untidy. At their controls pilots and co-pilots tried as best they could to ignore the confusion of battle, whilst behind them the young crews sweated behind their guns.

Intent upon adding to this chaos were the pilots of *'Elbe'*. In his Messerschmitt, *Oberfeldwebel* Werner Linder, one of the pilots who had volunteered from *EJG 1*, made his selection and pointed the nose of his fighter towards his target. Ignoring the defensive fire, he flew towards the B-17s of the 388th BG. Spotting the danger, Lieutenant Leonard Kunz and Lieutenant Vernon Barto of the 504th FS, 339th FG, chased after the lone fighter. As the pair pushed their aircraft at full speed the gap between them and the *Luftwaffe* fighter began to diminish. Believing that the enemy pilot had noted their approach and was taking avoiding action in an attempt to foil their attack, the two pilots watched as the Bf 109 collided with the nearest bomber. The two aircraft, the fighter and a bomber from the High Squadron, were engulfed in flame and the wreckage plunged to earth. Despite having inflicted no damage to the Messerschmitt, the two Mustang pilots felt that their approach was sufficient to enable them to claim a share in its destruction. Even if it is true that *Oberfeldwebel* Linder had been aware of the Mustangs behind him, he was not to be diverted from his duty. His fighter finally splashed into the waters of the Hüttensee, from where his body was dragged several days later.

Forced to watch in horror as the B-17 had been ripped from within their formation, the other crews tried to make sense of what they had seen. But even before the dying bomber had left the sky a second bomber suddenly followed. This time the bomber was torn from the Lead Squadron. At the head of the bomber formation the loss of the two B-17s in quick succession made the position of the surviving aircraft even more lonely.

However, the attack upon the 388th BG had reached its peak with the loss of the two bombers, and attention turned to the following Group, the Deopham Green-based 452nd. Again the B-17 crews found enemy fighters attacking from every direction and every height. Because the initial attacks had drawn many of the defending 339th FG Mustangs into skirmishes or into giving chase, some of the loose *'Elbe'* formation from Mortitz/Delitzsch had an easier approach. One of the Bf 109s turned towards the leading B-17s, perhaps having decided upon an initial head-on attack, possibly attempting to force a bomber to break from its position within the formation. Adopting this approach, the pilot found himself under a hail of fire from every gunner who could bring his weapon to bear. As the Messerschmitt neared the bombers, he found streams of tracer rounds making for his fighter and it shuddered under a number of well-aimed bullets. The actual damage caused is uncertain, but, with the disconcerting effect of a continued barrage, the young fighter pilot wavered from his course. With the high closing speed any slight changes in course could have a dramatic effect, and the pilot began to make desperate attempts to correct his flight. As the shape of the weaving fighter grew larger and larger, the crew of the leading B-17 of the 452nd High Squadron watched its approach with dread. With only three seconds separating the two aircraft the pilot and co-pilot would have been willing the gunners to blast the fighter from the sky. The gunners failed in this task, the final movements of the Bf 109 placing it directly in front of the B-17, filling the windscreen. When the impact came it was horrifying. The big bomber appeared to come to a stop as the German fighter buried itself into the nose. Forward of the top turret the entire front fuselage of the Fortress had disintegrated, and within seconds what remained of the bomber and its attacker was plunging towards the ground.

As the attacks continued, the B-17 crews reported that several of the fighters which flew past them had their landing gear and flaps lowered. The high speeds of approach led some of 'Elbe' pilots to attempt to cut their airspeed as they neared their targets, allowing them to stall and, they hoped, drop on to the bombers. This particular variation had little success: any fighter which slowed too early before the guns of the bombers was placed in a dangerous position. It was likely also very quickly to attract the attentions of the escorts.

A further attack which more closely followed the planned method was launched against the Lead Squadron of the 452nd BG. This time the lone Bf 109 pilot was able to direct his attack against the rear fuselage of one of the B-17s. Although the powerful engine drove the propeller into the body of the bomber, the pilot was unable to stop his fighter from ramming into his target. As the fighter itself pushed into the gaping wound it completed the destruction. Whereas the first attack upon the 452nd BG destroyed the nose of a bomber, this second attack severed the tail section. In two neat portions the B-17 tumbled to earth.

Despite the severity of these collisions, both of the young *Schulungslehrgang 'Elbe'* pilots were somehow able to avoid being dragged down with their fighters, but escaping from their aircraft and then being able to open their parachutes was to use up their remaining luck. One of them was 20-year-old *Fähnrich* Eberhard Pröck, whose bullet-ridden body was found several days later near the village of Enghausen, north of the River Aller. It appears that he was shot by an enemy fighter as he floated defencelessly down. The fate of 23-year-old *Feldwebel* Reinhold Hedwig would remain unknown for seven months: it was not until October 1945 that his body was found, suspended by his parachute from the branches of a fir tree. Both pilots today share their final resting place: they are together in the war cemetery at Schwarmstedt. Both of these damaged fighters undoubtedly finally fell as victims before the guns of the 339th FG's P-51s. Because of the number of combats recorded by this Group, it has, however proved impossible to confirm the pilots responsible. As would be expected in such circumstances, pilots on both sides were unlikely to admit to having fired upon enemy airmen hanging beneath their parachutes.

13. ONE PILOT'S STORY

While the 452nd BG was finally recovering from a series of brutal attacks it was realized that two further B-17s had left the formation. Although exact detail of these losses are unclear, certainly *'Elbe'* fighters had been responsible. It is also possible to suggest which aircraft were responsible.

Delayed as they had prepared to take off from Delitzsch airfield by mechanical problems, *Unteroffizier* Werner Zell and his friend *Obergefreiter* Horst Siedel finally arrived over Schwarmstedt after taking a more direct route. It was this delay, however, which allowed the pair to gain some benefit from the attacks which had already been launched. Many of the American escorts which should have been covering the leading bombers of the 13th CBW had been drawn away in pursuit of the jets or were already attempting to deal with the first arrivals of *Schulungslehrgang 'Elbe'*. As this latest *Rotte* approached the bombers, with *Unteroffizier* Zell leading, it seemed as if the two Messerschmitt fighters had found themselves alone in the sky. Below their positions they had spotted the glistening metal stream which seemed to be flowing to the very centre of Germany. The two pilots had at last found their targets.

After first meeting during their period of training, the two young pilots had remained close friends and it seemed natural that they would volunteer together for *Schulungslehrgang 'Elbe'*. The time spent preparing for this mission had now ended: at last the moment had arrived for both men to steel themselves for the task ahead. With a final glance at his instruments, each pilot jettisoned his drop tank and checked that his seat harness was tightened. With no radio link between them it was impossible for these close friends to say any final words. Instead, with a glance through their canopies, they exchanged simply a brief wave of recognition. All that now remained was for each pilot to select his target and point his fighter towards it.

From almost 26,500ft Unteroffizier Zell pushed his fighter into a dive, towards the bombers which lay 6,500ft below. This steep dive upon his target was intended to carry the *Schulungslehrgang 'Elbe'* fighter at high speed through any escort fighters which may have appeared before he reached his quarry. Although his mind raced with questions and doubts, he forced himself to concentrate upon his target: the next few minutes would be dangerous enough without any negative thoughts. Now he had a mission, a duty, and he was also well aware that his friend was following behind. As the distance between fighters and bombers narrowed, *Unteroffizier* Zell thought that his first target choice was already showing signs of being wounded: the B-17 appeared to be trailing smoke from one engine. Knowing that he may only have one chance of making an attack, he decided that this was not a valuable enough target. Instead he made a slight adjustment to his course and aimed towards the left-hand side of the sail-like tail of another of the Fortresses which now loomed in front of him.

Although constantly scanning sections of the sky around them, the gunners of the B-17 had little opportunity to react when suddenly *Unteroffizier* Zell's dive ended only yards from one of their formation. The gunners who did react would have been unable to change the course upon which the Messerschmitt was now set. As the yards between the two aircraft rapidly became only feet, a collision was unavoidable. With the tail of the Fortress now seeming to tower above him and the rest of the bomber filling his vision, Zell prepared himself.

If he had been lucky the tail gunner of the Fortress would have missed seeing the propeller of the Messerschmitt pass his position, with barely inches to spare. However, he was perfectly placed to hear the horrific noise which followed as the blades sank like teeth into the tail and the fighter itself was then thrown against the bomber. The horrific noise had been firstly the vibration as the Daimler-Benz engine continued to turn each of the blades as they cut more deeply, followed a split second later by the noise of the fighter being pulled further on to its shuddering victim.

Even with his harness so tight that it bit into his flesh, the impact had shaken *Unteroffizier* Zell into unconsciousness, for which he should perhaps have been thankful. As the Messerschmitt fell away from the B-17 he at last regained consciousness, only to now find himself unable to control his aircraft and blinded by the layer of oil covering his canopy. At first unsure what had actually happened to him in the last minute, he quickly realized that he had little hope of flying his unresponsive fighter. Every minute he remained in the cockpit increased his chances of being trapped when his aircraft finally lost the remaining vestiges of powered flight and plunged to earth. Mechanically the young pilot followed instructions, grabbing and pulling out the magnetic ignition to kill the engine and prevent the risk of fire. Then, releasing the restricting harness and at last able to take several deep breaths, he reached to free his canopy. But the lever would not move. Again he tried and again, panic beginning to rise. It was at this moment, with anger and frustration driving the young German pilot's efforts to free the stubborn lever, that his saviour arrived in a very unlikely form.

Having only a very limited view of the sky around him, Zell was unaware of the P-51 which had closed upon his fighter. He was only alerted to the danger by the impact of 0.50-calibre rounds striking his aircraft. Fortunately for the pilot, the hail of fire seemed to have missed him, but the impact of the bullets had done what he himself had been unable to do: his shattered canopy suddenly flew free. With his harness already unfastened, the pilot had barely time to think before he was dragged from his cockpit by the slip-stream, his body brutally thrown against unyielding metal. Dazed and in pain, but at last free from his doomed fighter, he somehow followed the instructions to release his parachute. As the canopy opened above his head his aching body was again shaken as his fall was abruptly halted.

So much had been endured in the space of only a few minutes, but the danger was not over. As the Bf 109 fell to earth the Mustang circled back towards the pilot, now suspended beneath his parachute. Whether intending to kill the young German or merely wishing to confirm his victory with a photograph of him, the American opened fire as he passed. As bullets streamed above his head and the menacing shadow of the Mustang roared by in the freezing air, any thoughts the hapless pilot might have had that life was about to end as he hung powerless faded as he again blacked out. Within a few miles of *Fähnrich* Pröck and *Feldwebel* Reinhold Hedwig, the pilot narrowly missed sharing their fate.

After being abandoned by its pilot, the crippled Messerschmitt Bf 109K-4 had began to break up as it fell. The remains of the fighter finally crashed near the village of Grindau, the larger pieces demolishing a barn in which a group of Russian prisoners who had been drafted to help the local farmers had sought shelter to eat their meagre lunch. Ten of these former soldiers died amidst the wreckage of barn and fighter.

Some distance away the unconscious pilot landed heavily and awoke to see an elderly couple who had followed his descent and had seen the attack by the fighter. Approaching warily, the pair seemed unsure whether the crumpled airman was German or American, and they refused to come near until the aching pilot was able to produce his battered field cap and his pay book. Reassured that the injured man was indeed friendly, the farmer and his wife attempted to tend to his injuries, only to find that they were far beyond their abilities. The collision, the manner which he had abandoned his fighter and his landing had combined to inflict severe wounds. *Unteroffizier* Zell's left leg had been badly cut by shrapnel fragments, and the right side of his back and his neck had also suffered a number of cuts. Severe pain also told him that his right arm had been dislocated. After a time it was possible to summon a military ambulance to carry the pilot to the nearest military hospital at Schwarmstedt.

Despite his pain *Unteroffizier* Zell was confident that he had at least completed his mission. At the hospital, as nurses attended to his wounds, someone found time to examine the parachute which had been bundled into the ambulance with him. In disbelief they found that the remains of the shredded parachute held nineteen bullet holes—perhaps the reason his landing had been so heavy. Finding that *Hauptmann* Pesch had already established a telephone link between the hospital and the *Schulungslehrgang 'Elbe'* head-quarters at Stendal, Zell was able proudly to report his success to *Major* Köhnke. However, although he had succeeded in achieving a *'Herausschuss'*, the Fortress having indeed been 'cut out', he did not know if he had inflicted a mortal wound.

Having made his report, his next priority was to locate his friend. Sure that *Obergefreiter* Siedel had followed him against the bombers, his only thought was how badly he had been hurt. But none of his questions to hospital staff and ambulance crews at Schwarmstedt produced any answers. By the end of the day the hospital at Schwarmstedt would include amongst its patients several of the *Schulungslehrgang 'Elbe'* pilots. Despite each pilot's happiness at finding another *Kamerad* who had survived, Werner Zell was becoming more concerned about the fate of his friend. His painful wait for news was destined to last not for days but for years.

Three days after Zell's combat, as he still lay in bed recovering, the hospital suddenly became a scene of much confused activity. The cause was the approach of British forces. On 10 April the front line of the 2nd British Army had reached Schwarmstedt and then quickly passed by the hospital. All the staff and patients found themselves under British control. Zell and his fellow pilots were transferred to a more secure building in Celle a few days later, and by the beginning of May the young pilot found himself in Belgium. His period of detention was to last until 18 January 1946. Had he been able to leave hospital and search for his friend on 7 April it would have been a fruitless venture. Even the military units that had brought so many pilots for treatment or assisted them to return to their units would be unable to find *Obergefreiter* Siedel.

Several weeks after the combat, near to the village of Engehausen, to the east of Schwarmstedt, farmers were once again attempting to return to their centuries-old work of toiling in their fields. One day, as they moved between their fields, they came across the battered body of Horst Siedel. As on so many previous days during this latest bloody conflict, the cost of war was to be found littering the landscape. The young pilot was found with his parachute unopened: he was already dead, or had been mortally wounded, as he fell to the soil of the Ostenholzer Moor from his fighter. In his search for his friend, Zell was to be further frustrated as the confusion which reigned during the closing stages of the war led to Siedel's body being buried under the wrong name. When at last Zell was able to pay his respects to his friend it was to a grave in the military cemetery at Schwarmstedt marked 'Joachim Siedel'.

Even after finally finding his friend, Werner Zell did not know how he had met his fate. Had he been shot down by the bombers or by the Mustangs, and had he been able to accomplish his mission? Indeed, Zell did not know to which Bomb Group the B-17 he attacked had belonged. For many years these questions have remained unanswered. An examination of the available information may at last provide a partial answer to these questions.

Amongst the possessions which *Unteroffizier* Zell had carried with him to hospital had been his broken wrist-watch. Either as a result of the collision with the bomber or because of his landing, the watch had frozen at 1230. Therefore, it is possible to say that this was the latest time his attack could have taken place. The bombers of the 45th CBW had crossed over Schwarmstedt at 1228 on their way to Kaltenkirchen airfield. The first B-17s to report being attacked soon after this belonged to the 452nd BG, flying as the 45th's 'B' Wing. Because the trailing three elements of the 13th CBW did not come under attack for a further ten minutes, it seems most probable that it was this group of bombers, with twin yellow bands on their fins, which the *Rotte* had attacked. Combat reports from both the 339th and the 353rd FG assigned as the nearest protection to these bombers confirm that both Groups had already become involved with numerous *Luftwaffe* fighters, including Me 262s, which had drawn many of the fighters from their close escort. Although many combat reports were completed by the American pilots, none provides both a description and a time which agree sufficiently to allow their opponent to be identified as either Zell or Siedel.

One interesting report was filed by Captain Harrison Tordoff of the 352nd FS, 353rd FG, and should be considered. The time the pilot recorded for his combat was 1250, but he notes that the encounter began at 1230 when his escort, the 45th CBW, came under attack from Bf 109s making individual approaches. He remained in position until he spotted a Messerschmitt flying alone below him, beneath the bombers. He dived on this fighter, but his initial attack was frustrated by the slow speed at which the fighter was flying. He was forced to cut his speed to make a further attack, but the enemy fighter made no attempt to avoid the P-51, allowing Tordoff finally to get into a good firing position. As his bullets struck the target he saw the canopy fly free and the German pilot drop clear, his parachute opening almost immediately. A spray of coolant then covered the Mustang's windscreen and the pilot broke away to allow it to clear. Although Captain Tordoff's combat film was of poor quality, the sight of the pilot abandoning his fighter and the supporting statement of his wingman allowed the kill to be confirmed. It is possible that this claim records the end of *Unteroffizier* Zell's damaged fighter. It certainly represents the final minutes of one such *Schulungslehrgang 'Elbe'* fighter—one of many that appeared before the guns of the 353rd and 339th FGs that day.

Despite the loss of four bombers, and despite suffering numerous other attacks, the 452nd BG continued upon its mission to Kaltenkirchen. By enduring this series of attacks and completing their planned raid, the crews of the Group were awarded a Distinguished Unit Citation.

14. 9¹/₂G IN A P-51

Throughout the day's encounters, those involving Bf 109s had been very much one-sided affairs. The inexperience of the *'Elbe'* pilots and the modifications to their fighters combined to place the latest recruits to the ranks of the *Jagdwaffe* at a distinct disadvantage. This balance was almost reversed during an encounter at the left-hand edge of the 3rd AD's route. After a brief encounter with a pair of Me 262s which again easily outpaced their Mustangs, 1st Lieutenants Henry R. Slack and Richard K. Corbett of the 84th FS, 78th FG, sighted a Bf 109 level with them at 23,000ft. As the fighter began a shallow dive at the bombers, the two Mustangs split, Corbett chasing at full power while Slack attempted to cut off the fighter at the other side of the bomber formation.

The path chosen by Lieutenant Slack proved to be the less dangerous. As Corbett's P-51 began to catch the Messerschmitt, the pilot opened fire on the bombers. Being so close behind, the Mustang became the centre of attention of the return fire from the bombers. Ignoring the hail of bullets aimed at him, Lieutenant Corbett maintained his pursuit, opening fire as the Bf 109 passed through the bomber formations. Although he saw his bullets striking home, by now his fighter was diving at over 500mph and drawing level with its quarry. Finding himself about to pass the Bf 109, the American was forced to break off the chase, hauling the Mustang away to the right. At this moment Slack had the Messerschmitt in his sights and he opened fire. At first certain that he had caught the Bf 109, he watched in disgust as his bullets flew wide: the *Luftwaffe* pilot had turned into him. At this point the combat was broken as the Bf 109 entered a cloud, but the pair of Mustangs opted to fly underneath, intent upon resuming the fight once the Messerschmitt reappeared. Suddenly the grey shape of the Messerschmitt burst clear of the clouds in front of Lieutenant Corbett, the fighter turning so hard that by the time Corbett reacted the two fighters were almost head-on. In the split second before the two aircraft passed, Corbett hit the firing button and glimpsed strikes on the forward fuselage, before he was again forced to haul his fighter around in pursuit.

Following closely behind his Flight leader, Slack saw the Bf 109 pass Corbett's Mustang. At almost point-blank range he opened fire and was at last rewarded with the sight of his bullets catching the Messerschmitt. By now all three fighters were flying at less than 500ft and the *Luftwaffe* pilot, almost certainly injured by the final hail of fire, had no time to escape. As the American pilots watched, the Bf 109 rolled and then crashed into a small lake below. The combat had been so aggressive that it had taken a great deal of skill for Slack and Corbett to make their kill. The brutal manoeuvres had affected both pilot and machine, the accelerometer in Lieutenant Corbett''s cockpit silently recorded the facts. When the readings were examined it was found that during the combat his body had been under a pressure $9^1/2$ times greater than gravity.

Such forces are a common feature of modern air combat, but in 1945 pilots were less protected than their modern-day counterparts. Despite the huge advances made in aircraft design since the 1914–18 period, the pilot, although now protected from the elements, had to endure combat operations wearing the same basic clothing. It was only in the autumn of 1944 that the first 'G-suits' had appeared. The tight-fitting suits were designed to inflate around the lower body, stopping a pilot's brain from being deprived of the supply of blood during severe combat manoeuvres. The introduction of these suits, especially the Berger-designed version, bestowed upon the Eighth Air Force pilots an advantage comparable to that gained by the introduction of the K-14 gun sight. After initial doubts over the value of an additional piece of bulky, complex instrumentation, the K-14 had become standard fit from November 1944. The two items of equipment together at last enabled the pilot to exploit the full capabilities of his fighter, so paving the way for the high-speed, 'high-G' combat of the dawning jet age.

Although the Me 262s had, by and large, followed their orders and resisted the temptation to carry out further attacks upon the bomber formations, isolated attacks did occur. Flying fifth in the 1st Task Force formation, ahead of the 100th BG, the 390th had so far escaped the attentions of any of the *Jagdwaffe* aircraft. This situation changed in a dramatic manner at 1304hrs. Screaming in a shallow dive from the rear of the formation, from a 7 o'clock position, a lone Me 262 from *I./KG(J) 54* proved just how deadly these revolutionarily fighters were. With his battery of 30mm cannon ablaze, the pilot had selected his target B-17 and closed at high speed. The chosen bomber was flying in the 'number 10' position within the 570th Squadron, who were today leading the 390th BG. This attack was performed with almost surgical precision in the attempt to cut the B-17 from formation: no other bombers suffered even the slightest damage. As the gunners of the formation belatedly reacted to this lightning attack, the assault on their comrades had already been made. As the jet flew through the remaining formation, Staff Sergeant Allen, the tail gunner of one of the Fortresses, was able to score a number of hits with a well-aimed burst at the departing fighter. He was officially credited with damaging this Me 262.

Somewhat optimistically, the B-17 that had been attacked had been named *Hard to Get*, but after 55 previous sorties the damage caused today by the Me 262's cannon made the choice of such a tantalizing nickname appear ironic.

On his twenty-second mission 2nd Lieutenant Kotts eased his crippled bomber with great care between the two bombers to his right and slowly abandoned the formation. The trail of fire which had streamed from *Hard to Get*'s No 4 engine had been quickly followed by a fire which engulfed the entire right wing. By now in no doubt of the fate of his bomber, Kotts ordered his crew to abandon the aircraft. Despite the remaining danger from enemy fighters, many of their Squadron continued to watch the bomber. The longer the crew remained within the confines of the aircraft, the greater the risk. As one by one the crew left their positions and leapt from the bomber, those watching called out each sighting. When the count had reached nine a collective sigh of relief was released: at least each member of the crew had safely left his ship. The now crewless Fortress vanished from view as it was swallowed by the clouds below; its final moments would be hidden from those it had left behind. The nine members of its crew safely landed by parachute, to be captured and held for a brief time as prisoners-of-war.

Despite the skill of the Me 262 pilot, his effort was somewhat wasted. With an entire formation to choose from, over thirty B-17s each loaded with six 1,000lb bombs, the 390th BG bomber which had fallen from the sky had a bomb bay containing nothing more dangerous than leaflets. Nine men had almost lost their lives attempting to carry bundles of paper to their target and a young German had risked his own life in order to stop them.

15. FIRST ATTACKS ON THE 100th BG

Just as those bombers at the head of the formation felt vulnerable, so too did those crews bringing up the tail end. Today the tail of the 1st Task Force was being flown by the B-17s of the 100th BG.

Ever since a series of heavy losses during earlier raids had provided the 100th with the unofficial nickname of the 'Bloody Hundred', the Group had endeavoured to shake off their image. Preferring the name 'Century Bombers', by the end of the war the Group had proved itself. Whilst the high losses during single missions had attracted much attention, other Groups had sustained continued losses during their period of operation. Both the 91st BG, which lost 197 aircraft, and the 96th BG, which lost 189, suffered more than the 100th, who would eventually have lost a total of 177 bombers by the end of the conflict, having flown a total of 306 missions. However, missions such as that on 6 March 1944, when the Group lost sixteen B-17s during an attack on Berlin, served to leave a black mark against the Group and gave it an unenviable reputation within the Eighth Air Force. The crews of the 100th BG, today promised a 'milk run', must have said many a silent prayer and uttered a variety of curses as the other Groups around them reported enemy attacks and across the sky flashed fighters, both friendly and hostile.

It was the tail gunners of the rearmost B-17s which reported the first attacks aimed against the 100th. The speed of the attackers indicated the approach of jets, the Messerschmitts screaming in out of the sun. These attacks, which ran the length of the formation, appear again not to have been driven home with any commitment. The real danger to the bombers arrived with the conventional piston-engine fighters. These aircraft arrived in loose groups of three or four, then appeared to split before making their attacks. To the bomber crews the break-up of the attacking formations had been a result of the escorting P-51s: they were unaware of the tactics adopted by their enemy. When the solo attacks began, the ferocity became readily apparent, and even the concentrated defensive fire of the B-17s failed to divert the pilots from their task. Promises that the *Luftwaffe* fighter arm was a spent force now seemed to have a hollow ring. On his twenty-fifth mission Lieutenant William Howard found that the air around his B-17 had apparently filled with enemy aircraft. Although he and his crew had faced the *Jagdwaffe* before, they would estimate that they had seen more enemy fighters today than they had encountered on all their previous flights added together.

The inexperience of the young *'Elbe'* pilots proved their undoing as, unable to position themselves during their first pass, they flew through the formations and attempted to turn back for further passes. Often already damaged and unnerved by the gunners, the Germans found themselves facing P-51s as they levelled off and tried to haul their fighters around. Faced with the more experienced escorts, the *Schulungslehrgang 'Elbe'* men, unfamiliar with their own mounts, found themselves at a distinct disadvantage. For all their aggression, few of the young *Luftwaffe* pilots were allowed to make a second pass.

One Bf 109 elected to attack from below the bomber formation. Passing up through the narrow space between the bombers, it made a tight turn above the formation before diving upon a selected B-17. The American pilot must have thought it was to be his final mission as his bomber was shaken by the impact of the enemy fighter which crashed against the tail. But luck remained with the bomber. The wing of the *'Elbe'* fighter had torn into the horizontal stabilizer, severing it cleanly from the tail of the bomber. Although this was a frightening experience, especially for the tail-gunner, the rugged Fortress could survive such damage. On this occasion the German fighter had not finished its work. The sudden impact of the wing against the stabilizer caused it to be ripped from the fighter, which continued through the formation in a uncontrollable spin. The wing itself narrowly missed the nearest B-17 in the formation and collided with another bomber following behind.

To the crew of the second bomber, the sight of the first collision had been horrific. The gunners had been aiming at the fighter as it dived through the formation and they believed that their fire had caused the pilot to lose control. As the wing of the fighter was thrown clear and headed for their aircraft, they were powerless to take avoiding action. When the impact came it was at the rear of their bomber. The damage was again confined to one of the horizontal stabilizers, but this time the impact of the wing removed a sizable section without inflicting any further damage. Both of these B-17s were able to return to Thorpe Abbotts, the crew shaken, their aircraft damaged but repairable. The bombardier of the second B-17, who had carried out his important secondary task as gunner, was rewarded with the credit for the destruction of the Bf 109. Only after both bombers had returned home safely would he have been happy to accept the award, safe in the knowledge that he had not caused the destruction of another B-17.

In the sky to the north of Steinhuder lake the battle around the 100th BG continued. The escort fighters were gradually having greater success against the *Luftwaffe* fighters as the latter split for individual attacks and began to exhibit tell-tale signs of their lack of experience. For the bomber crews, any such failing in the German pilots was irrelevant: the Messerschmitts which passed through the formations continued to show a frightening level of aggression. In one of the older Fortresses taking part in the mission, Lieutenant Arthur Calder and his crew of eight were flying *Candy's Dandy* of the 418th BS (LD-P, 42-97071). Today *Candy's Dandy* was positioned in the lower formation of the 100th BG's Lead Squadron. With the battle raging around them, the crew were already on a high state of alert, the gunners firing at any fighter which posed a threat either to them or to their formation. Although the firepower of a B-17 could inflict a good deal of damage in the interests of self-preservation, when a dangerous shadow fell upon their bomber even the massed Brownings could offer little protection.

The attack upon *Candy's Dandy* came from above, a lone Bf 109 plunging through the upper formation from a 5 o'clock position. Having avoided the prowling escorts, the closest of which were from the 78th FG, the *Luftwaffe* pilot had pushed his fighter into a steep dive. Unable to approach his target in the prescribed manner, he passed the upper Fortresses without inflicting any damage. However, the speed of the fighter's dive and the position of the bombers of the lower formation placed the Messerschmitt on a collision course with Lieutenant Calder's bomber. Whereas other aircraft on this day suffered a protracted death, the end of *Candy's Dandy* was sudden and brutal. Both aircraft were consumed in a massive explosion as fuel and bomb load ripped apart what had become in an instant seemingly fragile machines. There was no hope of any of the crew escaping from such a blast—only fragments of twisted metal remained to shower the ground below.

The attacks upon the 100th had badly shaken the crews. When at last the sky around them finally began to clear of enemy fighters, they had been under attack for almost half an hour. Because of the enemy fighter activity the order had been given for all the Groups of the 1st Task Force to bomb in Group formation rather than the looser Squadron pattern. The events of the last half hour had already adversely effected the 100th BG formation: closing the gaps and cutting the distances between ragged formations would not be easy. Moreover, the bombers had not yet reached their targets. With the fighter attacks having stopped, the crews feared one thing—that the target would be defended by flak.

Under the protective cover of the American fighters, who were engaging the pilots of the *Jagdwaffe* as they approached the bombers, the 3rd AD formation had split into two task forces. Whilst the route of the 13th and 45th Combat Bomb Wings (the 1st Task Force) now took them towards their first targets which lay across the Elbe, the 93rd and 4th CBWs (the 2nd Task Force) had made a turn to the east. Selected to take the longest route of the day, the eight Bomb Groups of the 93rd and 4th CBWs headed towards their targets, which lay almost 300 miles from the point where they had first crossed into Europe.

Providing a part of the escort for the 93rd and 4th were the Mustangs of the 55th FG. Whilst it seemed that all around them fellow pilots were entering into combat, the 55th men had remained close to their bombers. Since the initial reports of clashes with the *Luftwaffe*, almost an hour ago, this group of pilots had scanned the sky for any sign that trouble was heading their way. Flying at between 19,000 and 20,000ft over the Steinhuder lake, pilots of the 38th FS, 55th FG, at last spotted the approach of enemy aircraft at about 1300. To protect the massed Fortress formation, the escort pilots moved closer, better prepared to react to any attacks. As the enemy neared it was possible to count fifteen aircraft in a loose formation. At first making no attempt to attack the bombers, the *Luftwaffe* fighters tracked the formation from a safe distance, at a height of between 25,000 and 23,000ft, for 30 miles until it reached the vicinity of Celle. At that point, as the American fighter pilots watched, single Bf 109s peeled off from the larger group and began solo diving attacks upon the bombers. It is likely that, having found the bombers still protected by their 'Little Friends', the German force had held back, hoping that their own 'escort' force would arrive to deal with the dangerous Mustangs. As the minutes ticked by and no assistance arrived, the pilots accepted their fate, each deciding to ignore the presence of the silver P-51s with their bright green and yellow noses and their recently painted bright red rudders.

As the first Messerschmitt made its dive towards the bombers, the escorts had been caught by surprise. The first to react was 'Hellcat White' Flight, led by Captain Donald M. Cummings. Ensuring that part of his formation remained to keep a watchful eye on the larger group of enemy fighters, Cummings dispatched his second element to pursue the first Bf 109. Needing no second bidding, 'Hellcat White 3' and '4', flown by 1st Lieutenant Donald T. Menegay and 2nd Lieutenant Dennis A. Cavanaugh, peeled off to give chase. As the German pilot passed the bombers without attacking, any thoughts of preparing for a second pass vanished as he found himself with two Mustangs uncomfortably close on his tail. The Messerschmitt continued to dive to 12,000ft before levelling out, and Menegay, sitting less than 200yds behind, immediately fired a concentrated burst which struck the enemy fighter with force. Receiving hits along the fuselage and on the wing roots, the *Luftwaffe* pilot decided that the best course of action was again to push his fighter into a dive. The first burst of fire must have inflicted damage to the Bf 109, for as the Americans followed they found themselves quickly catching their opponent. At one stage Lieutenant Menegay was able to draw level and see a stream of coolant trailing from the Messerschmitt. At this point the flight of the Bf 109 became erratic, the fighter twisting and spinning, forcing Menegay to cut his speed and follow from a safer distance. Attempting again to centre the Bf 109 in his sights, Menegay found that its manoeuvring made this impossible: once more his speed was bringing him closer to the German fighter, so he was forced to cut it again to avoid overshooting. Hoping to exploit this move, the *Luftwaffe* pilot pulled up and made a turn towards the safety of some clouds.

Watching his leader attempting to position himself for a good shot, Lieutenant Cavanaugh had seen the coolant trail from the Bf 109 turn into dense smoke. With his leader clearly having problems, Cavanaugh was looking for any chance to take his turn, and it came as the Messerschmitt made an attempt to reach the safety of the clouds. Although the German had escaped the attentions of the first Mustang, the pilot had unwarily placed himself in front of the second. From 300yds Cavanaugh let loose a three-second burst which ripped pieces from first the tail and then the wing roots of the enemy fighter. As the Bf 109 performed an uncontrolled snap and began to fall in a wild spin, the two Mustangs flew through a trail of smoke and debris. Neither of the Americans saw any trace of the pilot escaping from this fighter before they lost sight of the aircraft as it entered a solid layer of cloud at 4,000ft.

As the town of Celle drifted beneath the formations of bombers and fighters, the attacks continued. Holding his position while Menegay and Cavanaugh followed the first Bf 109, Captain Cummings had only minutes to wait for the next fighter to attack. This time Cummings and his wingman, 2nd Lieutenant Robert V. Bender, were able to drop their tanks and catch the Messerschmitt before it reached the bombers. After a short burst from 800yds Cummings stopped firing as they reached the bombers. This Bf 109 passed through the bombers without either selecting a target or being hit by fire from the gunners. Then the pilot began to turn back, perhaps having decided upon an attack from below. However, the pair of Mustangs were close behind, and before the turn could be completed Cummings again opened fire. From a distance of 400yds the bullets continued to rip into the Messerschmitt until the P-51 eventually overflew it. The damage inflicted was considerable: pieces of wings and fuselage were thrown free by the impact of the assault before the aircraft started to burn. The *Luftwaffe* pilot wisely decided that the time had come for him to abandon his fighter, and as Lieutenant Bender followed he saw the German leap free before his aircraft headed vertically to earth.

As the two Mustangs climbed back towards the bombers they spotted another Bf 109 entering a dive. On this occasion Captain Cummings followed the Messerschmitt too closely as it passed through the bombers and he found himself on the receiving end of an intense barrage from the Fortress gunners. Escaping unscathed, the Mustangs were able to catch their second enemy fighter at 12,000ft. Again Cummings took the lead and opened fire at 400yds as the Bf 109 began a turn to the left. With hits along the German's fuselage, wing roots and cockpit, Cummings made sure of his victory by flying his aircraft to within 20yds. At such a distance the Mustang was in danger from the debris being shed by the damaged Bf 109, a point emphasized with force as the aircraft suddenly burst into flames. Pulling sharply away from the inferno, Captain Cummings was lucky to avoid damage to his fighter. As the leading Mustang broke to the right the Bf 109 fell off to the left in front of Lieutenant Bender. From 10,000ft the latter followed the Bf 109 down, but this time the pilot failed to leave his cockpit and he never recovered from the fatal vertical dive.

As these clashes were being enacted other P-51s from the 38th FS were chasing their own Bf 109s. With the enemy formation continuing with solo attacks, it was proving relatively easy for the Mustang pilots to select the next Bf 109 and give chase. Positioned 3,000ft above the 93rd CBW bombers, Captain McCauley Clark put his fighter between the next Bf 109 and his 'Big Friends'. In his owns words, as he headed off the Bf 109 Clark fired 'a squirt from my guns to distract his attention. He dove under the bombers without hitting anything and I followed him, pulling in behind shortly after dropping my tanks.' From 300yds dead astern Captain Clark opened fire, his fire striking the fuselage and cockpit. Flying closer and closer to his target, he eventually pulled up just as the Messerschmitt entered a spin trailing dense smoke. As the damaged fighter passed through a layer of clouds, Clark turned back to confirm his victory. Passing through the clouds, he found before him a pilot floating beneath his parachute canopy. With no other combat nearby, Clark assumed this to be the pilot of the aircraft he had just attacked.

As the rest of his Flight was giving chase to a Bf 109—the one eventually caught by Captain Clark—1st Lieutenant John W. Cunnick had found himself suddenly alone. He had lost contact with everyone, including his own wingman. Having already dropped his tanks, Cunnick decided that it was safer to return to the bombers than to waste fuel searching for the remainder of his Flight. Just as he drew level with the bombers he saw another Bf 109 dive through the formation of Fortresses. It offered a target too good to miss, and Cunnick turned his Mustang around. The chase continued down to 10,000ft, where the Messerschmitt was pulled out of its dive. Sitting only 100yds from the rudder of his enemy, Lieutenant Cunnick fired, and in an instant shots struck the wing roots and shattered the canopy. In the space of only a few minutes the 38th FS had claimed five of the Bf109s.

Within a few minutes another P-51, which had become separated during the chase, added a sixth. Not wishing to follow some of his Flight through cloud, 1st Lieutenant Roger B. Mooers had pulled his fighter back up into the sun, rolling out to the south-east. Levelling his P-51, he caught sight of a Bf 109 400yds ahead, flying straight and level at 10,000ft. The sight must have surprised Mooers, as, despite the number of American fighters in the area, the pilot of this Messerschmitt appeared unaware of the danger and his fighter still carried the centreline tank. Increasing his speed until he sat directly behind the Bf 109, Lieutenant Mooers decided to open fire and his first two-second burst succeeded in scoring hits and producing a trail of black smoke. Once again the 38th FS pilot flew even closer to ensure his kill. From only 50ft two further bursts added to the initial damage, larger pieces of airframe now breaking free. By this time the smoke had increased, and just before the fighter disappeared within the dense trail Mooers thought he caught sight of the canopy fall free. With only the wing tips of the Messerschmitt visible, he broke off his chase to avoid the danger of a collision. Glancing back, he saw the mortally wounded Bf 109 being swallowed by the cloud layer below, only the trail of smoke and shower of debris marking its passage.

With the Mustangs of the 55th FG extracting such a high toll from the attacking *Luftwaffe* formations, it seems almost inconceivable that any attack could succeed. However, once again the aggression and determination of the young German pilots allowed some at least to escape from the protective escorts. Today the first bombers to suffer an attack were those wearing the bold red bands of the 493rd BG, flying second in the 2nd Task Force. A mixed formation of twelve fighters, thought to be an equal number of Bf 109s and Fw 190s, made a series of uncoordinated attacks upon the 493rd BG beginning at 1304hrs. Although the crews of the B-17s reported that these attacks appeared to fail due to the inexperience of the attacking pilots, one such attack did result in the destruction of a 493rd bomber. A few minutes later the leading formation, the 385th BG, saw enemy fighters approaching them. Even more boldly marked than the 493rd aircraft, the B-17s of the 385th BG, known as 'Van's Valiants', carried tails covered by a red chequerboard design which could be have provided a clear target for the *Schulungslehrgang 'Elbe'* pilots. However, when the attacks began few followed the intended method of approach. The first five Bf 109s approached from a 3 o'clock position but instead of a direct attack the fighters, in line astern, headed to the front of the 385th, where they circled at a slightly lower altitude, seemingly uncertain of their next move. When the fighters did approach they made head-on attacks, climbing towards the Low Squadron. On each occasion the pilots broke off their approach after closing to within 200yds of the Fortresses. A second formation, a *Schwarm* of four Fw 190s, also made a series of unenthusiastic approaches, the pilots ending their attacks some 800yds short of the bomber formation. The failure of any of these attacks to inflict severe damage to any bomber could have led crews to believe that they were not facing a very determined enemy.

After fifteen minutes of such attacks the real dangers became evident as a lone Bf 109 broke out of a patch of broken cloud at the rear of the 385th formation. Although the alert gunners of the High Squadron quickly reacted with a barrage aimed at this single fighter, it continued on its path, aimed directly at them. In the short time available to the gunners they succeeded in scoring a number of hits on their target. But, despite the trail of smoke streaming from the damaged engine, the pilot still had his fighter under control as he guided it though the High Squadron and plunged down upon an unsuspecting B-17 of the Low Squadron. As the two wrecked aircraft began slowly to drop below the formation, smoke and flames were very evident. But on this occasion the trails would not wind their way to earth. Having fallen only a few hundred feet, the bomber suddenly exploded, the detonation of the bomb load and fuel reducing the Fortress to little more than shrapnel.

Flying fourth in the bomber column were the 490th BG. The attack upon these bombers began at 1313 and was carried out by a single *Rotte*, the *Schulungslehrgang 'Elbe'* by now having become hopelessly split. Based upon the available evidence it would appear that one of the Messerschmitts approaching the 490th was flown by an older, more experienced pilot—28-year-old *Leutnant* Hans Nagel. One of the volunteers from *IV./JG 102*, Nagel had, like so many of his fellow pilots, felt powerless to stop the destruction of his homeland while based in Norway. At every opportunity he had requested a transfer to a unit under the control of the *Reichsverteidigung* (RVT), the home defence organization. The chance came with the plans of *Oberst* Herrmann. In his letters to his wife *Leutnant* Nagel expressed his frustration at having to hear of the reports of attacks upon his homeland of Schleswig-Holstein: his pride would be restored if he were able to fly against the American *'Terrorflieger'*. Despite his greater experience, the cost of defending his family and home would be high. Alone against the bombers, the *Rotte* approached the Low Squadron from the rear, the 6 o'clock position. Flying to within 100yds of the B-17s, the fighters then broke away to the right. This *Schulungslehrgang 'Elbe'* attack differed from others in that this first pass was a firing pass, one or both of the fighters having enough ammunition to attempt a 'standard' kill using gunfire. Although only speculation, it is possible that the more experienced *Leutnant* Nagel and his unknown *Rottenflieger* were allocated either unmodified Bf 109s or fighters retaining their weapons. Whatever the reason, the pilots made full use of their guns.

Turning back towards the bombers, the *Rotte* had become separated, and this time a single Bf 109 attacked the High Squadron from between 4 and 3 o'clock. The lone fighter completed one pass and again turned back to approach from 9 o'clock. After this pass a B-17 was seen to become detached from the safety of the formation and begin its fall to earth ablaze. The 490th crews at this point believed that their guns had scored hits on the Bf 109, for as it passed through the High Squadron the pilot seemed unable to take avoiding action as his fighter dived upon a B-17 of the Low Squadron. This unfortunate B-17 was flown by 1st Lieutenant Carrol Cagle, who must have feared the worst as his bomber was shaken by the impact of the Messerschmitt, the right wing of which smashed against the waist gunner's position. The aircraft's forward flight being so abruptly halted, the fuselage of the fighter then swung against the bomber, tearing down the fuselage and against the ball turret. The damage continued as the fighter dragged itself beneath the right wing of the B-17 before finally falling away. The initial impact and the brief seconds following had torn a six-foot wound in the B-17's fuselage near to the waist position, had smashed against the normally rugged ball turret, injuring the terrified gunner, ripped the supercharger from the inboard engine and finally torn away part of the outboard propeller. With the remains of the Messerschmitt falling away below, Lieutenant Cagle attempted to bring his bomber under control, but with only two engines now providing power his task seemed almost impossible. But again the strength and reliability of the Boeing design won through: the bomber continued to fly and to respond to the careful control movements. By gentle turns and adjustments the bomber was headed back towards the safety of friendly lines, eventually landing at a forward base in France. The only injury to the crew was a broken arm suffered by the shaken ball gunner, who had still been protected from the collision by the solid construction of his turret.

The Messerschmitt which had caused the destruction of the first 490th bomber and had so nearly accounted for a second had ceased to be a combat aircraft the instant its wing struck the fuselage of Cagle's B-17. A group of civilians had watched the entire encounter, following the small shapes of the fighters in their attempt to halt the entire formation by themselves. Unaware of the intended method of attack, they had followed the success of the fighter and witnessed its terrible fate. They now followed the descent of the Messerschmitt's twisted wreckage as it tumbled towards them, the pilot having no hope of escape. Although knowing the fate of the pilot, the group reached the crash site, finding little to indicate what had only minutes earlier been a formidable fighter. The body which they pulled free was identified from the papers it carried. It was *Leutnant* Nagel, and he had indeed paid the highest cost imaginable for the brief opportunity of defending his homeland.

The *Luftwaffe* pilot was buried with honours in the village of Berhof by the civilians who had witnessed this attack. Nagel's young wife received a letter from the village which said more than the official confirmation of her husband's death. The village recognized the sacrifice that *Leutnant* Nagel had made and felt that such courage, shown in the knowledge that the eventual outcome of the war had already been determined, should be remembered by generations to come. Only three days later the villagers themselves came face to face with the enemy, in the shape of the tanks belonging to the British 11th Armoured Division, part of General Dempsey's Second Army which had fought its way from the beaches of Normandy.

In the air the 93rd CBW formations were at last free from *Luftwaffe* fighters, and the 4th CBW's, following in their wake, would have been hopeful that perhaps they were to be spared. When an attack actually materialized it appeared to the crews of the 487th BG that it was limited to a lone Bf 109. However, if this attack had indeed been made by only a single fighter, the B-17s of the 487th did not escape lightly. Once again, when the fighter was spotted it was making a high diving attack from the 6 o'clock position, on this occasion against the Lead Squadron of B-17s. Yet again this fighter opened fire as soon as the Fortresses came within range and continued to fire as it closed with the formation. The damage which the gunfire inflicted would indicate that cannon rather than a single machine gun had been used. Only the top turret gunner of the No 6 aircraft was able to react in time to hit the enemy fighter. However, the gunners of this Fortress believed that their reactions had been quick enough. The enemy fighter, which they assumed to be damaged, made no attempt to avoid the bomber of 1st Lieutenant Wentz which was flying in the No 7 position. Suddenly the fighter collided with the B-17's tail and sheared off a large portion of the left horizontal stabilizer. Having torn through the control surface, the fighter then appeared to be thrown against the fuselage of the bomber, causing further damage near to the radio compartment before falling clear. The impact had knocked the Messerschmitt off course and it then fell beneath the No 6 aircraft. Despite the damage it had suffered during the collision, and any further damage sustained as a result of the gunners, the pilot of the Bf 109 appeared briefly to have regained control of his fighter whilst beneath this Fortress. His error was then to pull up in front of the nose gunner of the bomber, who opened fire at almost point-blank range. Under this fire the Messerschmitt was obviously badly damaged, large pieces of debris flying clear. Whichever of the gunners believed themselves responsible, this Fortress crew were able to celebrate a victory as the damaged Bf 109 began to spin, the pilot being seen to leap clear.

The damaged Fortress was to prove another lucky aircraft, for it remained with the formation for a further five minutes until the pilot decided upon the best course of action. The damage was serious enough to convince Lieutenant Wentz that he should head for an emergency landing site, so the bomber was eased from the formation and the bomb load jettisoned. He was able to guide his B-17 and his crew to a safe, if early, landing at airfield A-92. This was in fact St Trond in Belgium, currently home to the Ninth Air Force's 48th and 404th FGs but previously occupied by those hunters of RAF bombers *Nachtjagdgeschwader 1*.

If the Bf 109 which had attacked Lieutenant Wentz's B-17 had also been partly or even fully armed, it may have came from the same base as *Leutnant* Nagel's aircraft; quite possibly it had been the fighter of his *Rottenflieger*. The one interesting aspect of this attack is that in the gunnery report, filed several days later by the 4th CBW's gunnery officer Captain Charles Spare, mention is made of a number of 'self-inflicted battle damage reports'. The Fortresses which had flown in the Nos 2, 4 and 5 positions all received what was reported to be 'major damage' during the attack. Taking into consideration the positions in the formation of these aircraft, it seems highly unlikely that a single Bf 109, especially the one involved in the collision, would have been capable of bringing his weapons to bear upon these other B-17s. This raises questions. Was the damage entirely due to this one attack? Had the entire formation missed seeing another *Luftwaffe* fighter amongst their formation? Or were the gunners of the Group perhaps a little too keen and a little off target? In reacting to this one attack a total of 900 rounds of ammunition had been fired by the gunners of the 487th BG.

The 487th suffered no other fighter attacks, although several of the crews reported prowling enemy fighters. A loose formation of three Bf 109s stood off at a safe distance during the length of the previous encounter. They would have witnessed the fate of the courageous pilot, but they made no attempt either to follow his example or to attempt to complete the work started on the damaged B-17.

16. THE 486th BG

Although no other Bomb Group within the 4th CBW met any enemy fighters, the rest of their flight would not be uneventful. As they continued towards their first target at Fassberg the 93rd/4th CBW formations had passed the area of greatest danger. The escort fighters assumed their formations once again and returned to their covering positions alongside and above the bombers. Although the bombers were now heading even closer to the home bases of *Schulungslehrgang 'Elbe'*, the *Luftwaffe* force had been spread over a large area and had suffered a punishing introduction to combat at the hands of the Eighth Air Force pilots. The final encounters of a 3rd AD escort with what can be identified as *'Elbe'* fighters occurred at around 1320 when the 93rd/4th CBW formation had turned towards the north-eastern targets, beginning with Salzwedel airfield. In the penultimate combat Captain Ivan L. McGuire, of the 363rd FS, 357th FG, caught a Bf 109 probably attempting to return to its base at Parchim. This victory was followed closely by that of Captain James T. Windham, also of the 363rd FS, who met and promptly dispatched a lone Bf 109 in the vicinity of Salzwedel.

To the north-west of the 93rd/4th CBW formation the other element of the 3rd AD, the 45th/13th CBW, had reached its first target at Fassberg. Over the previous fifteen minutes the number of attacks upon these formations had dwindled, but the danger had had yet to pass. Suddenly a fresh attack materialized as Me 262s of *I./KG(J) 54*, finding some boxes of bombers without escort, chose to hit the Fortresses rather than seek out the American fighters. With no *Schulungslehrgang 'Elbe'* fighters in the area, it is likely that the Me 262s were finally freed from their previous supporting mission. The bombers suffering this latest attack belonged to the 13th CBW, their post-combat reports making reference to the 'thin support' resulting from their escorts' being busy chasing *Luftwaffe* fighters.

The jets streaked in towards their quarry at 25,000ft. One of the few American fighters able to react was a lone Mustang of the 505th FS, 339th FG. The attack began near Uelzen as the bombers turned on to a northern heading aimed at Lüneburg. Faced as he was by the sight of several Me 262s bearing down on him, Flying Officer John Joseph Rice was well aware that he could do little to protect the bombers. As the jets made their attack, Rice decided to carry out his mission to his best ability. As the nearest *Rotte* streaked past he turned in behind the trailing fighter. With the twin-engine jet only in a shallow dive, it was still obvious that the Mustang would be unable to match its speed. Letting loose a short burst while the Me 262 remained in his sights, somewhat to his surprise Rice saw hits on the wing of the jet. But there would be no opportunity to follow up these shots as the jet was easily outpacing the P-51.

Although the *Rotte* followed by Flying Officer Rice had not inflicted any damage upon the bombers, others were having greater success. Up to thirteen jets had been launched by *KG(J) 54* from Hagenow, and they had found the 45th/13th CBW as they approached the River Elbe. The escorts remaining close enough to the bombers proved, like Rice, unable to shield their 'Big Friends'. The jets were able to claim at least three kills from this bomber formation without loss. As was often the case, the jet units had few problems when carrying out their intended mission. However, once their mission had been completed and they attempted to disengage to return to base, their weaknesses often began to show. On this day *Hauptmann* Werner Tronicke had made a successful attack on the Fortress formation, destroying one bomber and inflicting damage on a second. It may indeed have been this jet which had earlier attacked the 390th BG and as a result may have suffered some damage. By this time it was certainly short of fuel and ammunition, and it was chased, caught and destroyed by Mustangs. It is possible that the destruction of Tronicke's jet can be credited to Major Vernon B. Hawthorn Jr of the 504th FS, 339th FG. An examination of Hawthorn's combat report reveals that his victory was not without problems. With the Flight he had joined breaking formation to chase after some of the high-flying enemy fighters, Major Hawthorn had found himself alone, without even his wingman. Joining two other P-51s who seemed to have singled out an Me 262, he followed them down from 25,000 to about 10,000ft. To his amazement, when the jet began a left-hand turn the other two Mustangs did not follow but seemed intent upon heading elsewhere. At this point Hawthorn admitted that his patience began to disappear, especially when both fighters then ignored his calls to them over the radio. Again alone, this time with an Me 262 ahead of him, he decided to continue with the attack without the help of anyone else. With the jet still in a turn and losing altitude, the P-51 followed until at 5,000ft the distance between the two aircraft had been reduced enough for Major Hawthorn to consider opening fire. When only 500ft separated the aircraft the American pilot did open fire, a long burst hitting the tail of the Me 262. To avoid the Mustang the German pilot pushed his fighter to the right and into a steeper dive, aiming at some low clouds. This dive allowed Hawthorn, who was already 'cutting the corner', time to make up more of the distance. With the Messerschmitt firmly in his sights, he poured a full ten-second burst of gunfire into its fuselage, cockpit and right-hand engine. The immediate effect was for the engine to burst into flames. The right-hand turn then became a very steep corkscrew, which continued until Hawthorn lost sight of the damaged fighter as it spun through a cloud layer at between

2,000 and 3,000ft. When the crash site of the Me 262 was finally found, not far from its home airfield, the body of *Hauptmann* Tronicke was found amidst the wreckage. So died another of the young pilots upon whom the survival of the *Luftwaffe* had depended.

17. THE 100th BG SUFFERS AGAIN

The bombers of the 100th BG had already been under attack from enemy fighters for over thirty minutes. Alarmingly, their escorts appeared to be giving the Group only sporadic cover and the mixed force of enemy fighters was still approaching from what seemed every possible angle. The bombers were now close to their IP (initial point), the last stage of their course aimed at the Büchen underground oil storage facilities. From now on the B-17s were to be held straight and level to enable the bombardiers to do their jobs. At this time the last thing they wanted was fighter attacks breaking up the formation—but of course still they came.

In his gleaming silver Fortress, 44-8334, sporting the black rudder of the 100th BG and the individual letter 'M', Lieutenant Howard carried out his usual ritual. Before ensuring that he had control of the B-17 for this stage of the flight, he had drawn his Colt .45 and placed it on the instrument panel in front of him. He then, as usual, told the crew that he was now ready to deal with any fighter that approached his position. Conscious of the tension the crew always felt nearing their target, especially so today, he always hoped that this would help lighten the atmosphere, even just a little. With only a minute or so to go to the IP and his ritual performed, Howard then switched his radio to the command channel to listen for final instructions from the leading aircraft. With a final check of his position within the formation, the pilot glanced to his right and looked across his co-pilot Lieutenant Gerry Delgano to see *E-Z Goin*, the B-17 of Lieutenant Joe Martin, off his right wing. Howard knew that the formation had their bomb-bay doors open and it was only minutes before the aircraft would unload their bombs on their targets. It was just at that moment, as the pilot made a final adjustment to his seat belt, that yet another Bf 109 broke through the formation.

With the sun behind this latest Messerschmitt, the crews manning the guns of the B-17s had little hope of spotting its approach in time. This *Schulungslehrgang 'Elbe'* fighter had made an almost perfect diving approach to its target. The unlucky B-17 that it had selected was *E-Z Goin*. Crouched in the rearward-facing tail position, the gunner had a split second to react and open fire upon the Messerschmitt now bearing down upon him, but with the fighter levelling out in the prescribed manner, the gunner seemed unable to move. Although no return fire came from the tail position, the *'Elbe'* pilot possibly decided that it was still necessary use his single weapon, and this may account for the damage inflicted upon the bomber nearest to his target. Seconds after the Messerschmitt had levelled out behind the B-17 it fell upon its chosen foe. The only comparable description of the damage caused by this fighter is that visible upon a victim of a shark attack. Metal skin, control cables and ribs were shredded like flesh, tendon and bone by the metal propeller blades. Having passed the crouched figure of the tail-gunner, the fighter continued to claw its way forward along the left-hand side of the bomber, the leading edge of its wing almost totally destroying the elevator and horizontal stabilizer which lay in its path. Only feet from the waist-gun position, its progress was cut short and the fighter was flung clear.

As the fighter fell away having completed its attack, in the cockpit of the nearest B-17 Lieutenant Howard found his co-pilot Lieutenant Delgano tapping him on the shoulder. Attending to the messages of the command channel, the pilot briefly looked up to see the damaged *E-Z Goin* off his right wing, and assuming that his co-pilot was drawing his attention to this he indicated that he had seen the troubled bomber. As he tried to turn back to his task, Delgano grabbed his shoulder and urgently pointed to his earphones. Correctly deciding that he should abandon his monitoring of the command frequency, Howard switched back to hear the voice of his co-pilot. Their own bomber had been damaged, perhaps by gunfire from the Messerschmitt or perhaps by debris thrown from the collision, but whatever the cause their No 3 engine was on fire. To get a better view of the trouble Howard unfastened his seat-belt and stood up to see his right wing in full. As the pilot later wrote, 'Sure enough, flames were sweeping back over the wing. One look was enough to convince me that we had a serious problem.' His major concern was for the fuel tanks which lay beneath the flames, covered by only a thin skin of metal. On previous flights he had witnessed at close quarters the death of B-17 and feared a similar fate. Having seen the damage to the aircraft to his right, he was sure that both bombers were now fighting for their survival. Following his instincts, Lieutenant Howard pushed his Fortress into a steep bank to clear the other aircraft in the formation and pulled the control which jettisoned his bomb load. He then alerted his crew to the danger posed by the uncontrollable fire engulfing their right wing. With the bomber still capable of being flown, Howard decided that they should aim for Allied territory, or at least get as near as possible in the time remaining. His navigator, Lieutenant Doug Jones, quickly provided a new heading at the same time that the pilot and co-pilot were attempting a variety of manoeuvres in an attempt to extinguish the engine fire. All of their efforts failed. Although they had been told that extinguishers fitted to each engine had not been designed to cope with such in-flight fires, they even tried this option, only to have smoke fill the flight deck. The fire was showing no signs of succumbing, and even as they watched it began to take a greater hold upon their wing. Very quickly the main wheel was set alight; this was located directly beneath the engine on fire and added black smoke and more flame to the inferno already raging.

Each second the fire continued to burn placed the aircraft and her crew in greater danger. Lieutenant Howard could already clearly see the wing leading edge ripple with the heat. Having decided that the risk had become too great, he finally ordered the crew to abandon their positions, his order reinforced by the sound of the warning bell. With his temperamental autopilot at last set, the pilot joined the other two crewmen at the forward hatch. When the pilot was sure that he was the last man aboard the stricken bomber, he too leapt clear. It was as he tumbled down and attempted to pull his ripcord that he had reason to curse the lighter than normal clothes that he wore: his harness had been adjusted for the standard fleece-lined gear and now slid across his body as he pulled. It required a determined effort finally to pull the cord free and release the parachute, but the effort was worthwhile as the reassuring jerk told Howard that his 'chute had opened safely. A glance around at the eight other silken shapes told him that all of his crew were also clear. After the last few minutes the young pilot attempted to relax, almost enjoying the unusual view. But his aircraft seemed intent upon spoiling things. His autopilot adjustments had put the bomber on a sweeping turn, and as he glanced up in disbelief he found the Fortress bearing down upon him. Although the turn was to carry the aircraft safely past him until it had faded from his view, it gave him a few moments of added anxiety.

Whilst in the last minutes Lieutenant Howard and his crew had fought in vain to save their Fortress, the crew of *E-Z Goin* had been involved in their own battle of survival. Although the damage to the tail surfaces of their bomber was extensive, much of it remained invisible to the crew; even the tail gunner, who was so close to the destroyed surfaces, could not gain a clear view. In the cockpit the pilot, Lieutenant Joseph Martin, considered his options. The bomber had wallowed in the air as a result of the torn tail surfaces, which failed to respond to his controls. Within the crew, shielded from the full extent of the damage to their bomber and finding the engines undamaged and wing controls still responding, any initial panic was replaced by hope. Although they knew that their Fortress was badly wounded, Martin and his co-pilot Lieutenant Henry Cervantes decided that they should stay with *E-Z Goin*: every minute that they remained flying brought them closer to friendly territory. With no tail controls, they experimented by shifting the rest of the crew between the nose and tail, and amazingly they found that the bomber could be nursed higher or lower. Unbelievably, this operation was to be repeated many times, and the Fortress gradually limped back across friendly territory, over the Channel and back home to Thorpe Abbotts. When the exhausted crew finally landed they were able to join the bewildered ground crews examining the damage inflicted by the *Schulungslehrgang 'Elbe'* pilot. All agreed that it was a miracle that the bomber had withstood the collision and that Lieutenant Martin and his crew had had the skill to bring the bomber home.

During their debriefing sessions the crew of *E-Z Goin* became convinced that the attack that they had suffered was a result of an unmanned Bf 109 crashing through the formation. The tail gunner was sure that he had caught a glimpse of the fighter without a canopy. But jettisoning the cockpit canopy before their attack was an option considered by the pilots of *Schulungslehrgang 'Elbe'*. Despite the fact that attack by this *Luftwaffe* fighter followed the exact technique adopted by the volunteers, the crew of *E-Z Goin* today still find it impossible to believe that the attack had been planned in this way. But it seems that a young German pilot had indeed flown his fighter against the 100th BG: he had been able to avoid the formidable escorts and carry out his attack as intended, and only the skill and luck of that particular B-17 crew had saved them from a fate similar that which befell Lieutenant Howard's.

An examination of official records initially appeared to indicate that three of Lieutenant Howard's crew had been unable to escape their bomber, the radio operator Sergeant Maty, the tail gunner Sergeant Thomas and the ball turret gunner Sergeant Lehrman appearing listed as 'killed in action'. Until the author was able to contact William Howard the actual events remained a mystery and the true horror of the crew's experiences on 7 April would have been unknown to any except the survivors of this B-17. As Howard described it, all of the crew had escaped from their aircraft: he had seen each member safely beneath his parachute. Thankful that they had escaped the crippled bomber, the crew faced the prospect of capture and imprisonment with both uncertainty and resignation. The war could not last much longer, so their confinement, and whatever conditions they found, would be short-lived.

However, even before Lieutenant Howard had landed he gained some indication of the hatred the Eighth Air Force bombing campaign had instilled in the civilian population. Drifting to earth, he crossed over a small village and saw beneath him a group of civilians, more than one of whom was pointing a shotgun in his direction. Although he saw the flash from the guns, thankfully the shots went wide. A further welcome awaited him on landing. His attempts to escape capture were hindered by a ankle damaged on landing and then by waterlogged boots which he was forced to discard. Running face to face into a large group of armed civilians, he was beaten before being paraded in the nearest village. As would the rest of his crew, the pilot would have cause to recall the information which accompanied each briefing, that any member of crew finding himself in a similar situation was to 'hide and wait for our troops. Avoid SS, Gestapo, Hitler Youth and civilians.' As the bruised pilot was led to the village hall, he found himself the target for any stone, stick or even piece of mud that could be found, hurled by the women and children. Once within the local hall he found his navigator Lieutenant Doug Jones, who had endured a similar welcome although his beating had resulted in a broken jaw. The two men were later moved to Uelzen, where they were eventually reunited with three more of their bruised crew. When the five men were again moved by car later the next day their journey showed them how great the fear of Allied air power had become. A lookout posted in a trailer would shout a warning at the first sign of any aircraft, the car would be quickly halted and driver, prisoners and escort would hide in the nearest ditch. Any aircraft was considered hostile, so their journey had many interruptions. Their destination was an interrogation centre, where they were separated and each man was questioned over a period of two days. Finally the crew were assembled, together with seven men from other crews, for the trip to a prisoner-of-war camp. Although the interrogation process itself had been quite civilized after the own encounters with civilians, Howard and his men feared for the remaining members of their own crew who were not amongst this group. Their journey took them by train to Hamburg, just in time to hear air-raid sirens. As the civilians hurriedly left the train in the search for shelters, the prisoners remained aboard. The guards told them that it was safer to remain in the train during a raid, but, sitting in the marshalling yards outside the station, the air crew did not agree. However, their concern proved unfounded as, inside the hour, the all-clear was sounded. The crew said that this had occurred on 12 April, and if this is correct then they were at least safe from their own bombs as no bombers left England that day.

On leaving the station they met the civilians who had spent the time huddled in their shelters, and it was obvious by their mood that, even having escaped bombs, they viewed the crew with hatred. As the guards tried to find transport to the next train station, the civilians began to surround the crew. After earlier beatings the crew feared the worst from this larger and angrier crowd. Luckily their guards rushed back to their rescue, although even they were forced to threaten the mob before they begrudgingly left the men. After over twenty flights the crew at last truly understood the hatred they had instilled in the civilian population. When their journey at last ended at Barth, near to the Baltic coast, the men again had to run a gauntlet of well-practised civilians who were armed with rocks, sticks and mud. At last finding some welcome shelter in their new home, Stalagluft 1, they saw another familiar face. The engineer and top-turret gunner Sergeant Ed Hall had already been there for two days, and after receiving similar treatment to the other man he had feared that only he had survived.

Six of the men were now together again, and they held on to the hope that they would eventually meet the remainder. Other such camps did exist, so perhaps they would see each other again after release. However, following their captivity Lieutenant Howard and his men did not find their missing companions. The bodies of Sergeants Maty, Thomas and Lehrman were all eventually traced: they had died after landing. Although the cause of their deaths remains unknown, the experiences of the other men left them with their own thoughts on the subject. As William Howard later recalled, the ball-gunner Sergeant Lehrman had been a last minute replacement for a sick crew member and Sergeant Maty was considered to be the cleanest-living member of their young crew. The radio operator left a wife and four sons at home in Minnesota. As William Howard wrote, and so many men felt on both 7 April and other days, 'Why them and not the rest of us? Who knows? The fortunes of war are cruel.'

The civilian population of Germany had endured a long and destructive campaign by the combined bombers of the RAF and USAAF. Whilst the British crews flew unseen by night, the American crews were the very visible enemy. When one of these terror-bombers fell from the sky, not only was it an event to be celebrated but it also brought the opportunity of coming face to face with the destroyers of families and homes. The natural hatred felt by the civilian population had been further enhanced through the work of the Propaganda Ministry. As an element of the 'total war' encouraged by the Nazi leadership, civilians had been urged to vent their hatred upon the American air crews. This was distasteful to many in the armed forces, and they did whatever they could to halt such brutal treatment. The reception given to Lieutenant Howard and his crew was by no means exceptional: a similar attack is described with distaste by Johannes Steinhoff in the second part of his biography. But the numbers of air crew who endured this ugly aspect of the war will remain unknown, as will the number of those listed as 'killed in action', like Sergeant Maty, Sergeant Thomas and Sergeant Lehrman, who may actually have met their fate at the hands of an angry crowd. Crew members such as Lieutenant Howard found not only the skies over Europe a dangerous place to visit: the towns and cities also harboured grave threats to Allied airmen.

18. FRIENDLY FIRE?

In less than half an hour the seemingly peaceful sky over the German countryside had once again become a battlefield. The white trails left by the passage of the latest flying armada were by now criss-crossed by the paths of American and German fighters. Black scars left by wounded or dying aircraft led away from the closed ranks of Liberators forming the 2nd AD. As the fighter pilots on both sides went about their duties, the bomber crews concentrated upon their task, maintaining position amongst the formation and ensuring that their bombs reached their targets. Behind their weapons the air crews scanned the sky, opening fire on any fighter which flashed past within range. Within the fuselages of the bombers shining spent cases had already began to gather and roll noisily as the turrets spewed their empty hot brass in brief showers. Beneath this life-and-death battle, alone in the silence, individual parachutes had begun to blossom in the cold April sky.

With over 300 bombers and 250 USAAF fighters now aware of the danger they faced from the approach of the *Jagdwaffe*, the confusion began to mount. At such times a pilot or gunner had only a brief instant to identify his target and fire his guns. As fighters peeled off to follow individual targets or lost contact with their colleagues in the twists and turns of a dogfight, any coordination was gone and units quickly became mixed. The airwaves had erupted with the cries of pilots and gunners, each having found a target before him and now urgently needing assistance.

In such a scene of chaos, amidst the heat of battle, mistakes could be made. In today's military phraseology such errors are reported as 'fratricide' but are more commonly referred to as examples of 'friendly fire'. For as long as man has chosen battles to decide his major conflicts such fatal mistakes have occurred, and with the abandoning of hand-held weapons in favour of fast-travelling projectiles such errors both multiplied and became more difficult to identify. It is far easier to identify the warrior who has cut a body with his edged weapon or pierced it with the point of a spear than to name with certainty the rifleman who with a misplaced shot cut down his countryman on the battlefield. Similarly, to view the scene above the German countryside on that April day and to name with certainty the pilot responsible for shooting down his comrade requires a measure of assumption and an examination of the available facts.

With a number of units becoming mixed, identification for the American fighters had to be accomplished in a matter of split seconds. At 1041hrs 51

Mustangs of the 78th FG had left their airfield at Duxford, today one of the best remembered Eighth Air Force bases. They reached their rendezvous position west of Dummer lake at 1205 to begin their escort of the 3rd Air Division B-17s. As the battle began to unfold around them, the 83rd FS positioned themselves at the trailing end of the bomber stream to offer protection against approaching fighters, the contrails of which could be seen rising to meet them. Once the loose formation of enemy fighters reached their altitude at 20,000ft, the P-51s attempted their interception. With the Bf 109s and Fw 190s seemingly spread out for their attack, the previously close escort being flown by the P-51s began to thin as pilots selected their target. To the north of their position the B-24s of the 2nd AD had turned to follow their course towards their targets. At the rear of this stream were the 359th FS, 356th FG, who had hurriedly been switched from their allocated escort of the 1st AD once the attack upon the Liberators of the 2nd AD had erupted.

As part of the 359th FS acted as close escort to the bomber formation, 'Farmhouse White' section was sweeping across the formation on their guard against further attacks. New reports were now being heard of 'bogeys' in the area around them. As they flew on a south-east heading, they caught sight of a fresh attack being mounted on the B-17 formation to the south of their position. Leading 'Farmhouse White' was 1st Lieutenant Harry R. Gosler in his P-51D, 44-15138. Like the rest of his Group, the nose of his aircraft bore bold red and blue diamond markings and carried the 359th FS yellow rudder and spinner. Without a second thought, Gosler called for the rest of his Flight to follow him as he pulled his aircraft towards the new combat. The speed of this manoeuvre caused the fighters of 'White' Flight to split up as they attempted to catch their leader and position themselves to face the *Luftwaffe* fighters.

Closer to the bombers, the 83rd FS had quickly become involved in a series of dogfights and were now scattered across the sky around the bomber stream. Amongst the 83rd FS pilots was 2nd Lieutenant Robert H. Talbot in a second-hand P-51K that had been his own for only five days. With the P-51s chasing any of the Messerschmitt or Focke-Wulf fighters within reach, they began to draw fire from the bombers as their gunners opened up on any aircraft diving through the formation. Whether the pair of fighters rushing past mere yards from their bomber's wing tip consisted of a *Luftwaffe* Bf 109 pursued by a P-51 was of little consequence to the gunners in the turrets or behind their waist positions. The hail of fire unleashed by the eleven .50-calibre guns of each B-17 offered their best defence against their enemy. That such a barrage, multiplied by the number of B-17s in the formation, could prove a danger to friend and foe alike received very little consideration from the often terrified young men manning the guns.

As Lieutenant Gosler neared the mêlée he centred his attention upon a pair of fighters already beginning their attack on the B-17s. Both fighters were drawing fire from the bombers, so he immediately classified both fighters as hostile. In his post-combat report Gosler wrote that the leading fighter, a Bf 109, became his target as it scored hits upon an already damaged B-17 which began to fall from the formation. Having completed his attack, the Bf 109 pilot turned away from the bombers, followed by the second fighter. The second fighter actually turned inside the leader and passed beneath him, ending up slightly in the lead and now positioned on his right wing. This manoeuvre had now placed the first Bf 109 closer to Gosler; only the bomber stream separated his P-51 from its target and he pushed his fighter into a diving right turn in pursuit. In the seconds that it took his fighter to cross through the rear of the bomber formation it became the centre of attention, as he reported he had to fly through 'a lot of tracer fire without being hit'. Even an aircraft as highly decorated as this 359th FS fighter was a potential threat to the gunners of the Fortress formation. To his relief he emerged unscathed from amongst the bombers and found that the Bf 109 had levelled out and was now only 150yds ahead. Without a second thought he opened fire and was somewhat surprised when after only a few rounds had left his guns the pilot abandoned the *Luftwaffe* fighter. This had been Gosler's target throughout the chase, and he positively identified it as an 'Me-109 with rounded wing tips'. The importance attached to this brief description can be judged as the combat continued.

Having seemingly dealt swiftly with the first fighter, the Mustang was now turned right through 10 degrees to centre upon the next fighter ahead. As the target swung into his sights, Lieutenant Gosler opened fire, the stream of bullets striking home along the wing root. The target immediately began to trail smoke and suddenly lifted a wing, the sight causing a now astonished Harry Gosler to catch his breath. The aircraft he had hit had 'squared' wing tips, just like his own Mustang; moreover, again like his own fighter, it carried no markings on its right wing. When he recalled this combat and his reactions, Gosler wrote that his instinct told him he had hit another Mustang from a Group other than his own. Having had time to dwell upon this horrifying prospect, and reinforced by the supportive comments of other 359th FS pilots, he continued his description by saying that it must have been an 'old-style Me-109, with square wing tips'. Eventually confident enough to make a claim for this second fighter, Harry Gosler had the support of two fellow pilots. However, each of these supporting reports contain comments which cast doubt upon the combat.

The first report was completed by 1st Lieutenant Leonard J. Hildebrand, who had flown 'White 3'. As his P-51 trailed during the initial stage of the attack he lost contact and only re-joined the mêlée as Lieutenant Gosler turned towards the second fighter. Certain that the Mustang would lose contact, Hildebrand himself turned into the second fighter, only to break contact when he spotted the same square wing tips. Although he thought the canopy of the fighter could possibly have been a frame type rather than the bubble canopy of the P-51, he had only a split second to view the fighter before Gosler scored his hits. The second report came from the pilot of 'White 2', 2nd Lieutenant Warren T. Edinborough, whose report was delayed as he had been forced to land his damaged fighter at an Allied airfield on the continent. Edinborough had concluded that both the aircraft attacked by Harry Gosler were indeed Bf 109s from the fact both had drawn fire from the bombers—although this was hardly a defining action as Lieutenant Gosler himself had been the target of the gunners during his chase. Again, Lieutenant Edinborough lost contact during part of this combat and was only able to gain positive sighting of the first fighter to fall to 'White' leader, which he confirmed as a Bf 109. At the very instant this fighter was struck, Edinborough's Mustang was itself hit from an unseen enemy and he was forced to half-roll to avoid further fire. The pilots of the 359th, as can be expected, supported each other after this combat; each had only a matter of fractions of a second to make their observations, but in these instants the square wing tips were a clear identification feature. On this April day no 'early model Bf 109s were being flown', but the sky did contain numerous Mustangs from many Groups.

As these three pilots of the 359th FS relived the moments of combat leading to the attack upon the second fighter, pilots of the 83rd FS were involved in their own combats. While attempting to score hits or avoid a dangerous foe, they heard over their radios the calls from Lieutenant Talbot. The frantic calls reported that he had been attacked by a Mustang and with his crippled fighter now losing altitude he was about to bale out. As the Mustang crashed to earth it was followed at a gentler rate by Robert Talbot, who spent the rest of his war as a prisoner-of-war.

Many reports of attacks by P-51s in *Luftwaffe* hands were filed during March and April 1945. Such reports must be viewed with some scepticism. The *Luftwaffe* still possessed its own supply of capable fighters but lacked the ability to maintain these aircraft because of the disintegration of the supply network. Bearing in mind such difficulty in maintaining home-built aircraft types, it would seem highly improbable that the *Luftwaffe* would make any effort to repair, rearm and fly a captured Mustang. In addition to the inherent dangers of flying a P-51 over a German airfield, it would also be foolish to think that any benefit could be gained in attempting combat operations. As has been seen, even flying a fighter wearing USAAF markings near a bomber box was at times a dangerous occupation.

It can therefore be judged as certain, no matter how distasteful such a conclusion, that Lieutenant Talbot was fired upon by a friendly P-51. From the post-combat reports, the Squadron most likely to have been at the wrong place at the wrong time was the 359th FS. Furthermore, the reports of 'Farmhouse White' Flight confirm their own element of uncertainty following the encounter. Given the available information, the positions of the aircraft and the times of the action, it must appear to be a strong possibility that one of the claims made by the 359th FS on this day was in fact an 83rd FS Mustang. Luckily Robert Talbot survived the day.

That such errors had become frequent occurrences is further illustrated by the report completed by the 339th FG when it returned to Fowlmere. Flying as escort to the 45th CBW, the fighters had found themselves involved in a number of clashes with what they described as very aggressive pilots. The determination of the *Luftwaffe* fighters to press home their attacks despite the opposition quickly forced the American pilots to split in an attempt to deal with as many as possible. A Flight from the 503rd FS had chased some of the attacking fighters which had flown the length of the 45th/13th CBW formation, from the leading 388th BG to the rear 100th BG. Finding the *Schulungslehrgang 'Elbe'* aircraft breaking away from the bombers, the Flight turned back to return to its escort position. As the aircraft curved across the rear of the 100th BG, from 5 o'clock to 9 o'clock, they paid the price for flying too close to the wary tail-gunners. When the Mustangs were 500yds from the bombers the gunners opened fire, one burst striking the undersides of the nearest fighter. This was the Mustang of Lieutenant MacKenzie, which quickly began to trail both smoke and debris. The rest of his flight slowed to maintain position with MacKenzie in his damaged fighter. With more of the P-51 seeming to be shed by the second, the pilot had little option but to pull the nose up, jettison his canopy and jump clear. Confirming that the parachute had safely opened, the rest of the Flight returned to their duties as Lieutenant MacKenzie drifted to earth almost half-way between Hamburg and Hanover. Once again the danger of approaching gunners alert to the threat of enemy aircraft had been clearly demonstrated.

The organization of such large and complex operations often added to the confusion experienced by pilots. With the battle around the 2nd AD, some of their escorts were forced to retire early because of low fuel. A decision was made to pull some of the escorts from the 1st AD formation to cover the space this early withdrawal created. The fighters from the 20th FG at the trailing end of the 1st AD split from the bombers, to be replaced by the yellow-nosed P-51s of the 361st FG, called into the air from their Belgian base of Chièvres at 1302. Having arrived late only to find the 1st AD escaping all but fleeting attention from the *Luftwaffe*, the 361st FG pilots made the most of any opportunity to chase the few Me 262s spotted above the bombers. This eagerness appears to have almost led two pilots of the 361st into trouble. Finding no *Luftwaffe* fighters attacking their bombers, the 359th FG were content to stick close to the B-17s. Suddenly a pair of fighters made firing passes upon a pair of Mustangs from the 369th FS, 359th FG. Although no damage was done, the pilots angrily recorded that their identification skills were certainly better than those of their attackers. The 359th FG pilots could easily identify the pair of yellow-nosed 361st FG Mustangs responsible for the attack; not only could they identify the Group, but they could also read the code 'E9', which indicated the 376th FS, and the individual letters 'L2' and 'H'.

Luckily this last failure in identification only resulted in anger and perhaps some embarrassment when the 376th FS pilots returned to the rear of the bomber formation. Of the five American fighters lost on 7 April, at least three were as a direct result of 'friendly fire'.

19. THE *'ELBE'* COMBATS

With so many Eighth Air Force escorts hunting in the sky around the bomber formations, the German pilots time and again found that their mission was not proceeding according to plan. A pair of fighters from Sachau had not even located their targets before the escorts fell upon them. *Gefreiter* Ernst Tetzel and his friend *Gefreiter* Rudi Ringhofer had very quickly lost contact with the other fighters from Sachau. Although keeping each other in sight for a time, the pilots had become disoriented and shortly after this each found himself alone. The first to fly into danger was Tetzel, who had been trying to pick out some landmark to help him on his mission. As he flew nearer to the ground his fighter suddenly shuddered from a number of direct hits. Scanning the sky, he could see no enemy fighters so assumed that he had been hit by an anti-aircraft unit—whether Allied or German it was impossible to tell. The damage was enough to convince the pilot that he had to find an empty field in which to land. After spotting a likely looking site he was able to touch down safely. As he abandoned his fighter he found that he had landed in an area already occupied by American forces. His brief career as a member of the *Jagdwaffe* had ended, but at least he could console himself with the knowledge that American flak had downed him and not, as was often the case, a supposedly friendly unit.

For his friend the danger came not from the ground but, as expected, from the sky. Having lost contact with those with whom he had started, *Gefreiter* Ringhofer then had his canopy begin to ice over. With his vision reduced, the pilot continued to fly his mission, pointing his fighter north in the hope of meeting the bombers. His route had indeed taken him towards his enemy: his fighter crossed the River Elbe close to Geesthacht. But his good luck then deserted him. Sensing danger, he turned to catch sight of a pair of Mustangs only yards from his tail. Instinctively he pulled his fighter to the left, away from his hunters. Before he had time to consider further avoiding action the first rounds smashed into the exposed side of his fighter. The Messerschmitt was caught in the centre of the fire from the American fighters, Ringhofer feeling the painful impact of several well-aimed rounds. Instantly his right leg seemed to have been set on fire. In his pain he knew that he had to abandon his aircraft: he was powerless to avoid the pair of fighters behind him. As he quickly prepared to jump clear he glanced down at his shattered and bloody right leg to find to his horror that one of the American rounds had completely severed his foot. Despite the shock, the young pilot was able to leap free and was lucky to land close to a farm. Seeing the wounds that the pilot had suffered, the owners of the farm were able to summon immediate medical help and *Gefreiter* Ringhofer's war was to end in a hospital bed. The remains of his fighter were recovered in 1986 from the wood where it had crashed.

Other pilots from Sachau had flown a more westerly route but again were found by the escorts before they had time to reach the bombers. The body of *Obergefreiter* Hugo Harms was found near Gilten, to the south-west of Schwarmstedt. He was still strapped within the cockpit of his fighter. This Messerschmitt was another which bore the marks of a savage attack by an enemy fighter.

One of the Focke-Wulf pilots who had forged his log-book to show the necessary Bf 109 experience had reason to regret his haste. After taking off from Sachau with the other pilots, *Fähnrich* Franz-Josef Schmidt had found that his assigned fighter, almost fresh from the production line, was far from perfect. As he attempted to gain altitude he found that the undercarriage refused to retract. With a curse he turned back to Sachau and was able to land safely. Leaping from the aircraft, he asked for any fighter that was still airworthy and was given what he later described as the last ancient Bf 109 on the airfield. Hurriedly taking off for a second time, he pushed his new mount at top speed to catch his fellow pilots. Again his haste brought frustration as he very quickly realized that he had no hope of joining the rest of his unit. Although he was heading in the right direction, he never saw another friendly aircraft. Instead, near to the Weser, he was attacked by an American fighter. Catching sight of a freshly ploughed field below him, he opted to attempt a forced landing. This time Schmidt's luck held and he was able to walk away from his badly damaged fighter, only to find that his landing had been watched by a group of American infantry. Perhaps as a reward for his skill he was given a cigarette by one of the officers before he being driven away as a prisoner.

The fighters at Sachau appear to have had their share of mechanical problems. The aircraft being flown by *Unteroffizier* Klaus Hahn was proving incapable maintaining its position within his *Schwarm*, the engine failing to respond to the demands for more speed. Rather than attempt to return to Sachau, which he feared would brand him a coward, the young pilot did the best he could to keep in contact with the other three fighters. As he began to drop further behind he found that his *Schwarmführer*, *Oberfähnrich* Schack, had drawn level with his wing and was trying to communicate in sign language. But without their radio link the two pilots were unable to make each other understood. Perhaps assuming that the trailing fighter would be forced to return to base, Schack gave a final wave and re-joined the remaining pair.

As the three fighters disappeared from view Hahn was alone but intent upon still trying to push his fighter on. With a sudden roar the Daimler-

Benz engine seemed to return to normal and the pilot climbed to find his *Kameraden*. Spotting a *Schwarm* of single-engine aircraft, he headed towards them: perhaps he could join them in their attack. But the aircraft proved to be a flight of P-51s which had already spotted this single Messerschmitt and wasted no time in attacking. Although he attempted to evade the fighters when faced with four opponents, Hahn had little hope of escape. Bullets began to rip into the Messerschmitt. One burst shattered the cockpit, a round hitting the pilot's left arm. With a damaged fighter and a now paralyzed arm, Hahn prepared to abandon his fighter. It was then that he saw below him the bomber formation for which he had been searching. Assuming that the damaged Bf 109 no longer posed a threat, the escorts had called off their attack; as they were drawing near to the bomber formation they also perhaps judged it safer not to follow. But the damaged fighter was still responding to Hahn's controls and he aimed himself at the tail of the nearest B-17.

The next seconds, which contained the crash and his escape from the fighter, were a mystery to Klaus Hahn. He blacked out at the moment of impact and did not regain consciousness until he was free-falling through the freezing sky. Although he remained conscious only for a brief moment before again passing out, it gave him the opportunity of releasing his parachute to slow his fall. When he awoke after landing he found himself attended by a group of civilians who had watched his fighter ramming the American bomber and followed his parachute. His injuries were extensive: as well as a dislocated hip caused by his landing, his wounded arm demanded immediate medical attention. A hospital capable of admitting him could not be found until later in the day, and the unpleasant memories of the time he was forced to spend receiving treatment have remained with Klaus Hahn ever since. Although his hip and numerous other injuries could be treated, his shattered right arm had to be amputated.

Having reached Schwarmstedt too early to meet the 3rd AD, those *Schulungslehrgang 'Elbe'* fighters that had taken off from Delitzsch continued to head in the general direction of Bremen. After reaching the outskirts of Verden they finally found the bomber stream, the Liberators of the 2nd AD. However, the escorts of this formation had remained near enough to their flock to fall upon the approaching *Luftwaffe* fighters in force. All the bomber groups of the 2nd AD later reported that they had received protection which they classified as being very good to excellent. Although the initial attacks by Me 262s were followed by those of conventional fighters, the American fighters did their job well. The largest group of *Luftwaffe* fighters, estimated to be up to 100 strong, approached the 14th CBW, but when the attack came it was limited to only 10–15 fighters which proved unable to inflict any casualties upon any of the Groups from this Wing.

Perhaps the best start to the day's operations had been at Gardelegen, where the *Schulungslehrgang 'Elbe'* fighters were able to take off free from the problems which marred the start at other airfields. Once take-off had been accomplished, however, similar problems began to materialize. Amongst those experiencing difficulties were *Oberfähnrich* Armin Thiel and *Oberfähnrich* Joachim-Wolfgang Böhm. Although the pair had followed the other Gardelegen fighters to their holding position over Dömitz, they had lost contact when they had been vectored towards the approaching bombers. Soon after this the pair themselves became split and then the engine of Böhm's aircraft began to prove troublesome. Even as he tried to nurse his fighter a stream of oil began to cover his windshield. Quickly his vision became severely restricted and his engine became a serious cause for concern.

Almost blinded by the oil and increasingly anxious about his engine, Böhm decided to land. But his attempts were hampered by the oil clinging to his canopy and his approach to what he thought to be a suitable field took him directly towards a stand of trees, into which he blindly stumbled. The Messerschmitt, its progress halted by the unyielding branches, was flipped on to its back and crashed down upon the trapped pilot. Luckily his accident had been witnessed and help was summoned to free the pilot. Even with the aid of a village blacksmith it took three hours to release the injured German, the attempt being halted as a Mustang flew low over the scene. On this occasion the American pilot must have judged the wreckage unworthy of his attention and left the rescuers to their task. Despite a prolonged rescue and transfers between hospitals, *Oberfähnrich* Böhm was eventually to recover from his injuries.

One of the more experienced *'Elbe'* pilots had also been positioned over Dömitz. A former *III./JG 300* pilot, *Oberfeldwebel* Heinz Müller had already scored five kills during his career and compared to many of those around him was now a seasoned combat veteran. This difference quickly began to tell as the already loose formation began to fall apart. Although up to 36 fighters had been positioned over Dömitz, it is impossible to describe the formation in normal *Luftwaffe* terms. This was not a *Gruppe*, a collection of *Staffeln* or even a strong formation of combat *Schwärme*, but at best a ragged collection of *Rotten*. When faced with USAAF escorts even these pairs often broke apart. Today Müller found this out to his cost. He was now on his own and heading for the bombers. But even his combat experience failed to bestow upon this pilot any greater chances of survival. Before he had the chance to reach the bombers he flew into airspace being patrolled by enemy fighters he identified as Thunderbolts. Although his previous combats allowed him to make the fight far from easy, with three enemy pilots out for his blood the outcome was as expected. Hit several times, *Oberfeldwebel* Müller had no option but to abandon his Messerschmitt. After leaving Dömitz his flight had taken him over 100 miles to the south-west, and when his fighter crashed it did so near to Bassum.

Despite knowing the location of this combat and the approximate time, just before 1230, it has proved impossible to identify with certainty the American fighters involved. If indeed *Oberfeldwebel* Müller had met Thunderbolts, then the only 56th FG claim at the approximate time when the *Luftwaffe* pilot was seen to abandon his fighter is the second of the Bf 109 claims by Captain Bostwick of the 63rd FS. Whichever pilot was responsible, the outcome was the same. Müller landed shortly after his doomed fighter. Unlike that of many of his fellow *'Elbe'* pilots, his landing was without problem, although he came down only a matter of yards from the front line of an advancing Allied armoured unit. Thankful to be pointed in the right direction by friendly troops, he was then amazed to be given a motorbike together with some bottles of wine to 'buy' any extra petrol he might need. After a dangerous journey which lasted three days, Müller finally returned to Stendal, intending to report to *Major* Köhnke, only to find that the remaining *Schulungslehrgang 'Elbe'* staff had already abandoned the base. It took several more days before Heinz Müller was finally reunited with his surprised unit, days which he later remembered for the taste of the wine which had made his journey more endurable.

Of all the men flying on 7 April, one of the most decorated was *Ritterkreuzträger Hauptmann* Ernst Sorge. His determination to take part in this mission had been as strong as any of the other volunteers and he had been horrified when he had heard that the *Reichsmarschall* had banned all such decorated officers from flying in the planned operation. He had immediately gone to *Oberst* Herrmann to plead his case. How could the young volunteers be expected to carry on when others such as he were to be protected? He was pleased to discover that his views reflected those of his senior officer and was relieved when Herrmann was eventually able to convince Göring of the error of the decision. Just before one o'clock, south-west of Geesthacht, *Hauptmann* Sorge finally sighted his enemy and aimed his *Schwarm* towards the bombers. The pilot had by chance selected a very congested piece of airspace to attempt his ramming mission. Not only were the bombers of the 2nd AD on the final run on to their targets at Düneburg and Krümmel, but less than twenty miles to the east the 45th CBW leading the 3rd AD were heading towards their target at Kaltenkirchen. With two bomber streams occupying what was a very small area of sky, the result was that Sorge found himself receiving attention from a very heavy concentration of Eighth Air Force fighters.

The *Schwarm*, which also contained *Hauptmann* Hugo Müller, initially handled itself well, despite the numerous enemy fighters. But no matter how many times they seemed to free themselves of P-51s, more appeared to stop them nearing the bombers. With only a limited amount of ammunition, *Hauptmann* Sorge knew that the chances of fighting his way through were becoming slight. It was then that his engine began to cause problems and a trail of smoke began to pour from beneath the cowling. Attempting to break free from the American fighters, he was perfectly placed to see the first bombs falling upon Krümmel and the black clouds of smoke rising into the air. Having no option but to attempt to land his Messerschmitt, Sorge was both angry and very sad that he had been unable to complete his mission. He was able to crash-land not far from Lüneburg, close to where *Hauptmann* Müller's damaged fighter also came to rest. This pilot had also been forced to abandon his mission in the face of overwhelming escort fighters. A further four *Schulungslehrgang 'Elbe'* fighters eventually crashed near to these two pilots, but each of the unlucky pilots was to die with his aircraft. Despite the bravery of these *Jagdwaffe* men, the bombs were once again raining down upon targets within the heart of the Reich.

20. THE BOMBERS REACH THEIR TARGETS

Despite the best efforts of the *Jagdwaffe*, the bombers of the Eighth Air Force had continued to fly towards their targets. Although in some places the formations were ragged and spaces indicated where aircraft had been torn from their positions, the remaining crews maintained course. The first aircraft to approach their targets were the Liberators of the 2nd AD, the 2nd/20th CBW being fractionally ahead of the other formations and the first to open their bomb bays. At 1257 the first bombs fell on the ammunition factory at Düneburg, situated on the western edge of Geesthacht. This target had in total 350 tons of bombs dropped upon it by 128 aircraft within a space of five minutes. Before the trailing bombers had turned from the target the site was visibly shaken by a huge explosion which appeared at the centre of what had been identified as the explosive distribution area.

Four minutes after the first B-24s released their loads on Düneburg the first of 452 tons of bombs were falling upon the other explosive production site at Krümmel, dropped by the leading Liberators of the 14th/96th CBW. Again the site was well targeted and a number of explosions followed the initial bombing. As the aircraft then swung north-west to commence their return flight, the last of the day's targets for the 2nd AD bombers, their secondary target at the railway yards at Neumünster, was shaken by the first of 70 tons of bombs which fell at 1327. At Neumünster the bombing was more widespread and the Eighth Air Force post-combat reports admit that the built-up housing area of the town received a number of hits. Interestingly, surviving German reports indicate that in these raids the greatest damage was inflicted upon the railway targets, a destruction which would be increased by the 3rd AD which would follow. In these initial raids the greatest loss of life had resulted from the bombing of Krümmel, where 108 people were killed.

The leading bombers of the 3rd AD reached their first target at 1322. The aircraft were the B-17s of the 45th CBW, which had encountered enough enemy fighter activity to convince the leading crews that they should remain in formation and bomb as Groups. At the head of the formation the 388th BG was encountering further problems on its approach to Kaltenkirchen. As the leading squadron released its bombs, the B Squadron following behind found its view of the target obscured by cloud. Rather than break formation and attempt a second run, the leading bombardier decided to gauge his release by measuring the time lag between his aircraft and the B-17s ahead.

This was an accepted practice, but today it resulted in his bombs and therefore those of the Squadron falling over a mile beyond their target. Also assigned Kaltenkirchen as their priority were the 95th BG, flying as 13C CBW. Although the first squadrons also found their view of the target hidden by smoke and cloud, both the C and D Squadrons were able to select their aiming points from a distance of eight miles. The largest load of the day, 375 tons of general-purpose bombs and 35 tons of incendiaries, fell upon the airfield of Kaltenkirchen and the site was devastated beneath this lethal rain. Although the airfield was unusable as a result of this attack, the bombers had lost the opportunity of striking a blow against their real enemy. Until recently the airfield had been home to the Me 262s of *JG 7*, but they had already abandoned the airfield for a new site. Despite the huge quantity of bombs dropped upon this target, the loss of life appears to have been limited to three *Luftwaffe* soldiers.

The important oil storage site at Büchen was the target for the 13th CBW at 1327. The impact of this attack was reduced by the smoke and cloud cover over the target. Instead of the intended attack by over 70 aircraft, half of the force were obliged to divert to a secondary target. The report filed by the 390th BG states that the turn on to the target had been rushed; they then found a 'large cumulus cloud sitting over the target' and could not release. As a result, only 36 of the B-17s dropped their bombs over Büchen, the total weight of their load being 108 tons. Each of the B-17s had released its six 1,000lb general-purpose bombs upon the facilities, the load having been selected to blast its their way into the underground storage facilities. When one of these bombs missed its target the result could be devastating: one is known to have fallen near a shelter within which a group of women and children had sought protection. When the wreckage was later cleared ten bodies were found.

Having experienced so much, the shaken crews of the 100th BG could perhaps have been forgiven for wanting this raid to be over as soon as possible. Opting to complete the run-in using dead reckoning, the leading B-17 was finally freed of its bomb load as the release button was at last depressed. As quickly as possible other crews followed, their bombs disappearing into the clouds below. Despite the expected danger from the flak units, the 100th's crews suffered little at this stage in their flight, the exception being another veteran aircraft of the 349th BS. This B-17, 42-37972 *Gold Brick*, had already completed 100 missions and was being flown today by Lieutenant Joe King. Over the target *Gold Brick* was suddenly rocked by a direct hit. As he struggled to regain control of his bomber, King called out over the intercom for a damage report. This did not take long as the damage was very visible. The burst had removed the entire right stabilizer, something the *'Elbe'* pilots themselves had been attempting to do only minutes earlier. Although *Gold Brick* protested about the sudden amputation, it continued to fly. The lucky bomber not only survived this raid and returned the crew to their base but went on to be repaired and saw out the war.

Despite the fighter attacks upon its bombers, the post-mission analysis of the 100th BG operation did not allow any leniency for the failures during the raid on Büchen. The breaks in the cloud that did exist had allowed at least some of the photographs taken by the bombers to be accurately plotted. The evidence was unmistakable: the bombs had fallen between two and three miles short of the target. The official report coldly states that 'This Group should have made a second run.'

The B-17s which diverted from Büchen headed towards their nearest secondary target, the smoking railway network at Neumünster. The aiming point for the bombers was the town's badly damaged railway station, the smoke making a visual sighting by the lead navigator possible from a distance of fourteen miles. But despite a clear run, without any flak defence and only a single pass by an enemy fighter, the bombs fell some distance from their target, the 111 tons falling mainly on residential areas. The combined death toll from the Büchen raid and the second attack on Neumünster was over 230.

As the 3rd AD's second task force approached its targets, the ground-based German defences had been able to extract a price for the attack. Within the 4th CBW formation the crews of the 486th BG, having escaped the attentions of enemy fighters, now found that a flak battery had opened fire upon them. This battery seemed to be aiming their sparse but well-guided fire directly at the Group. A single burst struck a B-17 belonging to the 835th BS and the aircraft was forced immediately to turn from its target and seek safety, heading for a base in France or Belgium. The 93rd/4th formation was now on the final leg of its journey to the targets and reached the first at 1351. This was the important jet field at Parchim, home to *III./JG 7*. In the space of half an hour the formation, with a strength of over 130 B-17s, dropped 324 tons of general-purpose bombs and a further 67 tons of incendiaries.

The attacks by both the *'Elbe'* fighters and their escorts had again prompted the task force leader, flying a B-17 of the 385th BG, to order the bombers to maintain group formation. The effect of the bombing was reduced by technical problems within the 490th BG. The leading B-17 of the B Squadron failed to release his bomb load over the target, and although five of the following bombers spotted his problems and bombed Parchim correctly a further three blindly followed their leader. Not willing to risk a second run because of the enemy fighters, the B Squadron leader apparently opted to jettison his full load as soon as the release problems were corrected. Seeing the bombs fall from their formation leader, the other three aircraft also released their loads, quite some distance from their intended targets.

Next in line, a B-17 of the 487th BG suffered greater damage as it prepared to release it bomb load. As the crew concentrated upon their task, the danger appeared not from an enemy aircraft or from ground-based flak, but instead from the bomb bay of one of their own aircraft flying in tight formation above. This Group's aircraft were each carrying a load consisting of thirty-eight 100lb M1A1 fragmentation bombs, and when these bombs were released their poor aerodynamics caused them to tumble and even collide. The close formation, adopted because of the continued fear of fighter attacks, caused the bombs to drift badly amongst the aircraft below. Whether it was the collision of two of these bombs which sparked an explosion or whether some uncontrollable projectiles simply struck the unfortunate aircraft remains uncertain, but the result was that the lower B-17, still with its own full load of bombs, was engulfed by an explosion which completely destroyed it. In the section of the post-combat report which examined the loss of this aircraft, the 487th concluded that the fragmentation bombs posed a danger to other aircraft within tight formations. It was stated that in future missions such experience would result in crews' being wary of such a bomb load, and they would undoubtedly be inclined to fly with a greater distance separating the formation.

After the 487th BG came the 486th BG. This Group, too, suffered technical problems as it attempted to bomb the airfield. The Group had opted to ignore earlier warnings and bomb by squadron. However as they reached Parchim the aircraft were unable to release the load using visual sightings, cloud hiding the ground from view. The bombers then headed towards their second priority at Schwerin, but here again the Group found cloud hiding their aiming points and only the D Squadron was able to bomb. In a very unusual move, bearing in mind the unsettling experiences of the previous hours, the crews decided to return to their first target. This time the clouds had thinned sufficiently to allow the lead crews to release their bombs. Problems did still continue: as the leading B Squadron aircraft tried to release its load the bombs clung determinedly to their racks. Luckily a lone smoke marker did fall free and the rest of the Squadron bombed on this. The leading bomber clung to its bomb load as it left the target area but the crew believed that the problems with the release mechanism had been solved, so for the third time the pilot turned his B-17 towards another target. Alone this aircraft released its load over the third priority target, Salzwedel airfield. Within the C Squadron more release problems were encountered, only half of the load of one B-17 falling on Parchim. This crew were not willing to risk a further run and the remaining load was released as soon as possible after a cure was found. Despite such problems the raid on Parchim did have the desired effect. The airfield and many of the buildings were devastated and remained beyond repair for the rest of the war.

Of the 4th CBW formations to hit Parchim on this day, one in particular was flying under special instructions. This was the trailing 94th BG, and its task was to fly the mission as if each B-17 carried beneath its wings a pair of

'Disney' rocket bombs. So far only three Eighth Air Force Groups had used these weapons in anger, and the 94th had been selected to join this rather élite band. The 4,500lb bombs were intended for use against heavily protected targets such as U-boat facilities and underground storage depots. Although the Group flew this practice mission without difficulty, it was, in the event, never called upon to carry a 'Disney' load in combat.

The final target to be hit by the 2nd Task Force was the ordnance depot at Güstrow, which was reached by the first of 104 aircraft at one minute before 2 o'clock. As well as the harmless load of leaflets released by the B-17s, Güstrow received a more lethal load of 300 tons of bombs, consisting of 198 tons of general-purpose and a further 102 tons of incendiaries intended to set fire to the buildings blown apart by the blast of the GPs.

Having flown its mission with little interference from any *Luftwaffe* fighters, the 1st AD approached its targets almost $2^{1}/_{2}$ hours after the first bombs had fallen free from the racks of the B-24s of the 389th BG. The first of the targets to suffer an attack was Kohlenbissen airfield, hit by the 1st CBW at 1519hrs. Over 261 tons of bombs fell upon the airfield and clear strike photographs were developed following the return of the bombers. These photographs showed that the damage had been centred upon the airfield itself: almost three thousand bomb craters covered the ground, although a strip 150 yards wide somehow escaped damage. Four of the buildings on the site were badly damaged and the dispersal area received a number of hits. The raid did not, however, destroy many *Luftwaffe* aircraft. Interpretation of photographs found 44 scattered around the airfield, but only three at most could be judged destroyed or badly damaged. The loss of personnel had been limited to three members of a *Luftwaffe* ground formation.

As Kohlenbissen was suffering from this attack a similar raid was unfolding above Wesendorf airfield as the 40th CBW unleashed its bomb load of 248 tons. Again the runway bore the brunt of the attack, photographs later showing up to 1,400 bomb strikes. Other strikes hit two large hangars, the control tower and several other buildings at the northern end of the site all receiving varying degrees of damage, including the airfield's radio transmitter. This time the raid did hit a collection of aircraft, up to 30 blazing fighters being counted.

Although the intended target of the 94th CBW had been the airfield identified at Reinsehlen, to the north of Soltau, the Wing was instead forced to fly to its secondary target, the rail network centred upon Lüneburg. At 1524 the first crews of the 94th CBW released their bombs over the target. Three Groups, the 457th, 351st and 401st BGs, each separated by two minutes, in turn released a total just short of 267 tons of general-purpose bombs. Once released, the bombs fell unguided towards whatever lay below. In contrast to the pin-point accuracy of today's guided weapons, the bombs dropped by the B-17s could not be aimed towards specific buildings. As a result the damage was spread, not only across the railway targets but also across other military and civilian buildings. By the time the bombers had left the area, slightly after 1530, the drone of their engines had already become lost against the sound of continued explosions and noise from fires raging around the town. The most visible sign of the impact caused by the raid was a pair of smouldering craters which lay within the rail sidings. One measured 55ft in diameter and the second 72ft, the blasts having severed nine rail tracks and destroyed or damaged numerous wagons; both would appear to have resulted from the destruction of trains carrying valuable munitions. It has been estimated that over 50 civilians died during the attack, which hit buildings including a military hospital. In addition, at Lüneburg station a train packed with prisoners had been caught by the raid as it passed through, and although accurate records have not survived the number who lost their lives has been estimated as upwards of 160.

As this attack was taking place the 41st CBW was beginning its own attack upon its primary target, the oil storage facilities at Hitzacker. The briefing notes for the mission had informed the crews that their target had last been attacked by the 2nd AD on 25 March, which had resulted in the site being out of action for ten days. The importance of the site had been indicated by the attached statement that the crews were about to give direct support to Allied troops of the 1st, 3rd and 9th Armies by denying the supply of oil to opposing German forces. Finding that their target was covered by a dense layer of cloud during the attack, crews had to trust that they had found it correctly using the H2X target radar which equipped the leading bombers of each squadron. The twelve B-17s of the Lead Squadron released their loads at 1528, followed at 1530 by the thirteen aircraft of the High Squadron and at 1531 by the thirteen bombers of the Low Squadron. The raid, as might have been expected, did add to some unrepaired damage from previous attacks, but fresh destruction was wrought on the adjoining rail yards and several trains of tankers were destroyed or derailed. Although over 280 tons was dropped on the site, nobody was killed during the raid.

In addition to the main targets for the 1st AD, two further sites received the attentions of the B-17s. The rail yards of Uelzen were hit by a total of thirteen aircraft which dropped 41 tons of bombs. This attack was not concentrated and damage was spread over a large area which did include the railway station but also an old part of the town itself. Reports show that twenty people died during this raid. A slightly smaller force of twelve B-17s attacked the airfield at Fassberg, which received a barrage of 456 bombs, in total almost 34 tons. The buildings on this airfield escaped lightly, the bombs being concentrated on the landing area. Any damage which was inflicted by this raid and by subsequent attacks aimed at rendering Fassberg inoperable was not decisive: when the airfield was finally captured by Allied forces they found that it had continued to be used as a safe haven for a collection of

Luftwaffe aircraft, including five Me 262s. Indeed, Fassberg airfield retained the ability to operate even these jet fighters.

By 1605 the final bombs had fallen from the racks of the trailing B-17s. The raids had ended, and all the Eighth Air Force crews could now look forward to the flight home. Throughout their missions the crews of the 1st AD had been well aware of the attacks upon the first two divisions. Initially it was believed that the danger posed by the *Luftwaffe* fighters had disappeared by the time that this Division approached its targets. In fact, although the gunners of the 1st AD were never given cause to open fire, it is clear that they did come under scrutiny from the *Luftwaffe*. After the B-17s left their final targets and headed south-west on the return leg of their journey, several of the crews spotted at least two Me 262s and a handful of single-engine fighters which approached the formation to the south of Bremen. This formation never attempted to attack the bombers, quite possibly because of the very visible escort of 222 P-51s, intend to ensure that the bombers did not suffer at the hands of the *Luftwaffe*.

And so the B-17s and B-24s of the Eighth Air Force headed for their bases. In total, 1,257 bombers had succeeded in releasing their bomb loads over or near to their targets, the vast majority of which were first priority. A total of 3,446 tons of bombs fell upon Germany and on the whole achieved their intended objective. Four *Luftwaffe* airfields suffered quite extensive damage, and although few aircraft appear to have been destroyed two of these airfields had been rendered inoperable. The rail network had again suffered extensive disruption, which was made worse by the number of munition and supply trains destroyed or damaged during the attacks. As well as the destruction of such urgently needed supplies, on their way to front-line troops, perhaps more important was the damage inflicted upon production facilities. Not only was the transportation system being systematically smashed but the means to replace the destroyed weapons and ammunition were also being removed. Whilst attempts were being made to reduce the arms industry to rubble, the equally important oil facilities had again been targeted. Although not decisively carried out on 7 April, the raids upon Büchen and Hitzacker disrupted any remaining production and added to the damage needing to be repaired. In addition, even before the costs to the bomber crews and fighter pilots are considered, these operations had already accounted for the loss of up to 850 lives on the ground.

As the American bombers returned to their collection of airfields in England, the initial reports of the attacks they had suffered began to be confirmed by the crews. As the debriefing sessions began, the crews who had found themselves under attack made a special point of commenting upon the ferocity of the *Luftwaffe* fighters. Whilst for some time the greatest danger had been posed by the jet fighters, the bombers had today found that the single-engine conventional force seemed to have proved themselves still capable of striking a severe blow. As the intelligence officers recorded details of the attacks, the number and method of these assaults began to give cause for concern. Later, as these reports were being coordinated, the attacks by the *Schulungslehrgang 'Elbe'* aircraft were highlighted amongst the *Luftwaffe* operations. It is unclear whether at this stage a determined effort was made to play down these attacks or whether more senior officers decided that it was simply the inexperience of *Luftwaffe* pilots which had accounted for the rammings. Whatever the reason, as the reports were being typed and distributed, the official interpretation of events had been decided upon.

It is quite obvious that, had the rumours of 'suicidal pilots' operating against the Eighth Air Force bombers had been allowed to circulate, *Oberst* Herrmann would have achieved an important success. Many of the crews had been shaken by the *Schulungslehrgang 'Elbe'* operations, and the news that ramming by enemy fighters had been intentional, successful or not, would have given understandable cause for concern amongst the crews. The reports prepared by the staff of Brigadier Charles Y. Banfill, the Eighth Air Force's Director of Intelligence, included the following analysis of the day's *Luftwaffe* action:

> After a lapse of several weeks during which conventional single-engined enemy aircraft have largely been non-active partners in the air war and even when encountered have shown very little fighting spirit, today in excellent flying conditions the *Luftwaffe* put up a force of some 115–130 single-engined fighters supplemented by 50-plus jets. From all reports it appears that this was a desperation attempt on the part of the enemy, and although enemy aircraft fought aggressively and made determined efforts to get through to the bombers our losses were comparatively light while more than half the enemy force was destroyed or damaged. Signs of desperation are evidenced by the fact that Fw 190 pilots deliberately rammed the bombers, bailing out before their planes went into the formations and making fanatical attacks through a murderous hail of fire. Tactics were thrown to the wind and attacks were made from all positions, mainly in ones and twos.

Mention of Fw 190s being involved in the attacks is of interest. When Brigadier Banfill forwarded his memorandum to his commander he commented further on this aspect:

> The desperation of the enemy attacks and the closeness and abandon with which they were pressed seemed to be evidence of 'suicidal ramming'. These were not suicidal ramming attacks, but in each case were aircraft clearly out of control either through injury to pilot or structural failure of attacking aircraft. The closeness of attack has given rise to rumors of ramming but review of complete Division experience fails to substantiate ramming theory.
>
> Evidence in the form of P.O.W. reports had previously indicated that a special *Jagdstaffel* of Focke Wulf pilots were experimenting with ramming. Reportedly they were practicing a maneuver whereby they could catapult themselves from their air-

craft after removing the canopy but prior to the actual ramming. This has never been substantiated.

Clearly, news of the operations and tactics of the earlier *Sturmstaffeln* had reached the headquarters of the Eighth Air Force. When the events of 7 April were examined it was naturally assumed that the ramming attacks were possibly from such a force. But despite the existence of intelligence reports suggesting that such a force may have existed, the official version was clear: the ramming had not been intentional. Any rumours to the contrary were being quashed.

With the *Luftwaffe* combat operations of 7 April having led Eighth Air Force officers to decide that it was necessary to halt the rumours of intentional ramming attacks, the stage seemed now perfectly set for the German propaganda machine to exploit the action of *Schulungslehrgang 'Elbe'*. Having been promised by *General* Koller that an initial success would be backed by a large-scale operation, *Oberst* Herrmann felt that his plans had been justified. Had his pilots not proved their courage and, despite their limited numbers, had they not succeeded in achieving a number of victories?

With his remaining pilots ready for their chance to fly against the bombers, and with news reaching him of his unit's successes, Herrmann awaited his new orders. When these orders did not arrive and the eventful day began to draw to its close, an increasingly impatient Herrmann forwarded another report to his superiors, requesting that resources be made available for the deployment of a larger force. But, yet again, his faith in his senior officers was to receive a savage blow.

The reports made by *Oberst* Herrmann were being supported by the confirmation of fallen bombers, but the news, no matter how good it seemed, was insufficient to convince the authorities that the operation should be followed up. Despite the fact that the propaganda apparatus had received news of the *Schulungslehrgang 'Elbe'* battle, neither the radio nor the remaining newspapers broadcast the information. At the head of this apparatus *Dr* Goebbels was also in receipt of the details, and although his staff did not make use of the operation he personally made mention of it in his diary. Had *Oberst* Herrmann been allowed access to these thoughts of the *Reichspropagandaminister*, he would perhaps have shivered at the description that his brave pilots had received: 'Our suicide fighters were in action for the first time during this Saturday when the weather was only semi-favourable. Great success is expected from these missions but we will wait and see.' It seems that Goebbels still viewed the force as an extension of the *Selbstopfermänner* concept. Had he been allowed any form of control of the plans, the pilots may have become involved in a far more dangerous mission.

With the High Command finally acknowledging that some success had been achieved, Herrmann again pleaded to be allowed to follow up the first operation. He had the men and he had some of the required aircraft, and they all had an example to follow. The reply he received was again negative: his commanders would not sanction a second mission. Whilst Herrmann felt betrayed by this stubborn refusal, it must of course be considered that each hour that passed added to the country's general decline. Had the necessary resources been readily available to support a second operation it could have achieved a further success. As it was, with every hour—and then, as the *Luftwaffe* commanders continued to hesitate, the hours grew to days— the hopes of a more forceful demonstration of these plans faded.

By the following day the remaining borders of the Reich continued to constrict upon those within. Allied armies continued to pour men and armour across the Rhine, bypassing the now trapped Army Group B of *Generalfeldmarschall* Model. Advance elements of the British 2nd Army, heading for Bremen, had at first reached Twistringen and then crossed the Weser to reach Verden, which only the day before had formed the edge of the hunting ground assigned to the pilots of *Schulungslehrgang 'Elbe'*. Units of the US Ninth Army, for which the 160th RCN Squadron had flown their reconnaissance mission, were now reaching Elze and the southern approaches to Hildesheim. Soviet forces also appeared unstoppable, now having Vienna firmly in their sights.

Despite the devastation of Germany and the destruction of her armed forces, the various elements continued their own feuds and pointed the finger of blame for failure at each other. After the failure of an SS division to provide the required defence of its assigned area, the entire division had been stripped by Hitler of its honour title and its personnel ordered to remove from their uniforms the armbands which carried this ornately embroidered wording. At this disgrace *Reichsführer* Himmler protested that the *Luftwaffe's* greater failure had not resulted in a similar punishment. Amidst the collapse of the combined defences, that such arguments could still continue is incredible. The deteriorating situation was duly recorded by *Dr* Goebbels, who wrote further of the *Schulungslehrgang 'Elbe'* mission:

> The first use of our suicide fighters has not produced the success hoped for. The reason given is that the enemy bomber formations did not fly concentrated, so that they had to be attacked individually. In addition our suicide fighters encountered such heavy defensive fire from the enemy fighters that only in a few cases were they able to ram. But we must not lose courage as a result. This is only an initial trial which is to be repeated in the next few days, hopefully with better results.

Having initially recorded his misunderstanding of the role of these pilots, he also clearly showed his failure to understand their planned mission.

What was now to become of Hajo Herrmann's pilots? In the skies above them the answer was abruptly written on 8 April. A force of over 1,100 Eighth Air Force bombers returned again to their targets in Germany, seemingly oblivious to the previous day's attacks by *Schulungslehrgang 'Elbe'*. It was clear that only a full-scale attack could have had any hope of stopping these *Viermöte*. As if to reinforce the point, B-17s of the 1st AD appeared over Stendal. Luckily they had come to bomb the rail yards and not the airfield. But it almost seemed as if the Eighth Air Force were out to show that they did not fear the pilots of *Oberst* Herrmann's force.

21. COLD STATISTICS

When the American fighters and bombers returned to their bases, the post-combat reports were completed. As had become standard, the various claims, by both fighter pilots and gunners, were exaggerated and inflated, mainly as a result of the confusion of combat and also in some cases from wishful thinking. The escort fighters claimed to have destroyed 59 single-engine aircraft and a further five jets. The infamous 'gunner multiplication table' (whereby many gunners within a formation may have been aiming at the same fighter, each believing that he had scored a hit and so recording a claim), produced a figure of 33 kills from the bomber crews, 26 from the 3rd AD and a further seven from the 2nd AD.

The often manic series of clashes that form any battle do not produce the ideal circumstances to examine and interpret such claims. The formations adopted by the Eighth Air Force bombers make the claims from gunners unreliable, and they had no gun cameras to support them. Fighter pilots often fired upon the same enemy aircraft and, as has been shown, even a pilotless and already doomed *Luftwaffe* fighter could be fired upon by another P-51 and claimed a second time. In addition, the enemy fighter destroyed by a P-47 or P-51 could also have been fired upon by the gunners and again claimed by them. There also exists the problem that a few bullets striking home was often taken as being conclusive proof of a kill being achieved.

The official reports completed by the participating fighter Groups on 7 April 1945 have been examined in an attempt to clarify as far as possible the various claims. In total the number of *Luftwaffe* fighters claimed on this day by USAAF fighter units was 82, this being compiled from both Eighth and Ninth Air Force figures. Of these, 67 were made by Eighth Air Force fighter units active as escorts during the mission against which the *'Elbe'* pilots operated. With further analysis it is possible to reduce this figure to approximately 47 victories against single-engine *Luftwaffe* fighters. This still represents a combined total for Bf 109 and Fw 190 kills; therefore the Eighth Air Force fighter claims against the *'Elbe'* force will be less than 47:

8th AF fighter claims	67
Less unconfirmed	3
Less probables	2
Less Me 262s claimed	7
Less Fw 190Ds	4

Less P-51	1
Less multiple claims	3
Revised total	**47**

Many of the claims made by the gunners of the various bombers have been discounted. Not only are these claims in the most part impossible to verify, but many have been duplicated within those made by fighter pilots. The particularly close escort mission flown on 7 April makes the possibility of fighters scavenging upon any damaged enemy aircraft an even more common occurrence than usual. The only claims which could be considered are those instances where the gunners believed that their fire had caused an *'Elbe'* fighter to collide with another bomber. Although the *Luftwaffe* fighters were undoubtedly already on their intended flight path, the defensive fire of the gunners can be judged to have had a detrimental effect upon the collision which took place. Instead of the precise method of attack that had been planned by the young German pilots, the defensive fire thrown out by the bombers caused them to crash with, very often, disastrous results. Of the 33 claims made by the gunners, only six can be said to represent enemy fighters that were destroyed before leaving the bomber formations as a result of defensive fire combined with collisions; even so, some of these *'Elbe'* fighters may still appear in the listing of fighter claims. It should be remembered that the nature of the air war being fought by the USAAF crews, with the bulk of these combats taking place over enemy territory, made the verification of many claims difficult. During previous operations the ratio of USAAF claims to actual *Luftwaffe* losses has been shown to have been as high as three to one.

Using these revised figures, it is possible to estimate the effect that the brief minutes of combat had upon the *'Elbe'* force:

Claims by USAAF escorts	47
Claims by bomber gunners	6
Approximate *'Elbe'* losses	53

Even had each of these aircraft losses also represented the loss of an *'Elbe'* pilot, this 44 per cent loss rate, although shockingly high viewed with the hindsight of more than fifty years, would appear to be a low figure for a unit considered by many to have been a suicide force. An examination of the operation shows that many of the *'Elbe'* fighters never actually came near to their target bomber formations; the inexperienced pilots had difficulty in navigating, some encountered severe freezing conditions which they were ill-prepared for, others found themselves flying temperamental aircraft incapable of combat operations and, of course, the Eighth Air Force fighters were still ready in force as protection. Few of the pilots who encountered the various Eighth Air Force fighter groups that day escaped unscathed.

Many died before the aircraft that they piloted reached their targets; others were trapped within their fighters as they crashed to earth. Even those who escaped their damaged fighters faced further dangers as they parachuted to earth. Almost all of those who survived these events of 7 April suffered injuries, often horrific. Nevertheless, some of these young pilots did escape. Although exact figures have proved impossible to establish, *Herr* Saft in his examination has estimated that at most 40 died, though the figure may be as low as 25–30. So from the 120 *Schulungslehrgang 'Elbe'* pilots who had been committed to combat, the worst estimated fatality rate equates to 33 per cent.

Clarification is difficult because of the state of near-chaos which existed by April 1945, both before the *'Elbe'* operation and during the weeks which followed. Many of those who died were buried either under the wrong names or in unmarked graves—as was the fate of many soldiers and airmen during these weeks. Some of the badly injured pilots crashed or landed in areas under Allied control, leading to additional confusion in trying to collate figures. Moreover, how many of these young men ended their war on 7 April, never returning to their unit or able to escape captivity, will remain forever unknown. But, even if it has proved frustratingly difficult to pinpoint the exact losses of *Oberst* Herrmann's force, it is readily apparent that as many as 67 per cent of his volunteers survived their mission. This is in stark contrast to the figures estimated during the earliest stages of the planning, when the volunteers themselves were warned that their chances of survival were as low as 10 per cent.

And what of the Eighth Air Force bombers that the *Schulungslehrgang 'Elbe'* pilots had flown against? The 2nd AD lost three of its B-24s during the period of combat and a badly damaged bomber had to be abandoned by her crew whilst still over the European mainland. The 3rd AD suffered the most concentrated series of attacks and as a result lost fourteen B-17 bombers. Of the total losses, one was to flak, one a result of bombs falling from another aircraft and possibly three from Me 262 units (although the jet units claimed six victories, only three can be confirmed). These figures suggest that for a maximum loss of 30–40 pilots the first operation by the fledgeling *Jagdwaffe* unit had been able to claim as many as thirteen USAAF bombers destroyed. Although the figures are still in favour of the American forces, the balance had swung back some way towards the German defenders.

In addition to the bombers lost, the skirmishes of the last hours inflicted considerable levels of damage upon those bombers which were able to return to their bases. A total of 188 bombers reported varying levels of damage, and, of these, 54 were categorized as being 'major'. To put these figures in some perspective, it is only necessary to view the trend that had developed by April 1945. Since the beginning of December 1944, despite almost daily operations, the USAAF bombers had only suffered losses of over ten bombers on eight occasions; on many, only one or two losses were recorded.

Of these eight missions, three were aimed at targets in or around Berlin, which was heavily defended by both flak and fighters. The mission mounted on Christmas Eve 1944 was the largest bombing operation of the war and involved 1,884 bombers—virtually 'every aircraft that could fly'. This mission suffered the loss of twelve bombers. A further nineteen bombers fell on 24 March when 1,714 aircraft were dispatched in support of the Rhine crossings, many units flying two missions during the day. The losses of 24 March were the last major losses until 7 April. It therefore becomes readily apparent that the operation mounted by the pilots of *Schulungslehrgang 'Elbe'* reversed the current decline in the effectiveness of the *Jagdwaffe*. As well as the tactics employed by the defending fighters, the results they had achieved marked 7 April as a notable day.

But even this success could ultimately mean little when the losses suffered by the Eighth Air Force are examined in their wider context. If we consider that the *'Elbe'* operation was the only major undertaking that the *Luftwaffe* could mount on 7 April and had been aimed at only the bombers of the 2nd and 3rd Air Divisions, the losses begin to take on their true perspective. The losses represented only 2.18 per cent of the bomber force. When the lost bombers are taken as a total of the *entire* Eighth Air Force mission, this percentage falls to only 1.42. By the end of 1944 American industry alone had produced 96,000 aircraft of various types. With these resources behind it the USAAF could continue to operate even had it been necessary to accept greater losses. When it is considered that the combined Allied air forces mounted over 5,000 sorties on 7 April, the loss of fewer than twenty aircraft equates to only 0.3 per cent of the day's operations. Such losses, whilst in themselves tragic, were easily accepted by those in command. By the end of the day nearly 4,000 tons of bombs had fallen upon targets in Europe, over 680 armoured vehicles and nearly 600 motorized transports had been destroyed and 40 trains had been wiped from what remained of the rail network.

22. THE FATE OF *SCHULUNGSLEHRGANG 'ELBE'*

By late afternoon the sky had at last returned to its former peaceful state. Only the ugly scars of the many columns of smoke gave any indication of the battle which had been fought. The land, however, bore witness to the full horror of the last hours. Across a wide tract of countryside the remains of both fighter and bomber aircraft now lay as useless scrap. In many such collections of metal the life of a young pilot or crew member had ended. At other sites the forlorn shape of a dead or dying man could be found near to his parachute. For those whose injuries would not lead to death, the next few days and the weeks that followed would allow a slow and often painful recovery to be made. For the young *Luftwaffe* pilots there would then follow many months of captivity in the hands of their enemies. Those who had survived the battles on both sides found that they had lost both comrades and friends. How great, then, had been the cost? Had the desperate gamble taken by *Oberst* Herrmann and his commanders paid off?

In judging the events of 7 April 1945 we must attempt to remember the existing circumstances. Was *Oberst* Herrmann guilty, as some would have us believe, of squandering his fledgeling *Jadgwaffe* pilots in this suicidal mission, doomed to failure from its inception? The answer must be no, for in his plans what Hajo Herrmann was attempting followed existing military doctrine—an improvised defence against a stronger enemy. Had these pilots been employed instead to reinforce the standard *Luftwaffe* formations, as suggested by some like *General* Galland, then their usefulness for this task must be questioned. By April 1945 Germany could not allow such pilots to benefit from the required training: even basic flying skills were being imparted within a constantly restricting timetable. These young men would without doubt have been thrown into front-line units at the earliest opportunity, where their chances of survival would have been no greater than they were in '*Elbe*'. For this was indeed the fate of many hundreds of young pilots during 1944 and 1945. Perhaps their first flight, certainly one of their first five, would have resulted in an encounter with a USAAF P-51 or an RAF Tempest, and before the guns of the enemy their lack of skill and training would have cost them dearly.

If, then, the lack of training inherent within this latest group of *Jagdwaffe* pilots is accepted, how else could Germany have employed them? It is probable that they would have found themselves drafted into one of the improvised *Luftwaffe* ground formations and given a steel helmet and a rifle. From here their survival chances would have been dramatically reduced, for whatever limited flying skills they possessed these certainly outnumbered their skills as infantry soldiers. Although it may appear harsh, to us, viewing these events from the safety of over fifty years, perhaps it is better that these young eagles were allowed to take to the air, albeit prematurely, to defend their homes rather than to have died before the advancing Allied armour, holding a gun that they barely knew how to use.

Finding himself without the support he had been promised, *Oberst* Herrmann had a number of difficult decisions to make. For every hour that was spent trying to obtain agreement from his hesitant leaders, his men remained becalmed at Stendal. With the course of the war continuing to run towards its close, this base was now increasingly at risk: as well as facing the threat of air attack, it was now also in danger of being overrun by Allied ground forces.

The courage that his pilots had displayed touched *Oberst* Herrmann deeply, and he would now do all within in his power to protect them. But if the men were to be to protected they had to be moved, and quickly: the remaining Reich territory was on the verge of being split apart by the advancing Allied forces. The former complex structure of the *Luftwaffe* was rapidly becoming more simplified. All forces were now to be subordinated to either *Luftflotte Reich*, based within the remaining northern half, or *Luftflotte 6*, in the south. The order for the staff of *IX Fliegerkorps* to transfer south arrived as *Oberst* Herrmann was desperately attempting to get the next stage of his plan organized. When the message was relayed to Stendal, *Major* Köhnke was quick to act. Having remained with his men, he was able to ensure that the move was rapidly put into effect.

The protection that the pilots and officers of *'Elbe'* were receiving from their senior staff was required in the face of another very real threat. Whilst the Allies attempted to capture the *Luftwaffe's* airfields or destroy its remaining aircraft from the air, elements within its own leadership were seemingly intent upon destroying the organization themselves. Already thousands of ground staff, technicians and even now air crews were being deemed surplus to requirements and organized into *ad hoc Luftwaffe* field formations, either to serve as ground troops or to man flak units. Once again the fear returned of losing the young pilots to the demands of the front line. By the time preparations to move had been made, 27 of the *'Elbe'* pilots who had taken off on the morning of 7 April had been able to report back to Stendal, and each was now guaranteed a place in the next phase of *Oberst* Herrmann's plans. Alongside these men were the 60 pilots who had been forced to return to their airfields and also some of the remaining volunteers who could not be included in the ramming mission.

After a journey of over 300 miles, which took three days to complete, the men, shepherded all the way by *Major* Köhnke, finally reached Pocking, fourteen miles south-west of Passau. Although this move was based upon a tactical decision, it has brought an additional aspect to the rumours which surround the *'Elbe'* force. With the remaining German territory being split north and south, the forces had two options if they were to regroup. Those who moved south—as did the *'Elbe'* force—arrived in an area which was rumoured to be the site of *'Festung Alpen'*, the 'Alpine Redoubt' from where the continued defence of the Reich was to be coordinated. In practice, the forces which did move would have been equally doomed whichever direction they had selected. This is clearly illustrated by the case of the staff of *IX Fliegerkorps*, which seems to have simply ceased to exist whilst en route to its new base. It would appear to be a sign of the resourcefulness and perhaps luck of both *Oberst* Herrmann and *Major* Köhnke that they were able to accomplish the move to Pocking. But the move itself finally sealed the fate of Herrmann's plans for a second *'Elbe'* operation. The confusion which existed even prior to their mission had by now dissolved into chaos. At airfields designated as collecting areas for the remaining *Luftwaffe* aircraft, very little fuel was to be found. Although aircraft arrived at their new fields, the vast majority were unable to leave.

In a last attempt to clarify his orders, Hajo Herrmann flew in person to see his *Reichsmarschall*, who had been encamped at Berchtesgaden since 21 April. Was he expected to mount his large-scale *'Elbe'* operation, an operation that he himself must have known to be hopeless, or were there other plans for his force as a part of the *'Festung Alpen'*? In fact the very reason for the existence of his force had already begun to bring to an end its campaign. On 20 April, the day of Adolf Hitler's 56th birthday, the Eighth Air Force returned to Berlin for the last time. With the beleaguered city already shaking beneath Marshal Zhukov's artillery, the final B-17s and B-24s unloaded their bombs on what remained of the rail network. Only one bomber was lost during this raid.

Oberst Herrmann had travelled with one of his successful *'Elbe'* pilots, only to be met by the SS—who seemed to hold so tightly the reins of power—when he landed at Salzburg. Requesting an audience with his commander, Herrmann was greeted with the news that Göring no longer held any position within the Reich. The *Reichsmarschall*'s final attempt to restore himself to a position of importance by assuming control from his besieged *Führer* had immediately backfired. Those who still influenced Hitler seized upon Göring's telegram of 23 April to show his treachery: the *Reichsmarschall* had finally played into the hands of his own enemies. On 24 April *Generaloberst* Robert *Ritter* von Greim had been flown into Berlin together with Hanna Reitsch in the back of a Focke-Wulf 190. The uncomfortable and dangerous trip into Hitler's last headquarters beneath the ruined Reich Chancellery had been necessary in order that he receive his new appointment to the rank of *Feldmarschall* and Commander-in-Chief of the *Luftwaffe*.

With the man who had supported the *Selbstopfermänner* proposals now leading the *Luftwaffe*, perhaps the distance Hajo Herrmann had put between Berlin and his men had been a wise precaution.

Although he admitted later that the news had finally convinced him that the end was indeed near, *Oberst* Herrmann decided that he should continue with the aim of his visit. He thus found himself before *General* Koller, the officer who had first scaled down his original plans and then refused to allow a second operation to be mounted. But even before Herrmann was able to discover what was to become of his force, *General* Koller was summoned to return to Berlin and the madness of the *Führerbunker*. Still remaining ignorant of the intended use of his force, Herrmann decided to make a final attempt to speak to Göring and drove to Berchtesgaden, only to have his belief in the chaos which surrounded him again reinforced. Not only had the former *Reichsmarschall* been stripped of all his titles and positions, but he was under house arrest on the direct orders of Hitler and awaiting a possible death sentence. Those he met with whom he was able to discuss events each appeared to have decided their own plan for survival—a fight to the death in the mountains, a surrender to the British or Americans, continued partisan warfare or even a quiet surrender of arms and a return to civilian life. The major remaining fear was of capture by the Soviet forces.

As well as his *'Elbe'* force, Herrmann had organized a special commando force named *Sonderkommando 'Bienenstock'* ('Beehive'). As originally envisaged, this force would complement the operations of *'Elbe'* by attacking the bases used by USAAF bombers in Italy from which they had launched their raids upon the important *Luftwaffe* jet bases in the south of Germany. He now found that his final instructions from higher command were for the *'Bienenstock'* force to be employed to sabotage Soviet supply lines and slow the progress of their forces. Whilst several raids were completed successfully by Herrmann's second force from Pocking between 25 and 28 April, its missions were not as he had intended. Rather than one spectacular assault upon a crowded Allied airfield by a number of teams who would leave explosive charges to wipe out a large number of bombers and their ground facilities, the *Kommando* was used to attempt to destroy several crossings over the River Donau. But such attempts could not alter the course of the war for long. On 29 April the final hopes ended of any German forces being able to break through the iron circle of Soviet armour which surrounded Berlin. The following day Hitler committed suicide and the Red Flag finally flew from the roof of the *Reichstag*. So ended one man's dreams of an enduring Third Reich.

Whilst the British and American advances had halted at the River Elbe, the Soviet assault continued: hour by hour and day by day the Red Army seized control of more and more of the rubble which covered Europe. It was in the face of this irresistible Allied advance that the pilots assembled by

Oberst Herrmann finally ended their service in the *Luftwaffe*. Faced with the breakdown of communications with the remaining elements of *Luftwaffe* High Command and finally the total loss of supplies by the beginning of May, the remaining operational units ceased to exist. Even the over-optimistic paper-strength of the *Luftwaffe* was unable to hide the truth: the *Luftwaffe*, its fighter forces and its pilots were at last consigned to history.

April 10 had witnessed what was to be the peak of *Jagdwaffe* jet operations when *JG 7* launched 55 Me 262s. The cost was high. By the end of the day 29 of the fighters had been destroyed and six pilots were dead, a further five wounded and fourteen reported missing in action. From that day onwards even the jet force entered a rapid decline. At an airfield on the outskirts of Salzburg a number of fires were lit on 3 May using the final drops of aviation fuel. The flames increased and quickly consumed up to sixty Me 262s which had assembled over the previous days and included the fighters of *General* Galland's *JV 44*. The final hopes of the *Jagdwaffe* were being symbolically destroyed by fire. Now even the revolutionary force which *Oberst* Herrmann had hoped to protect and the aircraft which so many had hoped could lead to a regenerated *Luftwaffe* had been reduced to twisted scrap at the hands of their own pilots.

Whilst many of those around him had been able to avoid capture, *Oberst* Herrmann was forced to surrender to Soviet forces at Budapest on 11 May. He was to spend the next ten years of his life as a prisoner. By the time he was finally freed the events of 1945 had already begun to become obscured with the passing of time. Many of those who had taken part wished only to rebuild their lives and to forget the horrors of war. As the actions of brave men became the subject of stories, many facts became confused and many events became surrounded by rumours. This is what had happened to the story of those young volunteers assembled by *Oberst* Hajo Herrmann. Now the true story is known—the story of *Schulungslehrgang 'Elbe'*.

24. 7 APRIL 1991

The events described throughout the previous pages have of course been remembered by those who survived. From time to time as the years passed the men who had united in the defence of their homeland gathered to talk of their experiences and to salute their fallen *Kameraden*. They discovered, as had many former soldiers before them, that shared experiences during a time of war had created a formidable bond. After the passing of nearly half a century they found that, whilst the actions of others had been remembered and honoured, only rumours of their operation existed.

In an attempt to rectify this omission the group decided that it was time that a fitting memorial to their mission be erected. Although donations quickly appeared from the veterans themselves, the fund also began to grow thanks to the contributions from civilians, including those who had assisted the injured pilots in 1945. An application to build on a site at Schwarmstedt, near to where some of the fallen pilots had been buried, ran into initial difficulties. The plans were, however, rescued the following year by a former member of the *'Bienenstock'* force, Karl-Heinrich Langspecht, who donated his own land at Celle, a site which marked one of the boundaries of the designated hunting ground of the *'Elbe'* pilots.

On 7 April 1991 a memorial was finally unveiled. In his welcoming speech to those who attended the unveiling, *Herr* Langspecht said that by whatever means men had fought in defence of their homes, it was only fitting that they should be remembered: after all, they all shared the same love of their Fatherland. Amongst those who listened were former *Schulungslehrgang 'Elbe'* pilots who also felt that it had been their duty to defend the memory of their fallen *Kameraden* against the various misrepresentations which had been made following their flight. They did not seek to be considered as equals to the other *Luftwaffe* pilots, but only a recognition that their courage allowed them to be considered worthy of inclusion within the ranks of the *Jagdwaffe*, who had all shared a common goal.

They had been promised in 1945 that their courage and determination to defend their homeland would be remembered, but it was not until their forty-sixth anniversary that a memorial was finally created. It is perhaps an indication of the fortunes of war that the only reference to the courage, bravery and determination of this group of pilots lies within the official records of the Eighth Air Force, prepared by the very crews they fought against. The inscription on their memorial reads: 'For the remembrance of the fighter pilots, Rammkommando Elbe 7 April 1945, Sonderkommando Bienenstock April–May 1945.'

It is our duty as a part of the generations which follow to listen to such stories and record such events, remembering the sacrifice which so many were prepared to make.

APPENDICES

APPENDIX 1. KNOWN *SCHULUNGSLEHRGANG 'ELBE'* PILOTS

Anton, *Leutnant* Karl-Heinz
Bohm, *Oberfähnrich* Joachim-Wolfgang
Bohnke, *Fahnenjunker-Feldwebel*
  Gerhard
Bott, *Leutnant* Hans
Breinl, *Obergefreiter* Henfried
Brockelschen, *Leutnant*
Eitle, *Obergefreiter* Hans-Dieter
Funk, Erich
Fussinger, *Feldwebel* Hans
Grabinger, Anton
Hahn, *Unteroffizier* Klaus
Hansen, *Oberleutnant* Olaf
Harms, *Obergefreiter* Hugo
Hedwig, *Feldwebel* Reinhold
Herbold, *Flugzeugführer* Walter
Jansen, Gerhard
Korner, *Unteroffizier* Walter
Kraul, *Flugzeugführer*
Kruchem, *Feldwebel* Heinrich-Mathias
Linder, Werner
Loscher, *Leutnant* Hans-Ludwig
Marktscheffel, *Oberfähnrich* Fritz
Meya, *Fahnenjunker-Feldwebel* Fritz
Molly, *Unteroffizier* Klaus
Müller, *Oberfeldwebel* Heinz

Müller, *Hauptmann* Hugo
Nagel, *Leutnant* Hans
Pesch, *Hauptmann* Roman
Prock, *Fähnrich* Eberhard
Ringhofer, *Gefreiter* Rudi
Rosner, *Unteroffizier* Heinrich
Rummel, *Oberfeldwebel* Ernst
Schack, *Oberfähnrich*
Schmidt, *Fähnrich* Franz-Josef
Schrader, *Fahnenjunker-Oberfeldwebel*
  Heinz
Schulz-Sembten, *Leutnant* Dietrich
Seidel, *Obergefreiter* Horst
Sorge, *Hauptmann* Ernst
Stauff, *Obergefreiter*
Stumpf, *Obergefreiter* Otto
Tetzel, *Gefreiter* Ernst
Thiel, *Leutnant* Armin
Thiel, *Fähnrich* Jurgen
Uhlich, Georg
Wienkotter, *Unterfeldwebel* Manfred
Winter, *Fähnrich* Franz
Zapp, *Unteroffizier* Jakob
Zell, *Unteroffizier* Werner
Zens, *Leutnant* Franz

APPENDIX 2. COMPARATIVE RANKS

	Luftwaffe	Royal Air Force	USAAF
	Reichsmarschall	–	–
	Generalfeldmarschall	Marshal of the RAF	General (5-star)
Genobst	Generaloberst	Air Chief Marshal	General (4-star)
Gen der Flg	General der Flieger	Air Marshal	Lieutenant-General
Genlt	Generalleutnant	Air Vice-Marshal	Major-General
Genmaj	Generalmajor	Air Commodore	Brigadier-General
Obst	Oberst	Group Captain	Colonel
Obstlt	Oberstleutnant	Wing Commander	Lieutenant-Colonel

Maj	Major	Squadron Leader	Major
Hptm	Hauptmann	Flight Lieutenant	Captain
Oblt	Oberleutnant	Flying Officer	1st Lieutenant
Lt	Leutnant	Pilot Officer	2nd Lieutenant
Stabsfw	Stabsfeldwebel	Warrant Officer	Warrant Officer
Ofhr	Oberfähnrich	(Senior Officer Cadet)	–
Hptfw	Hauptfeldwebel	–	Sergeant-Major
Obfw	Oberfeldwebel	Flight Sergeant	Master Sergeant
Fhr	Fähnrich/Fahnen-junker	(Officer Cadet)	–
Fw	Feldwebel	Sergeant	Technical Sergeant
Ufw	Unterfeldwebel	–	–
Uffz	Unteroffizier	Corporal	Staff Sergeant
Hptgefr	Hauptgefreiter	–	–
Ogfr	Obergefreiter	Leading Aircraftsman	Corporal
Gefr	Gefreiter	Aircraftsman First Class	Private First Class
Flg	Flieger	Aircraftsman Second Class	Private Second Class

APPENDIX 3. 3rd AIR DIVISION, FIELD ORDER 1914A, 7 APRIL 1945

CBW		BG	Call-sign (fighter–bomber)	Call-sign	Escort Group	Call-sign (bomber–fighter)
1st Task Force						
45th	A	388th	Vampire Leader	Vinegrove 1-1	339th 'A'	Balance 1-1
	B	452nd	Vampire Love	Vinegrove 1-2	339th 'B'	Balance 1-2
	C	96th	Vampire Charlie	Vinegrove 1-3	353rd 'A'	Balance 1-3
13th	C	95th	Fireball Baker	Vinegrove 1-5	353rd 'B'	Balance 1-4
	A	390th	Fireball Leader	Vinegrove 1-4	78th 'A'	Balance 1-5
	B	100th	Fireball Dog	Vinegrove 1-6	78th 'B'	Balance 1-6
2nd Task Force						
93rd	A	385th	Clambrake Leader	Vinegrove 1-7	55th 'A/B'	Balance 1-7, 1-8
	B	493rd	Clambrake Victor	Vinegrove 1-8	55th 'A/B'	Balance 1-7, 1-8
	C	34th	Clambrake Sugar	Vinegrove 1-9	55th 'A/B'	Balance 1-7, 1-8
	D	490th	Clambrake Tare	Vinegrove 1-10	357th 'A'	Balance 1-9
4th	A	487th	Hotshot Leader	Vinegrove 1-11	357th 'B'	Balance 1-10
	B	486th	Hotshot William	Vinegrove 1-12	352nd 'A/B'	Balance 1-11, 1-12
	C	447th	Hotshot King	Vinegrove 1-13	352nd 'A/B'	Balance 1-11, 1-12
	D	94th	Hotshot Able	Vinegrove 1-14	352nd 'A/B'	Balance 1-11, 1-12

Note: 55th FG forced to withdraw early because of low fuel. Additional escorts from 20th FG (77th and 79th FS). Arrived over Steinhuder at 1430 to assist support of 4th CBW.

APPENDIX 4. 2nd AIR DIVISION, FIELD ORDER 1914A, 7 APRIL 1945

CBW		BG	Escort group
2nd	A	389th	355th 'A/B'
	B	445th	355th 'A/B'
	C	453rd	479th 'A/B'
20th	A	93rd	479th 'A/B'
	B	446th	4th 'A/B'
	C	448th	4th 'A/B'
14th	A	44th	356th 'A/B'
	B	392nd	356th 'A/B'
96th	A	458th	56th 'A/B'
	B	467th	56th 'A/B'
	C	466th	56th 'A/B'

APPENDIX 5. 1st AIR DIVISION, FIELD ORDER 1914A, 7 APRIL 1945

CBW		BG	Call-sign (fighter–bomber)	Escort group
94th	A	457th	Vinegrove 3-1	359th 'A'
	B	351st	Vinegrove 3-1	359th 'A'
	C	401st	Vinegrove 3-2	359th 'B'
41st	A	303rd	Vinegrove 3-2	359th 'B'
	B	379th	Vinegrove 3-3	364th 'A'
	C	384th	Vinegrove 3-3	364th 'A'
1st	A	381st	Vinegrove 3-4	364th 'B'
	B	398th	Vinegrove 3-4	364th 'B'
	C	91st	Vinegrove 3-5	20th 'A'
40th	A	92nd	Vinegrove 3-5	20th 'A'
	B	305th	Vinegrove 3-6	20th 'B'
	C	306th	Vinegrove 3-6	20th 'B'

Note: When the 20th FG moved to cover the 3rd AD it was replaced by the 361st FG.

APPENDIX 6. EIGHTH AIR FORCE TARGETS, 7 APRIL 1945

Priority	Target	Sorties	Effective	Tonnage GP	Tonnage IB	Results
3rd AD						
Primary	Kaltenkirchen A/F	153	143	375.5	35.0	Good
Primary	Büchen oil storage	76	36	108.0	–	Unknown
Primary	Gustrow ordnance depot	108	104	198.0	102.0	Unknown
Primary	Parchim A/F	192	134	323.7	67.0	Unknown
Secondary	Neumünster M/Y		37	111.0	–	Fair
Secondary	Schwerin M/Y		48	117.9	–	Fair
3rd priority	Salzwedel A/F		1	5.0	–	Unknown
Totals			503	1,239.1	204.0	

2nd AD

Primary plant	Krummel explosive	148	128	350.0	–	V good
Primary plant	Düneburg explosive	192	168	452.8	–	V good
Secondary	Neumünster M/Y		26	70.0	–	V good
Totals			**322**	**872.8**	**–**	

1st AD

Primary	Reinschler A/F	113	Not attacked	–	–	–
Primary	Hitzacker oil storage	116	115	284.0	–	Unknown
Primary	Kohlenbissen A/F	105	93	261.4	–	Good
Primary	Wesendorf A/F	108	107	214.0	34.0	Good
Secondary	Lüneburg M/Y		92	266.9	–	Good
Opportunity	Ulzen M/Y		13	41.6	–	Good
Opportunity	Fassberg A/F		12	33.9	–	Unknown
Totals			**432**	**1,101.8**	**34.0**	
Grand totals			**1,257**	**3,213.7**	**238.0**	

Information based upon extracts from Eighth Air Force Headquarters summary No 342.

APPENDIX 7. EIGHTH AIR FORCE LOSSES BY FORMATION, 7 APRIL 1945

3rd AD

45th CBW, 388th BG, Knettishall

Sqn	A/C no	Name	Pilot	Fate
561st	42-97105		2/Lt Lewis A. Hickham	Ramming attack; crashed
563rd	43-38869	*Paula Sue*	2/Lt Robert F. Bars	Ramming attack; crashed
562nd	44-5874			Damaged; landed Sweden

45th CBW, 452nd BG, Deopham Green

731st	42-31366	*Snake Eyes*	· 2/Lt David L. Owens	Ramming attack; crashed
	44-8634	*Ida Wanna*	Lt Dabney W. Sharp	Fighter attack; crashed
728th	43-38868		2/Lt William Richardson	Fighter attack; crashed
	44-8531		2/Lt William H. Gill	Fighter attack; crashed

45th CBW, 96th BG, Snetterton Heath – No losses

13th CBW, 390th BG, Framlingham

570th	44-8225	*Hard to Get*	2/Lt William Kotta	Me 262 attack; crashed

13th CBW, 100th BG, Thorpe Abbotts

349th	44-8334		Lt William E. Howard	Damaged; crashed
	42-37972	*Gold Brick*		Damaged; RTB
351st	43-38514	*E-Z Goin*	Lt Joe Martin	Rammed; RTB
418th	42-97071	*Candys Dandy*	Lt Arthur R. Calder	Rammed; exploded

13th CBW, 95th BG, Horham – No losses

93rd CBW, 385th BG 'Van's Valiants', Great Ashfield
550th	44-8744		2/Lt George E. Burich Jr	Rammed; crashed

93rd CBW, 493rd BG 'Helton's Hellcats', Little Walden
860th	43-39070		2/Lt Warren P. Whitson Jr	Fighter attack; crashed

93rd CBW, 34th BG, Mendlesham – No losses

93rd CBW, 490th BG, Eye
850th	43-38002	*Lady Helene*	Lt Richard L. Druhot	Rammed; crashed
?	43-38058			Rammed; landed Continent

4th CBW, 487th BG, Lavenham
839th	43-37987	*Mean Widdle Kid*	Lt Richard L. Althouse	Reported as crashing nr Havelberg 'April 1945'; possibly lost 7 April
	Unidentified B-17		Lt Wentz	Rammed; landed A-92 St Trond, Belgium

4th CBW, 486th BG, Sudbury
834th	44-8528	*Flack Sack*	2/Lt Carl M. Knez	Unknown
835th	43-39163	*Happy Warrior*	Lt Walter G. Center Jr	Hit by flak; crashed

4th CBW, 447th BG, Rattlesden — No losses

4th CBW, 94th BG, Bury St Edmunds – No losses

2nd AD

2nd CBW, 389th BG 'The Sky Scorpions', Hethel
?	44-49254		Lt Bob C. Dallas	Rammed; crashed
566th	44-49533		Lt-Col Walter R. Kunkel	Unknown

2nd CBW, 445th BG, Tibenham
702nd	42-94870	*Axis Ex-Lax*	Lt Bruce O. Kilburn	Me 262 attack; crashed
?	44-48854			Crash-landed on fire, cause unknown

2nd CBW, 453rd BG, Old Buckenham – No losses

20th CBW, 93rd BG 'The Traveling Circus', Hardwick
Three unidentified B-24s damaged, one of which was a result of ramming; all RTB

20th CBW, 446th BG 'Bungay Buckeroos', Bungay
704th	44-48830			Crash-landed Continent on fire

20th CBW, 448th BG, Seething – No losses

14th CBW, 44th BG 'The Flying Eightballs', Shipdham – No losses

14th CBW, 392nd BG, Wendling – No losses

96th CBW, 458th BG, Horsham St Faith – No losses

96th CBW, 467th BG 'The Rackheath Aggies', Rackheath

| 789th | 42-94931 | *Sacktime* | | Possibly the B-24 abandoned on 7 April |

96th CBW, 466th BG, Attlebridge

| 787th | 42-95194 | *The Flying Witch* | | Crashed following take-off accident |

VIII FIGHTER COMMAND LOSSES

3rd AD
66th FW, 55th FG, Wormingford

| 338th | 44-72296 | | 2/Lt Harold J. Konantz | Shot down by *Luftwaffe* fighter |

66th FW, 78th FG, Duxford

| 83rd | 44-72217 | | 2/Lt Robert H. Talbot | Shot down by P-51; pilot POW |

66th FW, 339th FG, Fowlmere

| 503rd | 44-11325 | | 1/Lt David A. MacKenzie | Hit by B-17 gunners; crashed |
| 504th | | | 1/Lt Leonard A. Kunz | Damaged; forced to land Brussels |

2nd AD
65th FW, 355th FG, Steeple Morden

| 354th | 44-15346 | *Bobbie Socks* | 2/Lt Gilbert M. Plowman | Shot down by *Luftwaffe* fighter |
| | 44-72306 | | 1/Lt Newell F. Mills Jr | Shot down by *Luftwaffe* fighter |

1st AD
67th FW, 356th FG, Martlesham Heath

| 359th | ? | | Lt Warren T. Edinborough | Flying escort to 2nd AD |

APPENDIX 8. ALLIED AIR SORTIES, 7 APRIL 1945

Eighth Air Force	Total	Effective
Heavy bomber attacks	1,311	1,257
Fighter escort	844	778
Photo recon	37	34
Weather recon	41	41
Air/sea rescue	15	15
Special operations	25	24
Totals	**2,273**	**2,149**

Photo recon	**12 × F-5, 25 × P-51**
	10 × F-5 'dicing' missions to Central/Western Germany
	2 × F-5 mapping missions to Chemnitz area
	25 × P-51 as escort to bomber force (23 effective)

Weather recon		**29 × P-51, 5 × Mosquito, 7 × B-17**	
		2 × B-17 routine flight to NW of Land's End	
		2 × B-17 routine flight to position 13 and return	
		5 × Mosquito special weather recon over UK, Holland, Denmark and Belgium	
		29 × P-51 and 3 × B-17 weather scouts for bomber force	
Air/sea rescue		**14 × P-47, 1 × OA-10**	
		Routine search and patrol	

Ninth Air Force

9th Bomb Division	274	Northeim/Gottingen marshalling yards
9th TAC	413	Armed recon ahead of First Army
19th TAC	395	Armed recon Magdeburg, Leipzig, Chemnitz and Halle; air–ground support to VIII, XII and XX Corps
29th TAC	432	Armed recon to Stadthagen; air patrols, bomber escort and air–ground support to XVI Corps
Total	**1,514**	

Second Tactical Air Force

Armed recon	517	Zuider Zee/Emden area
Immediate/prearranged support	335	Support to 1st Canadian and 2nd British Armies
Interception/ASR	272	
Recon	198	
Total	**1,322**	

Fifteenth Air Force

Heavy bomber attacks	668	116	Adige/Mezzacorona RR bridge
Fighter escort	214	214	
Dive-bombing, P-38	84	82	Tannachstein RR bridge
Dive-bombing, P-38	74	–	S Austria; mission abandoned
Totals	**1,040**	**412**	

First US TAF

1st French Air Force	2	2	Weather recon
42nd Bomb Wing	–	–	
12th TAC	?	?	
Western French AF	?	?	
Totals	**2**	**2**	

RAF Bomber Command *Daylight operations*

Lancaster	15	15	Ijmuiden Sperr Brecher
Mosquito	2	2	Ijmuiden Sperr Brecher
Mosquito	3	3	Weather recon
Totals	**20**	**20**	

RAF Fighter Command

Escort	52	52	Bomber/Coastal Command escort
Totals	**52**	**52**	

Based upon information contained in 'Intops summary No 342, Period 0001hrs 7 April to 2400 hours 7 April 1945'. Prepared by 'Headquarters Eighth Air Force, Brigadier-General Charles Y. Banfill, Director of Intelligence'.

GLOSSARY

Abschuss	Air victory
Erganzungsgruppe	Advanced Training Group
Flugzeugführer	Pilot
Geschwader	Wing (largest *Luftwaffe* unit)
Geschwaderstab	*Geschwader* Staff
Gruppe	Basic *Luftwaffe* unit
Herausschuss	'Pickout', 'cull' (damaged bomber forced from formation)
Jagdflieger	Fighter pilot
Jagdgeschwader	Fighter Wing
Jagdwaffe	Fighter arm of *Luftwaffe*
Katchmarek	Wing-man
Kampfgeschwader	Bomber Wing
Kette	Flight (of three aircraft)
Kommandeur	Commander (a position, not a rank)
Kommodore	Commodore (a position, not a rank)
Luftflotte	Air Fleet (covered an operational area)
Nachwuchs	'New generation', 'new growth' (replacement pilots)
Oberkommando der Luftwaffe (OKL)	*Luftwaffe* High Command
Reichsluftfahrtministerium (RLM)	Air Ministry
Reichsverteidigung (RVT)	Air defence organization for Germany
Rotte	Two-aircraft tactical formation
Rottenflieger	Second pilot of *Rotte* (wing-man)
Rottenführer	Leader of *Rotte*
Schwarm	Four-aircraft Flight (standard *Luftwaffe* fighter formation)
Staffel	Squadron
Viermot	Four-engine bomber (abbreviation)

BIBLIOGRAPHY

PUBLISHED SOURCES

Adams, Paul M., and Andrews, William H., *Heavy Bombers of the Mighty Eighth*, Eighth Air Force Museum Foundation, 1995

Barbas, Bernd, *Aircraft of the Luftwaffe Aces II*, Schiffer, 1995

Baumbach, Werner, *Broken Swastika*, Robert Hale, 1960

Bekker, Cajus, *Luftwaffe War Diaries*, Macdonald, 1968

Cordts, Georg, *Junge Adler*, Bechtle Verlag, 1988

Erickson, John, *The Road to Berlin*, Grafton Books, 1983

Fiest, Uwe, *The Fighting Me 109*, Arms & Armour Press, 1988

Foreman, John, and Harvey, Sid E., *Messerschmitt Me 262 Combat Diary*, Air Research, 1995

Freeman, Roger A., *B-17 Fortress at War*, Ian Allan, 1977

——, *The Mighty Eighth*, Doubleday, 1970

——, *The Mighty Eighth War Diary*, Jane's, 1981

——, *The Mighty Eighth War Manual*, Jane's, 1984

Fry, Garry L., *Eagles of Duxford*, Phalax/Ian Allan, 1991

Galland, Adolf, *The First and the Last*, Methuen & Co, 1955

Gerbig, Werner, *Six Months to Oblivion*, Ian Allan, 1975

Gilbert, Martin, *The Second World War*, Weidenfeld & Nicolson, 1981

Green, William, *Warplanes of the Third Reich*, Macdonald & Jane's, 1979

Hahn, Fritz, *Deutsche Geheimwaffen*, Eric Hoffman Verlag, 1963

Hastings, Max, *Bomber Command*, Michael Joseph, 1979

Held, Werner, *Battle Over the Third Reich*, Air Research, 1990

Herrmann, Hajo, *Eagle's Wings*, Airlife, 1991

Hess, William N., *American Aces, World War II and Korea*, Arco Publishing, 1968

Hollingdate, R. J., *Nietzsche*, Routledge & Kegan Paul, 1973

Irving, David, *The Rise and Fall of the Luftwaffe*, Purnell Book Services, 1973

Jung, Robert, *Auf Verlorenem Posten*

Keegan, John, *A History of Warfare*, Pimlico, 1993

Le Strange, Richard, *Century Bombers*, 100th BG Memorial Museum, 1989

Lucas, James, *Kommando*, Grafton Books, 1986

Middlebrook, Martin, *The Nuremberg Raid*, Penguin Books, 1973

Murray, Williamson, *Luftwaffe*, George Allen & Unwin, 1985

Olynyk, Frank J., *USAAF Credits for Destruction of Enemy Aircraft*, Frank J. Olynyk, 1987

Parker, Danny S., *To Win the Winter Sky*, Greenhill Books, 1994

Price, Alfred, *The Last Year of the Luftwaffe*, Arms & Armour Press, 1994

Richards, Jeffrey, *Visions of Yesterday*, Routledge & Kegan Paul, 1973

Ries, Karl, *The Luftwaffe*, B. T. Batsford, 1987

Trevor Roper, Hugh, *The Goebbels Diaries*, Secker & Warburg, 1978

Saft, Ulrich, *Das Bittere Ende der Luftwaffe*, Militärbuchverlag Saft, 1994

Schliephake, Hanfried, *Flugzeugbewaffnung*, Motorbuch Verlag

Scutts, Jerry, *Mustang Aces of the Eighth AF*, Osprey, 1994
Shirer, William L., *The Rise and Fall of the Third Reich*, Secker & Warburg, 1960
Speer, Albert, *Inside the Third Reich*, Weidenfeld & Nicolson, 1970
Steinhoff, Johannes, *The Last Chance*, Hutchinson & Co, 1977
Streetly, Martin, *Confound and Destroy*, Macdonald & Jane's, 1978
Williamson, Gordon, *Aces of the Reich*, Arms & Armour Press, 1989
Various, Extract from *Jägerblatt* (inc. 1/91 and 3/91), Gemeinschaft der Jagdflieger

UNPUBLISHED SOURCES
Air Ministry, AIR 22/503 W/T Intelligence Summaries 7/4/45, Public Record Office, Kew
'German Aircraft Armament and Ammunition 1939–45', Ministry of Defence, Pattern Room, 1946
'Development of Aircraft Weapons' (1948 translation of report prepared by Unterluss Work Centre), Ministry of Defence, Pattern Room
Eighth Air Force, 4th Combat Wing operation 7th April '45, US National Archives, Maryland
———, 4th CBW, 'Disney' operation 4/7/45, US National Archives, Maryland
———, 45th CBW, 384th BG mission 4/7/45, US National Archives, Maryland
———, 390th BG, report of 7/4/45, 390th BG Memorial Museum
———, 100th BG, selection of records 7/4/45, 100th BG Memorial Museum
———, various 'Encounter Reports', VIII Fighter Command
———, Master Mission Report 4/7/45, microfilm B5027, USAF Historical Research Agency

OTHER SOURCES
Asbury, Lieutenant-Colonel Richard (correspondence with author)
Fry, Garry L. (extracts from personal archive)
Howard, William E. (correspondence with author; personal records)
Mason, Ian F. (correspondence with author)
Rall, *Generalleutnant* Günther (correspondence with author)
Zell, Werner (extracts from personal archive; correspondence with author)

INDEX